# A HISTORY OF
# THE TORBAY LIFEBOATS

# A HISTORY OF
# THE TORBAY LIFEBOATS
## With Pride and Dedication

### ALAN SALSBURY

HALSGROVE

First published in Great Britain in 2002

**British Library Cataloguing-in-Publication Data**
A CIP record for this title is available from the British Library

ISBN 1 84114 166 6

**HALSGROVE**
PUBLISHING, MEDIA AND DISTRIBUTION

Halsgrove House
Lower Moor Way
Tiverton, Devon EX16 6SS
Tel: 01884 243242
Fax: 01884 243325
email: sales@halsgrove.com
website: http://www.halsgrove.com

Frontispiece photograph: *The* James and Eliza Woodall *(1889–1902) on her arrival in Torquay,
11 November 1889. Note The Terrace dominating the skyline.* RNLI

Printed and bound in Great Britain by Bookcraft Ltd, Midsomer Norton.

# FOREWORD

## by Pete Goss

It is always a pleasure to be associated with the Royal National Lifeboat Institution and to be given the opportunity to express the high esteem in which I hold the crews of the RNLI lifeboats. I therefore had no hesitation in writing this foreword to *A History of the Torbay Lifeboats*.

Since 1866, a lifeboat service has operated from Brixham. Additionally, between 1876 and 1923, a lifeboat also operated from the Torquay Station. For 135 years, under the auspices of the RNLI, lifeboat men have provided the seafarers of Torbay and its adjoining waters, with a service that is second to none. The bravery of these men can not be overestimated. Their gallantry has been acknowledged in the fact that over the years the crew members of the Brixham/Torbay lifeboat have been awarded an Albert Medal, one RNLI Gold Medal, six RNLI Silver Medals and nineteen RNLI Bronze Medals, in addition to numerous letters of 'Thanks on Vellum'.

In sailing the seas off our coastline, be it purely for leisure or in preparation for an event such as the 'Goss Challenge', I am always comforted and reassured in the knowledge that should an unforeseen circumstance arise, or accident occur, the bravery and expertise of the lifeboat crew is never in doubt and only a radio call away. This book has set out to record some of the services, rescues and acts of bravery and heroism performed by the crew of the Torbay lifeboat; these acts they carry out daily with pride and dedication.

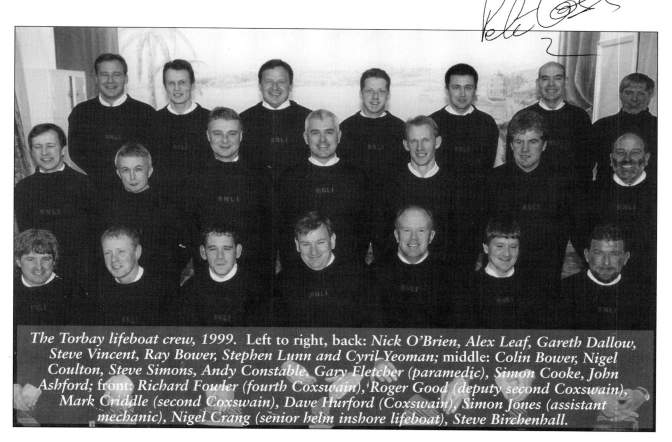

*The Torbay lifeboat crew, 1999. Left to right, back: Nick O'Brien, Alex Leaf, Gareth Dallow, Steve Vincent, Ray Bower, Stephen Lunn and Cyril Yeoman; middle: Colin Bower, Nigel Coulton, Steve Simons, Andy Constable, Gary Fletcher (paramedic), Simon Cooke, John Ashford; front: Richard Fowler (fourth Coxswain), Roger Good (deputy second Coxswain), Mark Criddle (second Coxswain), Dave Hurford (Coxswain), Simon Jones (assistant mechanic), Nigel Crang (senior helm inshore lifeboat), Steve Birchenhall.*

*The Torbay crew put the* 47–002 Sam and Joan Woods *through rough-weather trials off Berry Head, Brixham, 1982.*

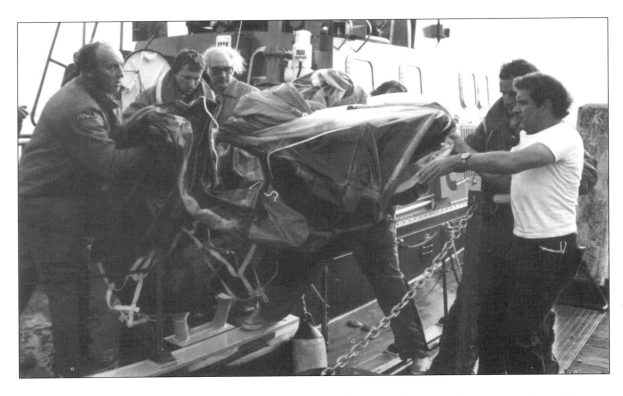

*The recovery of the liferaft from the* Majorca, 18 September 1982. *Left to right: Brian Caunter, Colin Bower, Second Coxswain Ernie Fradd, Russell Brown and Clive Moores.*

# Contents

# ACKNOWLEDGEMENTS

In compiling this book, I wish to acknowledge the help and assistance that I have received from: the staff of the Royal National Lifeboat Institution, Poole, Dorset; the *Herald Express*; the *Western Morning News*; the *Express and Echo*; Torbay News Agency; Torbay Reference Library; the Torquay Museum; the Brixham Museum; the West Country Studies Library, Exeter. My thanks are also extended to Mrs Fry, Mrs Soper, Arthur Curnow, Dave Hurford, Ken Gibbs, Simon Littlewood, Ken Thomas and Nigel Coulton for their photographic and memorabilia contributions.

I extend my sincere appreciation, and respect, to those persons who have put up with many months of my intrusion into their homes and constant barraging; those persons without whom a story such as this could not be told. I thank, and wish God's speed to:

The coxswains, officers and crews, past, present and future, of the RNLI lifeboats, Torbay Station, Brixham.

*The* Mary Brundret *at the Torquay Lifeboat Station, c.1880.* RNLI

# INTRODUCTION

**P**oets, authors, songwriters and philosophers have described her from time immemorial. Each has reflected upon her varying moods: romantic, enticing or volatile, unforgiving and dangerous. She means all things to all men, a provider of food, recreation and, often, the sustainer of life itself. For many she remains their final resting place. She covers two-thirds of the surface of the planet Earth, and remains one of the great forces of Mother Nature which man may harness, but cannot tame... she suffers no fools... she is the Sea!

Throughout the ages the sea has set the background for many tales of heroism and adventure. Here in the West Country we have inherited the legendary stories of the deeds of Drake, Howard and Raleigh. Our links with the sea continue today with the fishing fleets of Brixham and Newlyn together with our inextricable link with the Royal Naval Base at Devonport. In a tourist haven such as Torbay, it is for recreational purposes that the majority of people enter the sea's watery bosom. There will be a time when even the most experienced sailor, professional or amateur, will encounter difficulty at sea. In many cases the circumstances requiring assistance are beyond the individual's immediate control, whilst some are of their own making.

Some people have little or no regard for their own safety, let alone the safety of others. Likewise they show little or no respect for the sea. It is gratifying and reassuring to know that when assistance is needed, whatever the circumstance, without judgement of the individual and with unquestionable bravery and dedication, help is readily at hand from the brave men and women of the Lifeboat Service.

In this short history it is clearly not possible to chronicle in detail every launch of every boat during the 130 plus years that the RNLI has served the seafarers of Torbay; indeed not every launch is recorded upon the Station's service boards. This book, however, in a small way, attempts to record some of the acts of heroism and bravery of the crews of the Royal National Lifeboat Institution, Torbay Station.

*The yacht* Moonshine *which was dismasted off Hopes Nose, 29 December 1968.* RNLI

## ABBREVIATED BURIAL RECORDS OF THOSE WHO DIED IN THE STORM OF 10–11 JANUARY, 1866

| Name | Abode | When buried | Age | Ceremony Perf. by: |
|---|---|---|---|---|
| Geo. Hunger Found naked | Of the Brig. Zoe of Deal, Kent. Drowned in Torbay in hurricane on morning of 11 Jan. | 16 January | About 21 | A.F. Carey Vicar |
| Mariner unknown | Found drowned nr Churston Cove – with one boot on otherwise quite naked. | 16 January | About 32 | A.F. Carey Vicar |
| Mariner unknown | Found drowned nr Churston Cove quite naked, the letters WS and a heart marked on right arm. | 16 January | A young man | A.F. Carey Vicar |
| Sailor boy unknown | Found drowned nr Churston Cove, quite naked. | 16 January | About 15 | A.F. Carey Vicar |
| Dutch Mariner ship's cook | Drowned in the storm on 11 Jan. | 19 January | A young man | A.F. Carey Vicar |
| Mariner unknown | Drowned in the storm in Torbay. One shoe on his foot, no hair on his head. | 19 January | | A.F. Carey Vicar |
| Mariner unknown | Drowned in the storm in Torbay. Found without head, legs or arms! | 19 January | | A.F. Carey Vicar |
| Mariner unknown | Found drowned off Brixham, the great and smallest toe only on left foot (born so). Supposed by clothes to be French. | 20 January | | A.F. Carey Vicar |
| Mariner unknown | Found drowned between Churston Cove and Elbury. A smallish man, naked, no hair. | 21 January | | A.F. Carey Vicar |
| Mariner unknown | Found drowned off Brixham. | ? January | | F. May ? |
| Mariner unknown | Found drowned off Brixham. | 23 January | | F. May ? |
| Mariner unknown | Found drowned, much decomposed. | 24 January | | A.F. Carey Vicar |
| Mariner unknown | Found drowned off Brixham, naked. | 26 January | | A.F. Carey Vicar |
| Pierre Le Savouroux of French ship *L'Occidental du Havre.* | Found drowned, without his head, recognised by nuptial ring and initials on his stockings (P.L.S.). The ring was divided into two parts, one with his name on it, the other with his wife's 'Sophie Godfrey'. Burial service read in French. | 27 January | | A.F. Carey, Vicar Funeral attended by French Vice Consul frm London & 15 or 16 French Captains. |
| French mariner | Drowned in storm off Torbay, thought to be Guittard from a letter found in his pocket. | 27 January | | A.F. Carey Vicar |
| Mariner unknown | Drowned in storm in Torbay. | 30 January | | A.F. Carey Vicar |
| Mariner unknown | Drowned in storm in Torbay, found without his head. | 30 January | | A.F. Carey Vicar |
| Mariner unknown | Found drowned off Brixham. | 31 January | | A.F. Carey Vicar |
| Mariner unknown | Drowned in storm off Torbay | 31 January | About 13 | A.F. Carey Vicar |
| Mariner unknown | Drowned in storm, no particular marks on body, found floating in the middle of bay. | 1 February | | A.F. Carey Vicar |
| Mariner unknown | Drowned, found naked, a stout man with strap around his wrist, to which was fastened a case with a marline spike in it. | 2 February | | A.F. Carey Vicar |
| Mariner unknown | Drowned in the storm in Torbay, found naked. | 2 February | | A.F. Carey Vicar |
| Mariner unknown | Drowned in the storm in Torbay, found with a boot on with coffee berries in it. | 3 February | | A.F. Carey Vicar |
| Mariner unknown | Drowned in storm in Torbay. | 4 February | | A.F. Carey Vicar |
| Sam. Crocker | Drowned in storm, found Lower Brixham. | 7 February | 32 | Hubert M. Patch |
| Mariner, alle. Isaac Clayton | Drowned in storm with letters I.C. on stockings, recognised by friends, a Master mariner. | 7 February | 56 | F. May |
| Mariner unknown | Drowned in storm, found with waistcoat shirt and sailor's knife. | 10 February | | A.F. Carey Vicar |
| Mariner | Drowned in storm in Torbay, name unknown. | 17 February | | A.F. Carey, Vicar |
| Mariner | Drowned in storm in Torbay, name unknown. | 19 February | | N. Elrington |

# 1

# THE GREAT STORM

## *10–11 JANUARY 1866*

On the evening of Wednesday 10 January and the morning of Thursday 11 January 1866, the 'Great Storm' struck Torbay and wreaked unprecedented death and devastation upon the unfortunate vessels which had sought the shelter of the Brixham roads and, to a lesser extent, the fishing fleet of Brixham. Words cannot describe the horrors of that night, the tragic loss of life or the grief felt by those families who made desperate bids to rescue their loved-ones as they lost their lives within view of their homes. No household in the port of Brixham was untouched by the events which unfolded, the horror and despair being perpetuated in the aftermath of the Great Storm, as corpses and cargo continued to be given up by the sea.

Numerous were the accounts and stories of that night which were printed in the national and local press. These accounts vary in detail, particularly in respect of the number of ships and lives lost, and no two renditions agree. The scene was, however, captured in a contemporary account, which appeared in the *Torquay Directory and South Devon Journal* of Wednesday 17 January 1866, extracts from which read as follows:

### APPALLING WRECKS IN TORBAY, AND THE LOSS OF NEARLY ONE HUNDRED LIVES

*The destruction along our coasts during the last few months, great as it has been, has been reduced to comparative insignificance, by the number of ships wrecked, on Wednesday night and Thursday last, and the awful loss of human life by which these disasters have been accompanied. For some weeks past the weather has been very unsettled, there being a succession of violent gales chiefly from the southwest. On Wednesday there was a severe storm from the North, with snow; at night the wind rose to a hurricane, and veered about, at short intervals to the south-west, south, south-east and north-east, the wind, from the last named quarter, worked all the mischief in Torbay. As a roadstead Torbay has a high reputation for being a good anchorage ground for vessels requiring shelter from the south-westerly gales; and during the last few weeks a large number of vessels have sought its friend-ly shelter. But whilst riding at anchor in security from the south-west gales the mariner must ever have a watchful eye on the dog-vane, and should this give the slightest indication of the wind changing to the eastward, he must lose no time in weighing his anchor and getting out of the bay; for, with the wind in that quar-ter the danger is imminent. This seemed to be the case on Wednesday night; the wind sud-denly chopped round to the north-east, and before the vessels could fairly get under weigh, they were blown ashore. Indeed, one of the skippers whose vessel was wrecked, told us that nothing could stand against the storm; as soon as he attempted to make sail, the canvass was torn to atoms like so much brown paper.*

*On Wednesday night, there were seventy-four vessels, we were told, at anchor in Torbay. Many were large ships, outward bound; and others were of the collier class; some of them reached the Cornish Coast weeks ago, but were driven back by adverse winds.*

*The wind rose at nine o'clock and increased to a hurricane from the southward; the whole fleet attempted to work out of the Bay, but it is feared that only a few succeeded. The storm was so severe, and the change in the wind so sudden that all seamanship was unavailing. Vessels began to drag their anchors, and anxious spectators ashore, could see occasionally through the rain, glimpses of the masthead lights flitting onwards to the terrible lee shore.*

*The majority of the inhabitants of the lower part of Brixham turned out and proceeded with lanterns to the quay, while some went on to Furzeham Common. The coastguard under Mr. Milton were conspicuous in their noble exertions, and they were nobly seconded by the hardy seamen and fishermen of the port. Towards mid-night the hapless vessels drove towards the Brixham pier.*

*The inner harbour at Brixham was already crowded with trawlers that had previously run in during the day; and in the outer harbour, between the pier and the breakwater, there was also a large number of trawlers and small vessels at anchor. As soon as the ships began to drive, their only chance was to run for the already over-filled harbour, and where so many vessels large and small were striving to gain one narrow entrance, it was no wonder that the utmost confusion prevailed, or that so much destruction of life and property followed. With a pitchy black night, and the sea leaping over the piers, it would have been a hazardous experiment to the most experienced, and boldest pilot to attempt the task. But with*

*certain death before their eyes, if driven on the rocky shore to the west of the town, their only chance was to make for the harbour if possible. Only a few succeeded in reaching the much coveted refuge, and amongst these were the* Tangerine, *and the* Florence Nightingale. *It was an exciting scene as the vessels drove onwards to the pier; and hundreds of spectators watched their movements with suspense. On, on, they came, to inevitable destruction. The brave seamen of Brixham clambered on the parapet wall, and with lights directed the vessels to the harbour entrance. The harbour master, Mr. Scivell, with several pilots took the post of danger on the pier head, and shouted to the masters of the advancing ships to port or starboard their helms, as circumstances needed. Two ships passed the terrible ordeal in safety, and a great shout of joy was set up by the anxious spectators as they sped past the pier heads into smoother water. But, alas, the others that came crashing on, were not so fortunate. They missed the entrance, and ran against the solid pier; other vessels came on after, and in a few minutes, seven or eight vessels, were inextricably commingled together, grinding against the pier and each other. The parapet was instantly swarming with adventurous sailors and fishermen of Brixham, who, regardless of all danger to themselves,*

**Brixham Harbour after the Great Storm of 10–11 January 1866.**
COURTESY TORQUAY MUSEUM

sought to rescue the crews from a watery grave. In many instances, as the masts and yards were driven against and overhung the wall, the crews were rescued by passing along them; but it was a work of great peril, for as the spars swayed about, they had to watch for the favourable moment to drop on the pier, or to seize one of the hundreds of hands outstretched to help them. It is believed that the majority of the crews of the vessels that were wrecked by the side of the pier were saved. The cries of the poor fellows were heartrendering, and some it is believed were crushed to death either between the vessels themselves, or between the ships and the pier.

The Cæsarewitch, it would seem, foundered in the gale. We saw three men saved from her, and they could not account for the way in which they were saved. They declared that they knew no more than that they found themselves on board the Jesse, with which vessel she probably came in to collision. On asking one of the men where his vessel was, he replied, 'Sir, I can't find a stick belonging to her.' There is reason to believe that some ships went down with all hands on board.

At Goodrington, a small schooner was driven ashore, nearly at the same spot where a vessel was wrecked a few weeks ago.

The Broadsands, so well known to the inhabitants as the resort of picnic parties, was the scene of much devastation. At the northern point, where the rocks run into the sea in shelving ledges, two schooners were totally wrecked; further on seven vessels were beached, all within the compass of about five hundred yards. In driving ashore, a barque ran into a schooner, and both sunk, their upper works and masts being above water. There was the Fortitude, schooner of Exeter; the Stately, a fine barque laden with corn, from the Danube for Swansea; a French brigantine; and the Dorset, of Falmouth.

An eye witness says that the Stately broke from her anchors at eleven o'clock, on Wednesday night, and drove ashore at five minutes after one o'clock. Two of her crew got out the boat, and made for the shore before she struck, but they had not gone far before the boat upset, and they were left struggling in the water; fortunately this happened near the shore, and the coastguard, wading into the water, rescued them. The men still on board were anxious to land, fearing that the ship would go to pieces. They accordingly threw out a spar with a rope attached to it, in order to effect a communication with the beach. A Brixham man, Mr. Jeffrey Searle, volunteered to swim out and bring the spar ashore, but a

brave young fellow named James Nicks, of Paignton, would not allow him, declaring that as he was the youngest he had the most right; and so he plunged into the sea, and after a hard swim, at length brought it ashore, though much exhausted by his arduous work. It is gratifying to learn that the crews of all these vessels on Broadsands were saved.

Of the nine vessels here, five are total wrecks; the shore was strewn with spars, casks, mats, cushions, beams, planks, rope, and a vast quantity of wood churned into such small fragments that it was impossible to say to what part of the ship they belonged. The crews were landed by the friendly aid of the coastguard, who brought them ashore by means of mortar apparatus; lines were thrown across the rigging, and being fastened at both ends, a framework capable of holding one person was secured to it by blocks, and thus a communication was established, and the shipwrecked mariners released. It was not until late in the afternoon of Thursday that the last man was thus taken off.

Further on, at the southern extremity of the sands, a Dutch galliott was ashore, totally wrecked; all the crew were saved with the exception of the master who, it was said, was drowned in his cabin.

As the writer pursued his way along the cliffs towards Brixham, he observed indications of the terrible storm at almost every step; not far from the shore were to be seen spars upright in the water, apparently the masts of some vessel or vessels which had foundered.

Proceeding on to Churston Cove, more terrible wrecks came to view; at the entrance were to be seen the remains of a hull of some ship, which had gone to pieces; the beach in the Cove was covered with fragments of wood and spars; the sea was a floating mass of tangled and pounded wood. Of the crew of this vessel it is stated that only four out of ten were saved. Higher up the Cove was the brig Blue Jacket, not much injured – the damage being confined to the loss of her rudder.

The fearful havoc at Brixham is indescribable. Two ships were driven ashore inside the breakwater. From the point where the pier joins the land, to the pier-head, the scene is awful to contemplate. The sea along the whole length of the pier outside appeared as if it was covered by large floats of timber, and this was all that remained of ten or twelve ships which took the shore at that point. Close beneath the pier, and grinding against it was a large barque, her masts and spars still standing, but her upper works gone and apparently utterly wrecked, for the water was up to the combings of the hatchways; also a brig, two schooners and a large cutter, surrounded by the floating remains of those that had gone to pieces.

Twenty trawlers are wrecked, and of these twelve went down, the masts being still to be seen above the water.

The cries of the drowning men were heart-rending; the quays were crowded with strong hardy men ready to peril their own lives to save others, but all their efforts were unavailing; men met their deaths within a few feet of them. Many were the cries for a lifeboat, but alas, there was no lifeboat in Brixham.

Of the seventy vessels which were at anchor in the Bay on Wednesday night, there were not more than eight or ten that rode out the terrible storm.

A correspondent describing the scene says: 'The captains of some of the ships lying off the immediate entrance to the port of Brixham, endeavoured to take their craft into the harbour, but almost all these vessels were driven against the solid wall of the stone pier.'

When the effort was made to run into the harbour as the only chance of preservation, on dashed some of the larger ships, which struck several sloops and drove them against the wall, where a scene of indescribable confusion took place. Two large ships, the bark Wild Rose, and the Hamburg ship Leons, came down upon the sloops, and the result was that eight of them were driven from their anchorage; and before they also could make for the harbour entrance, they were dashed against the pier wall, and so completely pounded there, that now, excepting the two large vessels to which they acted as fenders, and which were therefore spared considerable damage, the water in front of the pier shows no trace of the shape of any one of them, and the sea was on Friday afternoon so extensively covered with beams, planks, masts, keelsons, stanchions, parts of heads and sterns of ships, bowsprits, ropes and chains intertwined, and even books, coffee, barrels of unfermented wine, boots and shoes and bags that floated on the surface, over all of which was spread broad cast such a vast quantity of chips and splinters that instead of resembling a pool of floating debris, the water so covered presented the appearance of being a large yard for miscellaneous ships' stores. As the vessels were flung with violence against the wall the sailors were rescued from them by dint of the greatest hardihood, the noblest and most fearless bravery on the part of those on the pier. The men on the pier wall ran imminent risk from falling spars and swinging blocks and chains; yet they courageously mounted the parapet, extended a light here, threw a rope or

hauled in a rope at another point, and stretched forward whenever occasion allowed of their grasping and rescuing any of the men. Some of the dangers to the saved were imminent, and the chance of rescue so small, that if the opportunities of but a few moments' duration had not been promptly taken advantage of they could not have recurred. Some were drawn ashore by hasty clutches at but very small portions of their dress, whilst others were hauled from their ships by ropes that were thrown from the quay over the vessels from which the escape took place. One man named Richard Mills, a fisherman, is stated to have been instrumental in saving no less than fourteen seamen, some of whom he dragged by main force out of the water in a state of nudity. A harrowing spectacle took place within thirty yards of the shore. The large ship Wild Rose, which now lies in front of the pier, was driven upon the smack Colonel Buller, and burst away the stanchions of the smack's stern, as well as a portion of her bulwarks. The crew, named respectively Crocker and Bucknell, with a boy named Blackmore, an apprentice on board, took to their boat, and had but a few yards to pull when their boat capsized, and they were immersed before the eyes of scores of their friends, who could render no help. They were speedily numbered with the victims of the storm. The two men each left a widow and four children. Crocker's wife has been confined but a few days and Bucknell, who was a fine young man, and who has left a very young wife, was heard to exclaim piteously, 'For God's sake save me, for the sake of my wife and family', when he was swallowed up by the dark water, and with his comrade and the boy was drowned. This was an instance in which the crew were drowned and the ship saved from destruction, but in the case of the trawler Telegraph, the craft was lost and the whole of the men were preserved. As the daylight appeared, it was seen that a vessel had struck on the breakwater; that the eight sloops in front of the Pier had been so thoroughly smashed, that there were no two planks sufficiently fixed together to indicate the character of the vessel of which they had formed part; and that from Brixham along the coast to Paignton, there were between twenty and thirty wrecks. Those who beheld the painful sight could not but feel that probably it did not by any means represent all the sad casualties that had happened on the angry waves in the Bay during the dark night that had passed. One terrible consequence of the storm is known to have occurred and left no trace. Two steamers were observed in the Bay in the evening, but one subsequently was seen with her bow towards the Channel, and it is believed that she steamed out; but the crew of one of the wrecked vessels, the name of which cannot yet be ascertained, have stated that during the night, as their ship was being dashed towards the shore by both wind and water, they struck an unknown steamer amidships, that the ship cut her instantaneously through the centre, and that she immediately sank with all hands. The ship that did this mischief in a few minutes after was broken up under the cliffs...

It was a mournful sight, in walking through the town to see house after house with its shutters closed, and the blinds drawn down, showing that death had been making sad havoc amongst its hardy population.

With so great a calamity happening at their very doors, the inhabitants of Brixham acted with the noblest generosity. Clergymen and ministers of all denominations, vied with each other in works of charity. Private homes were turned into receiving houses for the ship-wrecked seamen. Nothing could be more affecting than the motherly conduct of the fish-wives to the sailors. Mrs. Sheppeard, the wife of one of the proprietors of the trawlers that is lost, kept open her house the whole of the night, providing them with many suites of clothes (for some came ashore in a state of nudity), and distributing hot coffee and substantial food to all who entered. One poor fellow was brought in with his finger jammed. A surgeon was sent for, and it was immediately amputated. One Frenchman was carried to her house almost frantic at the loss of his ship, and the supposed loss of his son. Many of the inhabitants followed her example. Mr. Johnson, hairdresser, entertained the master and two of the crew of the Monda...

At the Assembly Rooms, eighty-five seamen were accommodated; the floor was covered with straw, and the sailors laid in rows. Hot coffee, bread and butter, and soup, were freely distributed. On Thursday morning, Mr. Elrington held a short service in the Assembly Rooms, which was much appreciated by the listeners. The whole of the gentlemen engaged in the work have worked together, without respect to sectarianism, all lending a willing hand to help in the good work. The committee have been able to dispatch seventy seamen to their homes.

The gentlemen and tradesmen aided with the utmost promptness, in assuaging the affliction of the sufferers. The drapers and others lent blankets and quilts for the men; and Messrs. Green and Brooking, surgeons, were indefatigable in their attendance. The Rev. J. R. Nankivell, the Chaplain to the Torbay and Dartmouth Missions, the Rev. Elrington, the Rev. Mr. Patch, the Rev. H. Cross, Mr. T. Lakeman, Rev. T. Whitmarsh, Mr. O. Bartlett, all lent their valuable aid in relieving the distress. Miss S. Brown, the Secretary of the National Shipwrecked Mariners' Society, exhausted her stock of "passes" – tickets by which the seamen were sent passage free to their homes; her efforts in this way were ably supplemented from the local funds hastily raised in a few hours. It should also be mentioned that about thirty distressed seamen met with a hearty welcome at Elbury Farm, occupied by Mr. Tully.

Eye-witness accounts and stories of this tragic and harrowing night are too numerous to recount here in full. One reported statement which stands out in the above account, must surely be: 'Many were the cries for a lifeboat, but alas, there was no lifeboat in Brixham.' As there was not a lifeboat stationed in Torbay, an appeal was made for the launch of the Teignmouth lifeboat, the China. Not surprisingly, the storm, which brought havoc to Torbay, also swept the Teign estuary and adjacent coastline. At Teignmouth the barometer fell fully one inch in the five hours between 18.00 and 23.00 hours, and the storm-force winds veered from southwesterly to easterly. Mr Burney, the Captain of the Coastguard, being bound by regulations, was not authorised to allow the China to go as far as Torquay, which was well outside the Teignmouth Station operating limits. Weather conditions being such as they were, it was anticipated that the services of the lifeboat might well be required in the Teignmouth area. Upon hearing of the total destruction of the shipping and the appalling loss of life, authority was given for the lifeboat to be taken to Torquay by road.

Local procedure provided a reserve crew of 16 men from whom 13 would be selected to man the lifeboat, excluding members of the Coastguard. On this fateful night insufficient men came forward to form a full crew, although a team of six horses was mustered and the lifeboat hauled some ten miles, to be launched at the Strand, Torquay, at 14.00 hours on 11 January. Despite the time lapse and the distance travelled, the gallant effort of the Teignmouth lifeboat crew saved seven men from the Liverpool-registered brigantine Cheshire Witch, and four men from the London-registered vessel Jessie (Master, Austin, of Brixham).

At a subsequent inquiry, held at the Coastguard Headquarters on 16 January, the Board of Inquiry recorded that the two Coxswains of the China (Bulkeley and Stuggins) and some of the men excepted, 'did show a readiness to volunteer their services on an occasion when it might have been expected of them.' None of those who refused would say anything in their own defence. It was said that they 'would not come forward for they were almost ashamed to walk through the town.'

In a letter sent by the Secretary of the Relief Fund to the Chairman of the Local Board, at Torquay, he reported:

*As far as we can ascertain, 62 merchant vessels were in the Bay on the night of the 10th. inst., besides trawlers. Of these, there were riding in the Bay after the storm, ten; got into the harbour, ten; wrecked on the coast, or sunk in the Bay, 42; besides eight trawlers sunk and wrecked. We think that the average number of crew per ship may be about seven, which makes 294 hands, leaving to be accounted for and supposed to have lost their lives in attempting to get on shore from wrecked vessels, or sunk in the bay, 73. In addition to these there were four fishermen drowned belonging to Brixham, making altogether 77 lives lost.*

In giving evidence at a subsequent inquiry, the Revd J.R. Nankivell stated that he was aware of 42 vessels having been wrecked in the southern part of Torbay, the number comprising: Goodrington Sands 1; between Goodrington and Broadsands 2; Broadsands 7; Warren Point 1; Elbury 1; Fishcombe 1; between Fishcombe and Black Ball 2; between Black Ball and the Pier 5; adjacent to the Pier 8; inside the harbour 2; off Dewdney's shipyard 1; outside the breakwater 3 and at anchor in Torbay 8.

The people of Brixham erected a monument, designed by the Revd A.F. Carey, to the memory of those who lost their lives in that terrible storm. It was therefore with sadness that they read *Trewman's Exeter Flying Post* of Wednesday 4 September 1867, which recorded that the monument:

*... had been maliciously defaced by some person who has erased from the inscription the name of Rev. Elrington, the Chairman of the Sailors' Relief Committee. It seems probable that the perpetrator of the malicious act was prompted by spite.*

*Memorial to those lost in the Great Storm of 1866, St Mary's Churchyard, Brixham.*
ALAN SALSBURY

The monument is situated in the churchyard of St Mary's Parish Church, Brixham. The inscription reads:

IN MEMORY OF
PIERRE LE SAVOUROUX
SAMUEL CROCKER
ISAAC CLAYTON
GEORGE HUNGER
AND 25 OTHER SHIPWRECKED
SAILORS WHO WERE NOT
IDENTIFIED, WHOSE BODIES
WERE WASHED ONSHORE
JAN. 1866 AND BURIED IN THIS
CHURCHYARD


THE BRIXHAM SHIPWRECKED
SAILORS RELIEF COMMITTEE,
HAVING FROM THE SUM OF
£3211.9.5 ENTRUSTED TO THEM
BY A GENEROUS PUBLIC RELIEVED
THE WIDOWS AND ORPHANS
AND OTHER SUFFERERS FROM THE
GALE OF JANUARY 11TH 1866
HAVE FROM THE SURPLUS RAISED
THIS MONUMENT


LORD SAVE US: WE PERISH

# THOSE THAT PERISHED

*Listed below are vessels known to have perished in Torbay as a consequence of the*
*Great Storm of 10–11 January 1866*

**ABEONA**
**Registered Port:** Brixham
**Captain:** Hellings
**Built:** Bideford 1851

**Lost:** Torbay, near Brixham. 50°24'.15N  03°32'W
**Type of Vessel:** Schooner (sail)
**Length:** 23ft.  **Gross Tonnage:** 128 ton

**ALONA**
**Lost:** Torbay 50°24'.15N  03°32'W
**Type of Vessel:** Brigantine (sail)
**Length:** 28ft.

**Cargo:** Currants
**Gross Tonnage:** 219 tons

**AMANDA**
**Registered Port:** Kingston-upon-Hull
**Type of Vessel:** Brigantine (sail)
**Crew:** 8      **Crew Lost:** 5

**Lost:** Torbay 50.25'N  03°33'.08W
**Cargo:** unspecified general

**BELLE**
**Flag:** France
**Type of Vessel:** Sailing trawler

**Lost:** Torbay 50°25'N  03°33'.08W
**Cargo:** Ballast

**BLUE JACKET**

**Lost:** Churston Cove

**BRITANNIA**
**Registered Port:** Aberystwyth
**Captain:** Clitton
**Built:** Greenock 1827
**Crew:** 6      **Crew Lost:** 1

**Lost:** Brixham Pier 50°23'.55N  03°30'.40W
**Type of vessel:** Brigantine (sail)
**Net Tonnage:** 100 ton
**Cargo:** Clay

**BRITON**
**Registered Port:** Brixham
**Type of vessel:** Trawler

**Lost:** Torbay 50°24'.15N  03°32'W

**CHESHIRE WITCH** [1]
**Registered Port:** Liverpool
**Captain:** Lowther
**Built:** Barnstaple 1838

**Lost:** Torbay 50°24'.15N  03°32'W
**Type of vessel:** Smack      **Cargo:** Copper Ore
**Gross Tonnage:** 138 ton

**CAMBRIA**
**Registered Port:** Exeter
**Captain:** Hayman
**Gross Tonnage:** 107 ton

**Lost:** Torbay 50°24'.15N  03°32'W
**Type of vessel:** Sailing
**Cargo:** Ballast

**COLONEL BULLER**
**Registered Port:** Brixham
**Crew:** 4      **Crew Lost:** 3

**Type of vessel:** Fishing vessel

**COURIER**
**Flag:** Prussian
**Gross Tonnage:** 147 ton
**Crew:** 8      **Crew Lost:** 2

**Lost:** Torbay 50°24'.09N  03°31'.17W
**Cargo:** Coffee

**DANIEL**
**Type of vessel:** Schooner

**Lost:** Torbay

*DORSET*
*Registered Port:* Falmouth

**Lost:** Torbay

*DRYAN* [2]
**Flag:** France
**Type of vessel:** Brigantine

**Lost:** Brixham Pier 50°23'.55N 03°30'.40W
**Cargo:** Ballast

*ELIZABETH LEWIS*
**Registered Port:** Aberystwyth
**Captain:** Lewis
**Built:** Aberystwyth 1857

**Lost:** Torbay 50°25'N 03°33'W
**Type of vessel:** Schooner
**Gross Tonnage:** 80 ton

*ELLEN EDWARDS*
**Registered Port:** Aberystwyth
**Captain:** Davies
**Built:** Aberdovey 1857
**Crew:** 8        **Crew Lost:** 2

**Lost:** Black Hole, Brixham 50°24'.15N 03°32'W
**Type of vessel:** Schooner (sail) **Cargo:** Sugar Beet
**Gross Tonnage:** 83 ton

*EMILE AND CHARLES*
**Registered Port:** Aberystwyth
**Type of vessel:** Brigantine

**Lost:** Torbay near Brixham 50°24'.15N 03°32'W
**Cargo:** Coal

*ERNEST*
**Registered Port:** Brixham
**Type of vessel:** Fishing vessel

**Lost:** Torbay 50°25'N 03°33'.08W
**Cargo:** Ballast

*FLORENCE NIGHTINGALE*
**Registered Port:** Padstow
**Captain:** Roach
**Built:** Padstow

**Lost:** Torbay 50°25'N 03°33'.08W
**Type of vessel:** Sailing vessel **Cargo:** Ballast
**Gross Tonnage:** 105 ton

*FORERUNNER*
**Registered Port:** Brixham
**Type of vessel:** Ketch

**Lost:** Torbay 50°25'N 03°33'.08W
**Cargo:** Ballast

*FORTITUDE*
**Registered Port:** Exeter
**Type of vessel:** Schooner

**Lost:** Torbay

*GRACE*
**Registered Port:** Brixham
**Type of vessel:** Fishing vessel (sail)

**Lost:** Torbay 50°25'N 03°33'.08W
**Cargo:** Ballast

*HANOVER*
**Flag:** Netherlands
**Cargo:** Vitriol

**Lost:** Broadsands, Paignton 50°24'.15N 03°32'W
**Crew Lost:** 1 (the ship's Captain)

*HELEN*
**Registered Port:** Brixham
**Type of vessel:** Ketch

**Lost:** Torbay 50°24'.15N 03°32'W
**Cargo:** Ballast

*HONOUR*
**Registered Port:** South Shields
**Captain:** Hodge
**Built:** Sunderland 1858

**Lost:** Fishcombe Pt, Brix. 50°24'.09N 03°31'.17W
**Type of vessel:** Brigantine
**Gross Tonnage:** 172 ton

**JACOBA**
Flag: Netherlands
Type of vessel: Brigantine
Crew: 9    Crew Lost: 1

Lost: Torbay 50°25'N 03°33'.08W
Cargo: Bone and horn

**JAMES**
Flag: United Kingdom

Type of vessel: Schooner

Lost: Goodrington Sands, Paignton   50°24'.15N
                                                              03°32'W
Cargo: Bulk flour

**JESSIE** [3]
Registered Port: Exeter
Captain: Mitchell
Cargo: Ballast
Gross Tonnage: 144 tons

Lost: Torbay 50°24'.15N 03°32'W
Type of vessel: Schooner
Built: Yarmouth 1842
Crew: 6    Crew Lost: 5

**LADY OF THE LAKE**
Registered Port: Brixham
Type of vessel: Smack

Lost: Brixham Pier 50°23'.55N 03°33'.40W
Cargo: Ballast

**LEONE** [4]
Registered Port: Antwerp
Type of vessel: Barque

Lost: Near Brixham   50°23'.55N 03°33'.40W

**LIVELY**
Registered Port: Brixham
Type of vessel: Fishing vessel

Lost: Torbay 50°25'N 03°33'.08W
Cargo: Ballast

**MARGARET ANN**
Registered Port: Beaumaris
Captain: Griffiths
Built: Beaumaris 1840

Lost: Brixham Pier 50°23'.55N 03°30'.40W
Type of vessel: Schooner

**MARY ANN**
Registered Port: London
Captain: Lee
Cargo: Ballast
Gross Tonnage: 182 ton

Lost: Black Hole, Brixham  50°24'.15N 03°32'W
Type of vessel: Brigantine
Built: Rye 1850
Crew: 8    Crew Lost: 3

**MONDA**
Registered Port: Kingston-upon-Hull
Captain: Fordyce
Cargo: General
Gross Tonnage: 200 ton

Lost: Fishcombe Point, Brixham
Type of vessel: Brigantine
Built: Prince Edward Island, 1862
Crew: 8    Crew Lost: 5

**MOSLEM**
Lost: Torbay

Type of vessel: Brigantine

**PRINCESS BEATRICE**
Registered Port: Falmouth
Captain: Johnson

Lost: Dewdney's Cove, Brixham
Type of vessel: Barque

**PROVIDENCE**
Registered Port: Brixham
Type of vessel: Fishing vessel

Lost: Brixham 50°23'.55N 03°30'.40W
Cargo: Ballast

**SALEM**
Registered Port: Brixham
Type of vessel: Fishing vessel

Lost: Torbay 50°24'.15N 03°32'W
Cargo: Ballast

**SCYTHIAN**
Registered Port: Exeter
Captain: Soloman
Cargo: Ballast
Gross Tonnage: 110 tons

Lost: Torbay 50°24'.15N 03°32'W
Type of vessel: Schooner
Built: Sunderland 1847

**SPY**
Registered Port: Brixham
Type of vessel: Fishing vessel

Lost: Torbay 50°25'N 03°33'.08W
Cargo: Ballast

**STATELY**
Registered Port: Shields
Type of vessel: Barque

Lost: Goodrington, Paignton

**SUSANNAH**
Lost: Torbay

Type of vessel: Brigantine

**TELEGRAPH**
Registered Port: Brixham
Type of vessel: Fishing vessel

Lost: Brixham Pier 50°23'.55N 03°30'.40W
Cargo: Ballast

**THOMAS and MARY**
Lost: Brixham

**WILD ROSE**
Registered Port: Whitby
Captain: Smith
Cargo: Wheat
Gross Tonnage: 280 tons
Crew: 11

Lost: Brixham Pier 50°23'.55N 03°30'.40W
Type of vessel: Barque
Built: Whitby 1856

**ZOE**
Registered Port: Deal
Crew Lost: 6 incl. a pilot

Type of vessel: Brigantine

**UNKNOWN VESSEL**
Lost: Churston Cove

Crew: 10     Crew Lost: 6

Notes:
1   Often reported as the *Cæsarewitch*
2   Also reported as *Drian*
3   Also reported as *Jessie* or *Jessy*
4   Also reported as the Italian vessel *Leonie*

In common with several other vessels, the brigantines *Moslem* and *Susannah*, together with the schooner *Daniel*, were lost without trace. It is believed that between these three vessels they carried a total crew of 30–40 men.

During the evening of the storm, two steamers were sighted in Torbay, one subsequently being seen to steam towards open waters. The crew of a wrecked sailing ship reported that their vessel had struck an unknown steamer amidships. The vessel was sliced through and sank with all hands.

# 2

# THE BIRTH OF THE TORBAY LIFEBOAT
## *1866*

In 1999 the Royal National Lifeboat Institution celebrated 175 years of saving life at sea. Today there are 227 lifeboat stations throughout the United Kingdom and the Republic of Ireland, all of which, with the exception of one, are manned by volunteers and financed solely by voluntary donation and legacies. But where and when did it all start?

It was in 1789 that a major sea tragedy occurred when, in a storm, the collier *Adventure* ran aground on the River Tyne; to attempt a rescue mission in such weather conditions would have meant almost certain death for the rescuers. Several thousand onlookers are reported to have watched in horror, as all the crew of the stricken vessel drowned. The tragedy so struck the members of a Gentlemen's Club in South Shields, that they sponsored a competition to provide a design for a lifeboat, offering a reward of two guineas. William Wouldhave, the Parish Clerk of South Shields, drew up the winning design. The design, modified by the judges, was given to Henry Greathead and from this he constructed the first purpose-built lifeboat, *The Original*. The boat was launched on Saturday 30 January 1790, was 30-feet in length and was propelled by 12 oars. Her high-rise design, at the bow and stern, provided cases that contained 7 cwt of cork buoyancy, the hull was lined with cork and a cork rail provided additional buoyancy. *The Original* served for 40 years on the River Tyne, whilst 30 other vessels, built to the same specifications, were placed throughout Britain. These lifeboats were operated independently but Colonel Sir William Hillary, a member of the Douglas lifeboat crew, Isle of Man, readily identified the need for a coordinated approach to saving life at sea, and the necessity of a national regulating body.

In 1823 Sir William Hillary published his paper 'An Appeal to the British Nation on the Humanity and Policy of Forming a National Institution for the Preservation of Lives and Property from Shipwreck', in which he highlighted the shortfalls, which he perceived, in the existing provision of lifeboat cover and outlined his recommendations for a national lifeboat service. His paper found wide spread support and sympathy for victims of shipwreck. On 4 March 1824, at a meeting in the City of London Tavern, the National Institution for the Preservation of Life from Shipwreck (NIPLS) was formed. King George IV became Patron of the Institution, the Prime Minister, Lord Liverpool, the President and Thomas Wilson MP, the Secretary. Hillary's Institution sought to alleviate the nation's loss and misery caused by shipwreck. He became the holder of no less than three RNLI Gold Medals, the lifeboat man's VC, a feat equalled only by the legendary Henry Blogg, GC, BEM, a former crew member and Coxswain of the Cromer lifeboat. Not surprisingly, Hillary's family motto was 'With courage, nothing is impossible'.

Initially the Institution received annual Government funding but this soon fell by the wayside. As with the RNLI of today, the Institution became reliant upon legacies and public donations, which in turn were most prevalent in the wake of a maritime disaster. One such incident, which served to raise public awareness, occurred on 7 September 1838 when in a storm the SS *Forfarshire*, on passage from Hull to Dundee, struck rocks in the Farne Islands. The vessel carried about 60 persons; nine of the crew and one passenger escaped in the only lifeboat but many of the passengers, who had been in their cabins below deck, drowned. The storm continued in its ferocity and as the day dawned,

*Former members of the crew.* Left to right: *Peter Easton, Harold Coyde, Dick Harris, Abe Bartlett, Harry Thomas, George Dyer, Dudley Stone.* KEN THOMAS

*Retired gentlemen of the Torbay lifeboat.* Left to right: *motor mechanic D. Harris, Frederick Sanders, H. Thomas, Abraham Bartlett, Harold Coyde, Dudley Stone.* RNLI

nine remaining survivors, five crew and four passengers, were spotted clinging to rocks, by the lighthouse-keeper of the Longstone lighthouse and his daughter. Battling against the storm and treacherous seas, the young girl and her father rowed out to sea to save the lives of the nine survivors. The girl became a national heroine – her name was Grace Darling. Tragically, she died, of consumption, only three years after this heroic rescue. A memorial in St Cuthbert's Chapel, on the Farne Islands, includes the inscription to her:

*Pious and pure,*
*modest and yet so brave,*
*though young so wise,*
*though meek so resolute.*

The plight of the National Institution for the Preservation of Life from Shipwreck was again highlighted in 1849 when, in the December gales, the River Tyne lifeboat *Providence* was lost, together with a number of her crew. The lifeboat had been launched to go to the assistance of the *Betsey*, which had run aground on the Herd Sands, at the mouth of the Tyne. The crew of the *Providence* had skilfully laid the lifeboat alongside the *Betsey* when a freak wave ran between the two vessels and overturned the lifeboat. One member of the lifeboat crew was pulled to safety by the crew of the *Betsey* whilst a further three crew members could be seen clinging to the upturned hull of the lifeboat. The crowds ashore immediately assisted in launching the *Tyne*, and she successfully landed the crew of the *Betsey* and the four lifeboat men, and then assisted her sister boat, the *Northumberland*, in searching for the *Providence* and her crew. The *Providence* was located and towed into shallow waters where the crowd waded in, thigh deep, to right her; she was completely empty; 20 of her crew of 24 had been lost.

In 1851, the Fourth Duke of Northumberland, then First Lord of the Admiralty, became President of the Institution. He identified the pressing need for advancement and instigated a national competition to elicit a new design of lifeboat. From the 280 designs submitted, that of James Beeching, a boat builder of Great Yarmouth, scoring 84 points, was judged to be the winning design. The boat was designed with a low waist and high cases at the bow and stern, which provided stability and this, coupled with the fact that it was also fast-draining, gave it self-righting capabilities in the case of capsize. Beeching built several lifeboats to this design before it was subsequently improved upon and modified by James Peake, Master Shipwright of the Royal Naval Dockyard, Woolwich. The self-righting boat, modified to Peake's design, became

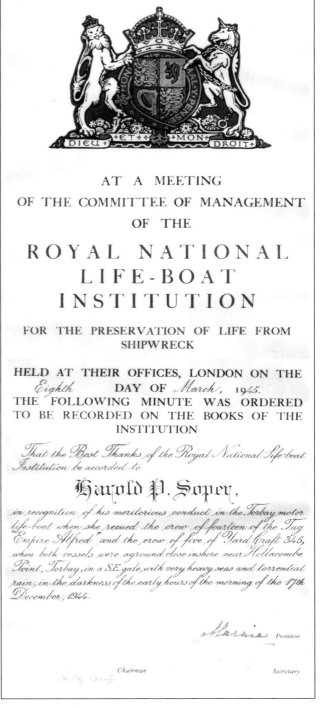

*RNLI's 'Certificate of Thanks' awarded to Harold Soper for service to the* Empire Alfred *and Yard Craft 345, 17 December 1944.*

the accepted standard for lifeboats throughout Britain.

The Institution's name had become shortened to the National Shipwreck Institution and in 1854 was changed to the Royal National Lifeboat Institution (RNLI).

When the NIPLS was originally founded in 1824, there were no lifeboats on the coast of Devon, those at Exmouth and Plymouth having

*Lifeboat men Toni Knights* (right) *and John Heale* (centre) *with rescued deer, 20 April 1995.* A. CURNOW

Below: *The Commemorative Boards at the Torbay Lifeboat Station are shown off by the artist Harry Diggins to Rear Admiral Graham, Director, RNLI.* A. CURNOW

*Brian Caunter winches a 'casualty' from the sea during a routine exercise.*

already fallen into disuse. With financial support from local businessmen and members of the gentry, the first true lifeboat on the Devon coast was founded at Bideford, North Devon, in October 1854. As public interest in the Lifeboat Service grew, a station was established at Ilfracombe; the Institution took over responsibility for the station at Appledore and increased funding allowed the establishment of further stations at Lynmouth and Clovelly.

Due to its geographical location and surrounding topography, the waters of Torbay have always provided a safe anchorage and haven for shipping; it therefore seems an enigma that Teignmouth was chosen as a location for a lifeboat station before Torbay. In 1843 work commenced, at Brixham, on the construction of a protective harbour breakwater, which now extends 3,000 feet in length. By 1866 the construction of only one-third of that length had been achieved. Construction was completed in 1916.

Records of the mid 1850s provide the first reference to a lifeboat at Torquay, but somewhat surprisingly, the boat was not providing active service. The *Exeter Flying Post* of 29 November 1855, reported on the 'celebrity status of the

Torquay lifeboats'. A local craftsman, Mr Amory Hawkesworth of Chestnut Cottage, Torquay, had patented a design for a lifeboat and been successful in selling a boat to the seamen of Hartlepool. It was reported that the sailors were so pleased with her qualities that further boats based on the same principle, but with differing lines, were likely to be built and furnished to other ports. The sailors of Sunderland engaged Hawkesworth to build for them a boat 40 feet in length and she was launched at Sunderland on Monday 3 December 1855. It was recorded at the time that:

*Captain Herd, commander of the coastguard, is so pleased, with her model and the principle of construction, that he has expressed a wish to be in her on her trial trip. She is built of the very best materials and will cost about £100 before she is thoroughly supplied with suitable gear. At Seaham the sailors are making subscriptions to get a boat of the same description.*

On Wednesday 4 February 1857 the lifeboat *Friend to all Nations*, which Amory Hawkesworth had built to his patented 'Torquay model' was launched at Torquay. The vessel was placed under the harbour crane for the purpose of testing her self-righting properties. It was reported that:

*The parbuckle and other necessaries being adjusted, she was with great difficulty hove bottom up; and, without any perceptible hesitation, she rolled over, righted, and freed herself entirely from water in about five seconds. The trial, which was regarded merely as preliminary to a more public exhibition of the boat's properties, was considered in every respect highly satisfactory, and its successful result was hailed with loud cheers from those who happened to be present on the pier.*

It was as the result of the Great Storm of the night of Wednesday 10 January 1866, when the barometer fell to 20 inches, and east-nor-easterly winds reaching hurricane force, that the need for a lifeboat in Torbay was fully realised. That night 94 vessels were at anchor in Torbay, and it is recorded that 'not less than 60 vessels were wrecked, and nearly 100 lives were lost.' Newspapers of the time report that those in distress had to await the arrival of the Teignmouth lifeboat for rescue. On the morning of Thursday 11 January, horse and carriage drew the Teignmouth lifeboat, the *China*, from Teignmouth to Torquay.

Paradoxically, it was in Exeter that a group of people who, hearing of the tragedy, formed a Lifeboat Fund and set about raising money. It is reported that the sum of £600 was raised, which was donated to the Institution for a Torbay lifeboat. It had been fully expected that the lifeboat station would be located at Torquay but, acting upon advice, the authorities established the lifeboat house at Brixham.

On 29 May 1866, the Secretary of the Royal National Lifeboat Institution wrote the following letter to the Reverend R. Fenwick Elrington:

> 14 John Street,
> Adelphi
> London, W.C.
>
> Dear Sir
> Will you kindly express the best thanks of this Committee to Mr Appleton for so kindly promising to superintend the erection of the Brixham new lifeboat-house.
>
> I remain
> Yours faithfully
> R. Lewis
> Secy.

The Secretary followed this correspondence with another letter, the following day:

> 30th May 1866
>
> My dear Sir,
> I have duly received your letter & the Estimates named in the margin for building the Brixham new Lifeboat House.
>
> I beg to acquaint you that this Committee have decided on accepting the lowest tender, & you will therefore have the goodness to order Searle to proceed with the house immediately after he has signed the accompanying form of Agreement which you will please then to return to me.
>
> At this period of the year our Lifeboat houses are usually completed in about eight weeks time & anyhow I think the Builder might be bound down to complete the house ready for the reception of the boat by the 8th August, which will give him ten clear weeks to do it in.
>
> I think you can safely give these directions to go on with the house for I feel sure that the Admiralty will grant this Institution the site of ground on which it is to be built
>
> I remain
> Yours very truly
> R. Lewis
> Secy.

The contract to build the lifeboat house was accepted by John Searle. He undertook to the specification:

*... for the sum of One Hundred & seventy five pounds, ten shillings (£175.10s.0d.) and to complete the work on or before the Twenty-Eighth day of August next or forfeit the sum of One pound (£1) per day for every day after such date as the works remain unfinished.*

The contract was witnessed by Edward Appleton and dated 27 July 1866. The first Royal National Lifeboat Institution lifeboat to be stationed at Brixham was appropriately named *City of Exeter*.

*The* Edward Bridges. *Bow to stern:* Steve Birchenall, P. Williams, ?, Cyril Yeoman, ?, ?, ?, ?, ?, Ernie Fradd, Brian Caunter. *Coxswain Arthur Curnow at helm.* A. CURNOW

*The launching of a new boarding boat by Coxswain Dudley Stone. Left to right: ?, Dave Taylor (boat builder), Dud Stone, Brian Caunter, Arthur Curnow, Michael Bower, Mike Mills, Ernie Fradd, Steve Bower, Derek Rundle, Derek Winning, ?, Dave Bubeer.* RNLI

# 3

# THOSE WHO FOLLOWED IN HER WAKE

## *1885–2001*

The Bolton Cross lifeboat house was replaced in 1872 at a cost of £396. The new boat-house was built immediately adjacent to the harbour and, being purpose built, provided a launching slipway direct into the harbour. Until this time, previous lifeboats had been kept on launch carriages. In 1873 the former lifeboat house was sold, for £50, to the ground landlords who intended to give the property to the Council for use as a fire station.

In the wake of the *City of Exeter* came the *Brian Bates*, which was on station from 1885–94. She was propelled by pulling/sailing; likewise were the two subsequent boats, the *Betsey Newbon* (1894–96) and a second lifeboat, also named the *Betsey Newbon* (1896–1922).

Following the establishment of the Brixham station, the RNLI was petitioned to provide a second lifeboat at Torquay. The petition was successful and on Christmas Day, 25 December 1875, Lord Haldon leased land at Beacon Cove 'for the building of a lifeboat house'. The lease was for a period of 30 years.

On 24 May 1876 the *Mary Brundret* was stationed at the new lifeboat house at the Ladies Bathing Cove, Torquay. The boat-house was constructed at a cost of £336. The *James and Eliza Woodall*, which in turn was succeeded, in 1902, by the *Wighton*, replaced her in November 1889. The *Wighton* was the third and last lifeboat to be stationed at Torquay.

It is recorded that in 1883 the Torquay Lifeboat Station 'was threatened by the encroachment of the sea' but remained operational until its closure on 31 March 1923. The demise of the Torquay Lifeboat Station was primarily due to the arrival, at Brixham in 1922, of the *Alfred and Clara Heath*, a motor-powered boat that could offer a greater and faster service than that provided by the Torquay boat. The boat-house was converted into a beach café and was ultimately demolished in September 1975.

In 1917, the Brixham Lifeboat Station was renamed the 'Brixham and Paignton Lifeboat Station' and since 1922 the lifeboats of Brixham have been known as the Torbay lifeboats.

The *Alfred and Clara Heath* remained in service for eight years until the *George Shee* succeeded her in 1930, to serve at Brixham for 28 years until 1958, the longest period for any Torbay lifeboat. She recorded a total of 245 launches.

In 1958 the *Princess Alexandra of Kent* succeeded the *George Shee* and remained in service until 1975. Whilst both boats were of the 'Barnett Class', each having a top speed of nine knots, the *Princess Alexandra of Kent* was powered by diesel engines as opposed to the petrol engines of her predecessor.

Perhaps the most well known of the Torbay lifeboats was *54-03 Edward Bridges*, (Civil Service and Post Office No. 37), Operational Number 1037, which was on station from 1975–95. She was a 54ft, high-speed, self-righting, offshore craft and the third 'Arun Class' lifeboat to be taken into service by the RNLI. Her wooden hull and two 460hp Caterpillar D343 diesel engines heralded the birth of the modern high-powered offshore lifeboat. From the 'Arun Class' stemmed the development of the Severn, Trent, Tyne and Mersey Classes, each with their own progressive development in navigation and rescue equipment.

The *52-19 Marie Winstone*, Operational Number 1076, succeeded the *Edward Bridges*. She was initially deployed as a relief lifeboat, prior to her confirmation as the Torbay lifeboat. Likewise she was an Arun Class vessel, but was built with a GRP hull. The proud service history

*The Arun Class lifeboat 54-03 Edward Bridges, Civil Service No.37 (1975–95).*
TORQUAY MUSEUM

of the Arun Class lifeboats closed its chapter at the Torbay Lifeboat Station, at 17.30 hours on Wednesday 31 October 2001, when the newest lifeboat in the RNLI fleet, the Severn Class *17-28 Alec and Christina Dykes*, replaced the *Marie Winstone*. The Severn Class lifeboat is a far cry from the *City of Exeter*. Today's modern boat is under the command of a Coxswain, assisted by the 2nd Coxswain/Station Mechanic. In all, the boat has a crew of six when she goes to sea.

There are 20 other crew members who come from all walks of life. The Station Mechanic is the only member of the team who receives a salary from the RNLI; all other members of the crew are purely and simply brave, dedicated volunteers, committed to the preservation of life and the provision of assistance to those in distress. Each member of the crew is trained on a regular basis, to ensure the maintenance of the highest standards in rescue techniques, first aid and the full workings and capabilities of the modern electronics fitted to the lifeboat (ALB)

and the inshore lifeboat (ILB). Training is carried out both locally and at the Training Centre, Royal National Lifeboat Institution Headquarters, in Poole, Dorset.

Now thoroughly modernised and refurbished, today's boat-house continues to occupy the site first occupied in 1872. Since 1964 the boat-house has provided accommodation and launch facilities for the ILB.

The RNLI has divided the country's lifeboat stations into six operational divisions. The Torbay Lifeboat Station is the third busiest in the British Isles, responding to in excess of 100 call-outs annually. The Launching Authority is the Station Honorary Secretary. It is either the Honorary Secretary, or one of the four Deputy Launch Authorities, who authorises the launch of the lifeboat, when a request is received from HM Coastguard, for assistance. The lifeboat is usually launched within ten minutes of the launch procedure being implemented.

In order to acknowledge bravery within the

*Relief Arun Class lifeboat 52-17 Sir Max Aitkin entering Paignton Harbour.* COURTESY TORBAY NEWS AGENCY

Above: *The* Marie Winstone *(1995–2001) at her mooring in front of Torbay lifeboat house, 23 June 1996.* COURTESY *HERALD EXPRESS*

Below: *Relief lifeboat 52-25 A.J.R. & L.G. Uridge.* A. CURNOW

Below: *The* George Shee *crossing Brixham Harbour. Note The Northcliffe Hotel on skyline.* MURIEL FRY

Lifeboat Service, the Royal National Lifeboat Institution awards Gallantry Medals and Citations. Gallantry Medals awarded to the crewmen of the Torbay lifeboats include one Albert Medal, one Gold Medal, six Silver Medals and 19 Bronze Medals, together with numerous Letters of Thanks and Citations on Vellum.

Since first entering service, the Brixham (Torbay) all-weather lifeboats have collectively recorded 1,029 launches and have saved 663 lives. During their period of service the Torquay lifeboats recorded 25 launches and saved 19 lives.

Throughout the 135 years during which the Royal National Lifeboat Institution has proudly provided a service from Brixham, there have been many occasions when vessels have sought the shelter of Torbay and adjacent waters. On many occasions hurricane-force winds, with velocities in excess of 63 knots (118km/h), accompanied by mountainous waves, have pounded our shores. At such times, pleasure craft are confined to harbours, fishing fleets head for the sanctuary of the ports, whilst larger vessels seek the lee of the bay. In conditions such as these quite often the only crew putting to sea, from Brixham, and heading deliberately into the teeth of the storm, unselfishly and valiantly, is that of the Torbay lifeboat.

To quote the poet Milton, 'They also serve who only stand and wait.' What words can pay a higher tribute to the partners and families of the RNLI crews who, not knowing what dangers their loved-ones face, patiently and unassumingly await the return to port of the Torbay lifeboat?

Although with the advent of modern technology, whereby the Coxswain and crew are summoned to launch by 'bleepers', the heart of every fisherman and sailor, and indeed the heart of the partner of every fisherman and sailor, must surely miss a beat when the sound of the maroons announce to the townsfolk of Brixham that their lifeboat crew are once again, for the benefit of others, volunteering to place their own lives at the mercy of the sea. This they constantly do, with pride and dedication.

*Line drawing depicting the lifeboat* City of Exeter *undertaking capsize drill, on the River Exe, at Exeter, during the inauguration ceremony, 1 October 1866.*
*ILLUSTRATED LONDON NEWS*

*A horse-drawn launch of the* City of Exeter.

# 4

# THE CITY OF EXETER

## 3 OCTOBER 1866–11 MAY 1885

**Type:** *Self Righting*    **Propulsion:** *Pulling*    **Oars:** *10*    **Crew:** *12*

**Length:** *34' 0"*    **Beam:** *8' 4"*    **Displacement:** *3T 12Cwt*

**Carriage Drawn:** *6–8 horses*    **Builder:** *Woolfe, Shadwell*

**Launches:** *5*    **Lives Saved:** *1*

**Coxswain:** *Charles Jackson*
*(former Chief Boatman to the Brixham Coastguard)*

Following the Great Storm of January 1866, many were the calls for a lifeboat to be stationed on the waters of Torbay. A General Meeting of the Shipwreck Relief Committee was held at the rooms of the Brixham Literary Institute, on Wednesday 24 January 1866; the Royal National Lifeboat Institution being represented by Captain Ward. There took place a far-ranging debate that considered the whole question of the provision of a lifeboat at Brixham. The Committee unanimously agreed to cooperate with the RNLI to effect the placement of a boat and boat-house. Following the meeting, Captain Ward accompanied by Dr Brooking, of the Local Committee, visited various locations in order to make recommendations in respect of a suitable site for the building.

The plea found support from all quarters, but primarily it was the people of Exeter who heeded the call. There was set up, within Exeter, a Lifeboat Fund, which in a matter of months, by way of fund-raising and donation, generated the sum of £600 (the equivalent of some £35,000 by today's standards).

For some time excitement and anticipation had mounted within the city, especially when, on Wednesday 26 September 1866 *Trewman's Exeter Flying Post* carried notification that the lifeboat, purchased from the funds raised, would be on view at Higher Barracks on Friday 28 September. The London and South Western Railway and the South Devon Railway Companies conveyed the boat to Exeter, free of charge. It was also declared that on Monday 1 October 1866 the lifeboat would be taken 'on a splendid parade' through the streets of Exeter and, at a service of dedication and naming, the Mayoress of Exeter, Mrs Head, would name the lifeboat *City of Exeter*. On that celebratory day the parade comprised: the band of the Royal First Devon Yeomanry Cavalry, the West of England Fire Brigade (No.1), mace bearers and a sword bearer, the Mayor and Aldermen in carriages, the Mayoress and ladies in carriages, the Town Council, the lifeboat and Crew, drawn by eight horses, the Lifeboat Committee in carriages, the Demonstration Committee in carriages, members of Exeter Amateur Rowing Club, the band of the Exmouth Artillery, Friends of the Cause, Norwich Union Fire Brigade, Sun Fire Insurance Fire Brigade, Royal Insurance Fire Brigade, members of the Ancient Order of Foresters, members of the Order of Odd Fellows, West of England Insurance Fire Brigade (No.2), the band of the Exeter Rifles and the Temperance Society Band.

*Trewmans Exeter Flying Post*, of 3 October 1866, reported on the event as follows:

### "CITY OF EXETER" LIFE BOAT

*Monday was kept as a gala day in Exeter. In the afternoon several of the large industrial establishments and other houses of business in the city were closed; and a procession numbering six or seven thousand persons, comprising the Right Worshipful the Mayor and Corporation, the Fire Engines of the principal Exeter offices, the bands of the Exeter and*

Exmouth Rifles and First Devon Yeomanry, representatives of the Foresters' and Odd Fellows, and the Temperance Society, was formed in the Queen street road, at two o'clock to escort the Lifeboat through the city to Gabriel's timber-yard, Shilhay. The boat was manned by Exmouth sailors, a crew representing the hardiest and most skilful coasters in England, and was drawn on its carriage by a magnificent team of eight horses. She is a beautifully built craft thirty-four feet in length, eight feet four inches wide, rows ten oars, is double banked, and weighs about fifty-six cwt. She is provided with a transporting and launching carriage, from which she is launched with crew, oars in hand, thus enabling the men to gain headway before the breakers have time to beat the boat broadside on the beach or rocks, and the hauling up of the boat is accomplished with equal facility. She is to be stationed at Brixham where a new and commodious life boat house has been built from the design of the architect to the Royal National Life Boat Society. The procession did not arrive in the yard till about three o'clock. This was thronged by thousands of visitors. The opposite bank of the river as far as the eye could reach in either direction was also swarming with spectators; and the river itself was covered with every variety of craft, from the eight-oared gig and Mr Brand's miniature steamer, to skiffs and punts. There was probably 10,000 to 12,000 persons present. The boat was christened by the Mayoress, and as it glided into the Exe fully manned and with colours flying the assembled thousands gave a succession of cheers which rent the air, the bands striking up 'Rule Britannia'. Under Captain Ward's orders the crew took a turn up and down the river, and some experiments afterwards followed to test the sea-going qualities of the boat in rough weather. They were of course perfectly successful and a little tedious. It had been announced by the Demonstration Committee that the boat was to be capsized with her crew in the river, but if this experiment was even possible it was very sensibly abandoned by Captain Ward, and the committee found no little difficulty in turning her over without the crew. The duty of formally presenting the boat to the National Society was very appropriately performed by the Right Worshipful the Mayor who, in the course of an interesting speech, paid a well deserved compliment to Mr. Brandreth Gibbs, the local secretary of the Life Boat Society, and to the proprietors of the Devon Weekly Times for the energy with which they had set themselves to work to collect subscriptions for the cost of the boat. Mr. Lewis accepted the boat as a noble and worthy contribution by the city of Exeter to the Royal National Lifeboat Institution; and at the close of his speech a succession of cheers was given for the boat, for the Mayor and Mayoress, and for the Institution. In the evening about thirty gentlemen dined together at the Clarence under the presidency of the Mayor. The dinner was served in Mr. Birkett's best style. In addition to the usual loyal and patriotic toasts, the Mayor proposed "Success to the City of Exeter Life Boat," which Mr. Tozer acknowledged on behalf of the committee. The toast to the National Lifeboat Institution was proposed by the Rev. Elrington, and responded to by Mr. Lewis. The health of the Mayor, proposed by Mr. Gard, was drunk with honours. It was followed by the health of the Mayoress, and several other personal and complimentary toasts. The subscriptions for the boat amounted to £600. The donor of £300, we believe, was Mr. J.C. Bowring.

The following letter accompanied the report:

### THE LIFE BOAT

Sir, - The affair of the Life Boat has passed off with éclat. Life Boats are very serviceable, and they ought to be stationed wherever they are wanted, although I question the policy of giving to people who can afford to buy. There is something amusing in the idea of the traders of Exeter presenting a Life Boat to the wealthy district of Torbay. But let that pass. When another liberal fit comes on, I hope the citizens will not forget the volunteers.

OBSERVER

Amongst the flags and bunting that adorned the streets of Exeter, was a banner, strung between the premises of Mr Thomas, Hatter, and the Higher Market, the wording on which read:

God speed the boat, our prayer shall ever be,
May she glide swiftly o'er the angry sea,
And bless the men who risk their lives to save
A fellow mortal from an ocean grave.

At this time in the Institution's history, the RNLI was responsible for 172 lifeboats, which during the first nine months of 1866 had reportedly saved 542 lives.

Following this spectacular inauguration, the City of Exeter was taken back to Higher Barracks and, the next day, to Brixham. Upon her arrival, she was initially kept under a makeshift cover, pending the construction of a boat-house at Bolton Cross, on the site latterly occupied by the Conservative Club, backing on to an old Naval reservoir. The first boat-house was designed by H. Cooke Esq., Honorary Architect of the RNLI, and stood on a tidal creek, which extended from the harbour, past the boat-house to what is now the site of the Catholic Church, at the junction of New Road and Lower Manor Road. Pulled by horse drawn carriage, the lifeboat was taken down Fore Street and launched from the old slipway.

The *City of Exeter* entered service at Brixham on Wednesday 3 October 1866 and the following comment appearing in the *Torquay Directory and South Devon Journal* of Wednesday 10 October 1866:

*As the frightful and heart-rendering circumstances attending shipwreck are so well known to all, and are so calculated to excite the sympathy of every humane person but especially of those who reside on the coast, the local Committee feel that they might only weaken their appeal by adding any reasonings of their own on the subject. They are, however, happy to be in a position to state that, through the National Lifeboat Institution, the cost, amounting to £450, of the Torbay new lifeboat, its equipment and transporting-carriage will be presented to the locality by some of the residents of Devon, and of the city of Exeter, and that the life-boat will bear the name of that city, on condition that some assistance towards the cost, say £200, of a substantial and commodious boat-house, and subscriptions of about £25 a year to meet the purely local expenses of the coxswain's salaries, and of the crew for practising in the life-boat every quarter, be collected in our neighbourhood. The parent institution in London will pay all expenses of rewards to the crew... for saving or attempting to save life; also the cost of repairs, painting, replacement of gear etc. on the life-boat establishment.*

*The local Committee, having received the promise of such valuable assistance from the parent institution in London in aid of their own exertions, are anxious that the inhabitants of Torquay, Brixham, Paignton, and the neighbourhood should, so far as possible, have the satisfaction and the credit of helping to provide and maintain, by their own exertions and from their own resources, a life-boat for affording succour to those unfortunate persons who may be cast away on their shores. Without, however, the pecuniary assistance and the hearty general co-operation of the people of the neighbourhood, and the community at large, their objects*

*and those of the Society cannot be carried... The local Committee, therefore, earnestly appeal to the benevolent people of the neighbourhood generally, to aid them in this necessary and philanthropic undertaking...*

Both the *Torquay Directory and South Devon Journal*, and the *Exeter Flying Post*, of Wednesday 14 November 1866, briefly reported upon the official launching ceremony of the *City of Exeter*, at Brixham. The former publication reported thus:

*The Life-boat so generously presented by the citizens of Exeter, has been fairly launched on the waters of Torbay. The interesting ceremony took place last Saturday, at Brixham, and was the occasion of great festivities at that town. It was originally designed that the towns along the shores of Torbay should participate in the holiday, in order that a greater number of friends might thereby be induced to give their support towards the maintenance of the boat. Brixham, however, was inexorable in the determination to confine the demonstration to that town alone. As Torquay has thus been deprived of a holiday, the inhabitants must have their revenge on Brixham, and the best way to do that is to make up a liberal subscription list, in order to defray the annual expenses.*

The *Exeter Flying Post* carried this report:

BRIXHAM. – The City of Exeter *lifeboat was launched on Saturday at Brixham, when the town put itself into its merriest mood. Triumphal arches with suitable mottoes were erected... The procession, formed by Volunteers, Artillery, and Engineer Corps, with band, the Rational Sick and Burial Club, Members of the Temperance Society, the Local Board and Harbour Commissioners, the boat drawn by six horses, the Coastguard, the Mayor of Exeter and other guests, the Lifeboat Committee, the Naval Reserve Fishermen, boys of the Seamen's Orphan Home, the Ancient Order of Foresters, and the trades and other inhabitants, passed through the chief streets of the town; and the lifeboat was afterwards successfully launched, amidst the approving shouts of the spectators and firing of guns by the Engineers. The* City of Exeter *was then rowed out into Torbay, where her sails were set; and when she returned preparations were made to test her self-righting powers. The boat was brought up alongside a smack, and she was capsized with her coxswain on board. The boat was capsized the second time with the*

*City of Exeter, at Higher Barracks, Exeter, 28 September 1866, prior to her inaugural launch and dedication ceremony.*
COURTESY WESTCOUNTRY STUDIES LIBRARY, EXETER

*whole of the crew: and the result was highly satisfactory. The proceedings terminated with a dinner at the Bolton Hotel. R.T. Head, Esq., Mayor of Exeter, was amongst the company...*

The first recorded service launch for the *City of Exeter* took place on Friday 19 March 1869, as Brixham was pounded by severe north-westerly gale-force winds and heavy seas. At the height of the gale, the French smack *Jeane Veuve* was dashed onto rocks at the entrance to the harbour; her crew scrambled to the safety of the higher ground and were subsequently taken off by the Brixham vessel, the *Ida*. A distress signal was flown by the brigantine *Hitena*, of St Lucia, which, laden with salt, had sought the relatively sheltered waters of Brixham Harbour. Subjected to the full force of the gale, the *Hitena* dragged her anchor; one cable parted and she became in imminent danger of grounding against the Brixham breakwater. The lifeboat was launched by direction of Revd Elrington, the Honorary Secretary, with many 'landsmen' taking the place of the regular crew. The *City of Exeter* battled against the wind and sea until her oarsmen finally manoeuvred the lifeboat alongside the *Hitena*, which had cut loose sail and rigging in an attempt to reduce her speed of drift. One crew member of the brigantine had sustained a broken arm, and was immediately taken off by the lifeboat. The gale was of such ferocity that, within the immediate vicinity of Brixham Harbour, the *Freak*, a yacht owned by Mr Dewdney, sank whilst at her mooring and the *Saucy Lizzy* of Plymouth was smashed onto the rocks, as was the smack *Fisher*, owned by Mr Bartlett. The sloops *Vivid* and *Christian* collided and sank. Having landed the injured man from the *Hitena*, the *City of Exeter* immediately put to sea once more and stood by, for some two hours, until the storm abated and danger passed. An entry appeared in the *Dartmouth Chronicle*, which reported on the fate of the Brixham schooner *Courser*, which was on passage from Fecamp to Torbay. The newspaper reported that on Sunday 13 February 1870 the vessel was lost and her crew of five drowned, off Blackstone Point. Strangely the article contains a note of regret that there was no lifeboat or rocket apparatus at Torbay or Dartmouth!

The RNLI issued the Hon. Secretary of each lifeboat station with a lifeboat portfolio, containing gummed guards, into which were inserted correspondence and circulars. The RNLI circular, dated 29 May 1871, gave notice that:

*... between this date and the latter end of next Month, the usual biennial supply of Paint for the Lifeboat and Transporting Carriage will be forwarded to your Lifeboat Station.*

The circular also set out the price, and the amount of paint allowed for giving the boats one coat, inside and outside, together with the oars; that amount being:

| SIZE OF BOAT | ALLOWANCE |
|---|---|
| 40' plus | £2.10s.0d. |
| 34' to 39' | £2. 0s.0d. |
| 33' and 32' | £1.14s.0d. |
| 30' | £1.10s.0d. |
| 28' | £1. 6s.0d. |

*Carriage and roller-skids, belonging to boats 33 feet and upwards in length (one coat), 18s. Those for the smaller boats (one coat), 14s. The Coxswains are expected to clean and prepare the boats for Painting without extra payment.*

As a south-easterly gale swept across Torbay on Monday 30 September 1876, several ships were at anchor in the roads sheltering from the wind, which had previously blown from the south-west for several days. A little before 20.00 hours, two French vessels, a lugger *Marie Francoise* and the brigantine *Jules Bertrand*, were sighted off Elberry Cove; both vessels were in difficulty battling against the heavy rolling seas and, although under sail, were being blown towards the shore. The *City of Exeter* was launched, supported by the Torquay lifeboat, *Mary Brundret*, and the seine boat, *Mary Erskine*, which belonged to Mr C. Bartlett of Brixham.

The 48-ton lugger *Marie Francoise*, of Nantes, had left Swansea, bound for Nantes, on the 19 September but had been forced to shelter in Torbay. During the course of the gale, which had blown that day, all three of her anchors had parted. Master Tilley hoisted sail and let the vessel run before the wind until she came aground on Broadsands Beach. He and one crew member swam ashore whilst rocket apparatus took off the other two. The vessel settled down in the sand over the remains of a vessel, which, ten years previously, had sunk in the Great Storm. Efforts were made to lighten the lugger but on Sunday morning the *Marie Francoise* broke up. The 150-ton brigantine, *Jules Bertrand* of Dunkirk, in ballast, under Master Merlan, was bound from Dunkirk to Caspa Bianca when she was forced to seek the shelter of Torbay. Like the *Marie Francoise* she also parted her anchors; she was beached on Elberry Cove.

It being low tide, and the vessels being comparatively light, the waves drove both ships well up onto the beach; the water to seaward was so shallow that the lifeboat could not make an approach to offer service. The seine boat, however, had a shallower draft and made an approach to the *Jules Bertrand*. She was swamped twice and lost a member of crew overboard, who was rescued, and the *Mary Erskine* took off six of the crew. Rocket apparatus took off the remaining three crew members. Both lifeboats stood by throughout the incident, subsequently returning to their respective stations without having rendered service. The brigantine had suffered little damage and, weather conditions having moderated, on the next tide she was refloated and towed to Dartmouth.

Passing references have been found which tend to allude to a second lifeboat having been placed in Brixham, operating primarily within the confines of the harbour. At this time in the town's history, the Boys Home also doubled as a Seaman's Mission. The older boys at the home formed a crew, which took the Minister to the various visiting vessels at anchor in the harbour and Torbay. The original boat donated for this purpose was the *Sun Flower*. In 1877, the Committee of the Home was approached by Captain Hans Busk, the younger (1815–82), a Naval Officer and member of the Bar of the Middle Temple, who was among the first to advocate 'life-ship stations'. Captain Busk, who had been forced to abandon his Naval career, mastered the skills of Naval construction and design. He designed and built 'life-ships', at his own expense; one such boat he donated to the Brixham Boys' Home. Although constructed as a 'life-ship', the pulling boat, which was named the *Hans Busk*, was purely a replacement for the *Sun Flower* and was not placed at Brixham to perform lifeboat duties.

All day on Saturday 24 November 1877, the wind had been blowing at hurricane force, from the north-west, when suddenly it veered to the north-east, accompanied by a tremendous hail shower; the barometer fell at the rate of three- to four-tenths per hour. At about 19.00 hours the wind increased in strength and by 20.00 hours the 140-ton French brigantine, *Jean Celeste*, which had been sheltering in Torbay, began to drag her two anchors and full chain. By 20.30 hours she had struck Fishcombe Point and eventually broke up. Three crewmen scrambled ashore but the Master and his young son were drowned. The hooker *Polly* foundered in Brixham Harbour and a Portuguese schooner parted from her anchor and ran into the fishing smack *Promise*, carrying away her mast. The schooner then drifted ashore onto the rocks near Dewdney's Cove, at the entrance to the harbour, where she lost her bowsprit and damaged her stem. Four trawlers, *Dazzler*, *Presto*, *Nebraska* and *Lily of the Valley* were amongst other vessels damaged. As the gale subsided, the *City of Exeter* was launched at midnight, supported by the *Mary Brundret*. The two lifeboats went to the aid of the barque *Mary Chapman*, which had got into difficulty at 20.30 hours, in the extremely heavy sea, when her anchors failed to hold. She began to drift and came dangerously close to the Brixham breakwater. Unaided, the *Mary Chapman*, of St John's, New Brunswick, refusing assistance from the lifeboats, managed to regain the open sea. Both lifeboats returned to their respective stations without rendering service.

The only other launch on which the *City of Exeter* performed effective service was on Tuesday 18 January 1881. On this date Torbay was hit by yet another tremendous gale with winds of east-north-east F10 being reported. Many vessels, including those of the Brixham fishing fleet, had sought the protection of either Torquay or Brixham Harbours; there were 60 vessels in Brixham's Inner Harbour but it was those anchored in its extreme northern part that were most at risk. Many were driven from their moorings, resulting in a number of dangerous situations. Two vessels foundered; others were driven up the slips into the streets.

Early the next day the Brixham pilot gig attempted to return crew members to their boats which were at anchor, riding out the storm in Torbay. Heavy seas continued to run and the E-N-E winds continued to drive snow into blizzard conditions. The *City of Exeter* was launched to act as an escort to the gig, finally returning to harbour some five hours later. Allegations were made in the local press that, during the heaviest part of the gale, it was not the lifeboat that was forward in putting out to rescue the trawlers, but the gig from the fishing smack *Society*. It was further alleged that the lifeboat turned out only in the after part of the day. Mr Elrington, the Hon. Secretary of the Brixham Lifeboat Station, refuted the allegations in a written statement:

*I attended in the morning and unlocked the boat-house, and as soon as the gig passed us taking out the crews to the sloops in danger, we launched the lifeboat and attended the gig for the whole time, from soon after 11a.m. till 3.30. Lifeboats are not used for salvage work when the ordinary boats can go out. The lifeboat was manned by a crew of fishermen who would have gone wherever any boat could go.*

Towards evening the wind dropped off and it was possible to use the lifeboat to assist the damaged trawlers in the outer harbour. *Red Cross Knight*, *Emma*, *Lightning* and *Martha Ann* were lost. Among the damaged were *Primrose*, *Rose of Devon*, *Calypso*, *Vesper*, *Favourite*, *Sunbeam*, *Surprise*, *Polly*, *Sea Flower*, *Four Brothers*, *Comet*, *Souvenir*, *Whim*, *Kate*, *Bessie* and *Jane*.

In 1884 work was undertaken to lengthen and extend the existing lifeboat house in order to take a new lifeboat.

# 5

# THE *MARY BRUNDRET*
## *22 MAY 1876–15 NOVEMBER 1889*

*Type:* Self Righting   **Propulsion:** *Pulling*   **Oars:** *10*   **Crew:** *13*

**Length:** *33' 0"*   **Beam:** *8' 6"*

**Carriage Drawn**

**Launches:** *11*   **Lives Saved:** *19*

**Coxswain:** *William Henry Brown*

Following the provision of the *City of Exeter*, to Brixham in 1866, the RNLI received a constant barrage of pressure for the provision of a further lifeboat to be stationed in Torbay. The determination of the local townsfolk and local committee finally paid off when it was announced on Monday 31 January 1876 that, through the Manchester Branch of the RNLI, Mrs Mary Brundret of Withington, near Manchester, had donated £1,000 for the provision of a lifeboat and lifeboat station at Torquay. The new boat arrived in Torquay on Wednesday 24 May 1876 when, with much celebration, the new boat was paraded through the town from Torre Railway Station. The procession was headed by the band of HMS *Britannia*, who were followed by 'a large number of Coastguardsmen, the boys of the Torbay Seamen's Orphans Home, Brixham, and an Italian Band.' The lifeboat was carried on a carriage, which was drawn by six horses, belonging to the Torquay Brewing Company and Messrs Whiteway and Ball. The crew were seated in the lifeboat, fully equipped for service, and were followed by the crews of the Brixham and Teignmouth lifeboats, wearing their cork jackets. Then followed Mrs Brundret, the donor of the boat, and a friend, riding in a carriage. The procession further comprised members of the Odd Fellows, Foresters, National Sick and Burial Association, the Good Templars and Temperance Society and four brass bands. At the harbour slipway, the inauguration was conducted under the superintendence of the Chief Inspector of Lifeboats to the Institution.

Mrs Brundret formally presented the lifeboat to the RNLI. Admiral Ward then presented it to Mr L.B. Bowring, Chairman of the Local Board of Health, who accepted the boat on behalf of the town.

The Venerable Archdeacon Earle who, in a short address, exhorted the crew of the boat to be at all times ready to perform their duty, conducted a service of dedication. The assembled thousands sang the hymn 'Eternal Father Strong to Save' following which Mrs Mary Brundret formally named the lifeboat *Mary Brundret*, as the boat slid gracefully into the water. It was launched from a slipway on the Strand, to become the first RNLI lifeboat to be stationed at Torquay, and joined the Teignmouth lifeboat, the *China*, and the Brixham lifeboat, the *City of Exeter*, moored in the harbour. A transporting carriage had also been provided in order for the lifeboat to be taken to Paignton or wherever the launch place was most advantageous.

The *Mary Brundret*, which carried ten oars, double banked, had undergone harbour trials in the Regent's Canal Dock, Limehouse, before leaving for Torquay, on which occasion:

*... the usual qualities of stability, self-righting, self-ejecting of water, et cetera, were fully and satisfactorily tested. When the boat was capsized by means of a crane it immediately righted, and in twenty-five seconds it was free of the water shipped in the operation.*

On the day following the launch, the lifeboat was taken out by her crew under the command of

Admiral Ward, who drilled the men in the details of working the boat. It is reported that they handled her well, both with oars and under canvas, once or twice turning her completely around almost within her own length. After the practice was completed, Mrs Brundret, in company with Admiral Ward, Dr Gale, Mr Cove and some lady friends, 'went for a short pull in the boat'.

On Saturday 25 December 1875, Sir Lawrence Palk, Bart. MP, granted a 30-year lease for the provision of a lifeboat house at Beacon Cove. The lease was subsequently extended in 1906.

In all, the *Mary Brundret* was launched on three occasions during 1876 and 1877, but no effective rescues were made. Her first official launch was on Saturday 30 September 1876 in support of the Brixham lifeboat, *City of Exeter*. For several days the wind had been blowing from the southwest and several boats, being wind-bound,

*Torquay Lifeboat House (1876–1923) at the 'Ladies Bathing Cove' (Beacon Cove), Torquay.*
COURTESY *HERALD EXPRESS*

had sought shelter by anchoring in the roads. The wind gradually increased to gale force and, during the early hours of Saturday morning, backed to the south-east exposing the vessels to the full force of the gale. A little before 08.00 hours, two French vessels parted from their anchors and, being unable to beat out of the bay, their Masters hoisted sail in an attempt to seek out a suitable area where their respective vessels could be safely beached. Despite sail being hoisted, both vessels started a shoreward drift in the heavy seas. Their plight was noticed, and the *Mary Brundret* launched.

At the time of launch it was dead low water and great difficulty was experienced in getting the launch carriage into water sufficiently deep to float the lifeboat. The crew had boarded the lifeboat when a member of the Coastguard, who was assisting with the launch, inadvertently released a slip rope. With heavy surf breaking on the beach, the bow of the lifeboat was forced by the breakers towards the Bath Saloon, whilst the stern grounded. The lifeboat, now broadside on to the waves, was hit five or six times by the breakers causing her to drift towards the rocks below the Bath Saloon. Many of the bystanders waded into the sea to assist the lifeboat crew

who, to a man, had jumped into the sea in an attempt to push the bow of the *Mary Brundret* towards open water. After many minutes of strenuous activity, the lifeboat was manoeuvred into deep water, the crew then reboarded and went to the assistance of the French lugger *Marie Francoise* and the brigantine *Jules Bertrand*, which had run aground at Broadsands and Elberry Cove, Paignton, respectively. Upon their arrival at the scene, the crewmen found the *City of Exeter* in attendance. The *Mary Brundret* stood by throughout the incident.

The lifeboat was again launched on 24 November 1877. At 20.30 hours, in north-westerly gale-force winds, the barque *Mary Chapman* of St John's, New Brunswick, had dragged her anchors and was drifting towards the Brixham breakwater. The *City of Exeter* had been launched and, with several flare-ups having been sighted from Torquay, the *Mary Brundret* was also launched. Having battled across Torbay in gale conditions, upon her arrival at Brixham she found that her services were not required.

The lifeboat was launched, in her own right, during the gale of Tuesday 18 January 1881. The *City of Exeter* had previously been launched in support of the pilot's gig at Brixham, when the *Mary Brundret* went to the assistance of the French trawler *Ernest Eugene* which was apparently in trouble off Torquay. For most of the previous night a gale had blown from the southeast, accompanied by a heavy fall of snow, which covered Torquay to a depth of several inches. The gale continued into the next day and a large number of French and English trawlers sought the relatively sheltered waters of Torbay. Between 09.00 and 10.00 hours, Coastguards observed the French trawler, *Ernest Eugene*, endeavouring to make the Quay. All her aft sail had been carried away and it was seen that she would not 'stay' sufficiently to enter the harbour. Her crew struggled on bravely but it was evident that the vessel was drifting towards the pier where she would be dashed to pieces. At the request of the Coastguard, the *Mary Brundret* was launched but the crew of seven on board the *Ernest Eugene* declined assistance, declaring that they could save the vessel; the lifeboat returned to port. At 16.00 hours the lifeboat was called out to the *Ernest Eugene* for a second time, but again the crew refused to leave her. The lifeboat returned to port without rendering useful service. The fate of the *Ernest Eugene* is not known.

It was on Friday 14 October 1881 that the *Black Cat*, a fishing boat, working out of Paignton, was reported overdue in a north-westerly gale, which was producing a heavy sea and swell off Paignton. The fishing boat was spotted apparently entangled in her own nets. It took the *Mary Brundret* approximately 30 minutes to reach the stricken vessel where the crew of two were found to be suffering complete exhaustion. The men had remained in the same position for some 17 hours, knowing that if they had released their nets, the *Black Cat* was in imminent danger of being swept out to sea. The nets were made fast to a buoy and the *Black Cat* was cut free and taken in tow to Brixham.

Having landed the crew of the *Black Cat*, the crew of the *Mary Brundret* had to return to Torquay, pulling in to the direct force of the gale. They had reached mid-bay when the lifeboat was caught in a heavy squall and was hit by an exceptionally large wave, causing her to capsize. The *Mary Brundret* self-righted herself within seconds without injury or loss of life to her crew.

The *Mary Brundret's* finest hour came with the rescue of the Liverpool-registered barque *Eden*, on Sunday 5 November 1892. The vessel, owned by Hope Brothers of Liverpool, was under the command of Captain Macauley and carried a crew of 17. She was on passage from Liverpool to Valparaiso with a cargo of coal when, off Cape Finisterre, she sprang a leak. Part of her cargo and stores were jettisoned but despite the pumps being constantly in use, the vessel continued to take in water. Captain Macauley attempted to make for the Spanish port of Corunna but heavy seas, adverse wind and the state of the vessel prevented him from so doing. As the wind increased to near hurricane force the ship laboured heavily and settled lower in the water. More cargo was jettisoned but to no avail. At this point the Captain decided to run before the wind in an attempt to make the English Channel. The Lizard lights were sighted and the *Eden* was within three miles of the St Anthony light when she ran into a dense fog. Captain Macauley steered a course for Plymouth but, being unable to make port, proceeded on up the Channel. Many times during this passage the gunwales of the *Eden* were under water. Captain Macauley rounded Start Point at 04.00 hours but, with the wind coming from the south-west, was unable to make Dartmouth and bore away for Torbay.

On rounding Berry Head the *Eden* was met by the outward-bound Newcastle steamship, *Tharsis*. On seeing the plight of the barque, the Master of the steamship offered to tow her in to Torbay for a fee of £15. The offer was accepted but after five hours a towline was not forthcoming. There was a meeting on board the *Tharsis*, and a deal was made whereby she would tow the *Eden* into Dartmouth, for a fee of £65, exclusive of pilotage. When a hawser was secured between the ships, a further five hours passed without the vessels moving. The *Tharsis* then 'up anchored' and the hawser parted. The *Tharsis* then abandoned the *Eden*. Captain Macauley had requested that the *Tharsis* should leave one of her ship's boats, in case of emergency, but the request was refused.

Between 21.00 and 22.00 hours the Torquay Coastguard observed distress signals coming from the *Eden*. Volunteers were quickly mustered and the *Mary Brundret* was launched into heavy seas and a west-north-westerly gale. She reached the *Eden* just before midnight, some 11 miles offshore. Coxswain Brown put his men aboard the *Eden* to assist the efforts of the ship's crew, who were nearing exhaustion. After two hours of extremely hard work, during which they had manned the pumps and set sails, the *Eden* was got under weigh and headed for Dartmouth.

The crew of the *Mary Brundret* sailed the *Eden* into Dartmouth Harbour at 15.30 hours, towing two of their colleagues in the lifeboat. Having moored the *Eden*, and landed her crew of 17, the *Mary Brundret* returned to Torquay, arriving at 18.30 hours. She had been at sea for 20 hours.

Within an hour of the exhausted lifeboat men returning to their homes, the *Mary Brundret* was called out again, following a report that the Coastguard had spotted distress signals a considerable distance off Daddy Hole. Another crew manned the lifeboat, their search proved fruitless and she returned to Torquay at 21.30 hours.

The *Mary Brundret* was launched to assist the Norwegian barque *Vesta*, during a south-easterly gale, on Friday 2 January 1885. On this occasion no useful service was performed.

It should be noted that, at the time of the inauguration of the *Mary Brundret*, the Royal National Lifeboat Institution had 254 lifeboats under its management, 33 of which were stationed on the coasts of Devon and Cornwall, at Sidmouth, Exmouth, Teignmouth, Torquay, Brixham, Salcombe, Plymouth, Looe, Fowey, Mavagissey, Portloe, Falmouth, Portoustock, Cadgwith, Lizard, Mullion, Porthleven, Penzance, Sennen Cove, Scilly Isles, St Ives, Hayle, Newquay, Padstow, Port Isaac, Bude Haven, Clovelly, Appledore (two boats), Braunton, Morte Bay, Ilfracombe and Lynmouth.

# TORQUAY LIFEBOAT POEM
## By Henry Matthews, L.D.,
## DEDICATED TO MRS BRUNDRET, DONOR OF THE BOAT
## Set to music composed by Johnson Hicks

While visiting our far-famed town,
"LUCRETIUS"[1] did by chance walk down
Near the sea on a stormy day,
To view the beauties of the bay.

As he gazed on the scene so grand,
And watched the spray fly o'er the land,
As Rumour says, "Surprised was he
That here no Lifeboat could he see."

And while he thought the matter o'er,
The big waves rolled upon the shore.
He saw the dangers of the deep,
And wept for those compelled to weep!

The solemn past came o'er his mind,
With miles of wreck our coast was lined;
Of a noble fleet that at anchor lay,
Secure they thought in old Torbay.

That awful night was heard the cry
For help – alas! no help was nigh.
How sad no Lifeboat near to save
Our sailors from an ocean grave!

And shall this great neglect remain?
"Nay, nay," said he "a Boat I'll gain,
And place upon the Eastern shore
To rescue our poor Mariner!"

How strange it was, and yet 'twas true,
Of this design we nothing knew,
Until in all our great surprise
"LUCRETIUS" did the scheme devise.

At first our "Leaders" all withstood
"The Stranger's" plan so wise and good.
But soon he did their minds inform,
And hushed to calm their little storm.

In spite of men so blindly led,
Including "Admirals" alive and dead,
The truth advanced a rapid pace,
And left opponents in disgrace.

He laboured hard with might and main,
With brilliant pen and active brain;
His heart was in the noble cause,
Which brought him more than man's applause.

Our Volunteers, imposing host,
Equipped with steel, defend our coast;
They rally at the bugle's call,
For England's glory stand or fall.

And thousands more that we could note,
Who give their welcome to the Boat,
Embracing almost ever trade,
Including men of every grade.

Before this vast assembly grand,
I see a graceful LADY stand;
As she presents her noble Gift,
Our grateful hearts to Heaven we lift.

Amidst this mingled, gazing crowd,
Each auditor in silence bow'd,
She gives the Boat her worthy name –
"Mary Brundret", now known to fame!

May GOD the Donor bless, we pray,
And save from danger night and day;
When called to cross o'er Jordan's deep,
In that dread hour, oh, Jesu, keep!

With joy we launch the splendid Boat,
And pray that she may safely float,
When tossed upon the foaming wave,
As on she speeds the wreck to save!

Behold her brave and gallant crew
Have nobly pledged to die or do;
They haste away with bated breath,
To rescue from the jaws of death.

'Midst drenching rain or blinding snow,
Though hurricanes of wind may blow,
Though mountain waves the Boat may hide,
Undaunted, lo, they still abide!

Around him gathered an active Band,
Of those who dared for truth to stand,
Whose earnest toil was not in vain,
For soon they did the Lifeboat gain.

What makes our town appear so gay;
See flags and laurels line the way,
Triumphant arched reared so high,
While fiery meteors gild the sky.

Hark! bands are playing through the street,
All beat the tune with merry feet;
A grand procession march along,
Loudly singing the "Lifeboat Song!"

See cheerful Templars passing by,
Their golden banners proudly fly,
With emblems clothed, how grand the sight!
In scarlet, purple, blue, and white.

These are the noble men who swore
For life to wage a holy war,
Against our country's greatest foe,
Till they this kingdom overthrow!

We gladly hail the youthful Band,
The hope and promise of our land,
Trained to abjure a drink so vile,
Which doth the nations still beguile.

Our Sunday Schools, some thousands strong,
Of happy children swell the throng;
They learn to read the wondrous page,
Which blesses man of every age!

Freemasons, with their craft of old,
And secrets which they ne'er unfold;
Their precepts bright with lustre shine,
Based on the Book of Truth divine.

And Foresters, a stalwart race,
With brawny arm and manly face;
All clad in green, with axe and horn,
To cringe for alms such men would scorn!

Oddfellows, too, have mustered well,
See how our mighty ranks do swell!
Whose sick ones have their tender care,
Each other's burdens thus they bear!

While thus through raging surf they reach
The shattered bark upon the beach,
We on the shore, 'twixt hope and fear,
Their gallant acts will loudly cheer!

And as they bring their living freight
To land with safety and delight,
Our thankful songs on high we'll raise,
And spread abroad their well-earned praise.

Nor I forgot the worthy "Sec",[2]
Who shudders at the thought of wreck,
Or o'er look the genius, Gale,
Whose heart is touched at orphan's wail.

Or Barclay brave, and Ball sincere?
Moved by the mourning widow's tear;
With Cox, and Fradd,[3] and Godfrey, too,
Among the champions, ever true.

Hicklin and Kitson, too, I'm told,
Are zealous workers, waxing bold;
Sir Lawrence Palk, I hear with pride,
Has nobly come the Lifeboat side.

And others, too, I'd gladly rhyme,
But then, I cannot spare the time,
Though lest forgotten they should be,
Then names I give below you see.

Now as my modest verse I close,
I will three hearty cheers propose:
Because, "Lucretius," 'tis my due –
Thy name should be in marble, too!

## AUTHOR'S NOTES:

1.    The Gentleman who has adopted the nom-de-plume of "Lucretius", and to whose efforts we mainly owe our lifeboat, is Mr. JOSIAH HARRIS, of Tregiskey House, Cornwall, whose published Theological and other Works *breathe in every page the spirit of purity and philanthropy, and who is at this moment, as I learn by the newspapers, endeavouring to obtain a lifeboat for Dartmouth and Start Bay.*

2.    *Mr. W.H. Soper is the Hon. Sec., and displayed great energy in the cause.*

3.    *Mr Fradd, referred to in the verse, was the Editor of the* Torquay Times. *I am informed that the following gentlemen took a zealous part in the movement, viz., Messrs. Whiteway, J.H. Harris (son of "Lucretius"), King, Mounstephens, Rev. E.B. Davies, M.A., Mr Jefferies, Mr. G. Oake. They will readily forgive my inability to bring their names into my humble verse.*

*The Poet is of course obliged to write some of his verse in anticipation, but he has reason to believe that the main facts will be fully borne out, and that the Christening Ceremony will take place on 24th May.*

*Dated 15, Belgrave Terrace, Torquay, 18th April, 1876.*

## "MARY BRUNDRET"
## TORQUAY, 24 MAY 1876

*A ringing cheer for the Lifeboat,*
*And the Lady whose name she bears:*
*Hurrah! For the "Mary Brundret",*
*To-day be our benisons, prayers;*
*To-day may the choicest of blessings*
*O'erflow the humane donor's heart;*
*Hurrah! for the kind Mary Brundret,*
*She's acted the patriot's part.*

*A ringing cheer for the Lifeboat,*
*And cheers for her stalwart crew;*
*Success to the "Mary Brundret",*
*So buoyant, so taut, and so true.*
*Whenever the storm-fiends shall bluster,*
*And threaten the poor sailor's life;*
*Then prompt be her oarsmen to muster,*
*And God give success in the strife.*

*A ringing cheer for the Lifeboat,*
*A cheer as she kisses the wave;*
*Hurrah! For the "Mary Brundret"*
*How noble her "mission to save";*
*May Hope lift her prow o'er the billow*
*May Faith nerve her crew for the fray,*
*May Charity act as her helmsman,*
*And Mercy aye prosper her way.*

*A ringing cheer for the Lifeboat,*
*A cheer for each seafaring son;*
*Hurrah! for the grand "Institution",*
*Whose Lifeboats such wonders have done.*
*May none on our seaboard e'er perish*
*For the lack of the Lifeboats prompt aid:*
*Our nation that Institute cherish*
*By which such provision is made.*

*A ringing cheer for the Lifeboat,*
*Whenever she floats on the main;*
*Hurrah! for the "Mary Brundret",*
*We'll shout it again and again.*
*May God be her shield when in danger,*
*And prosper her path o'er the wave;*
*May many a perishing stranger*
*Be snatched by her crew from the grave.*

23, Brunswick Square, Torquay.
W.J. COOKSLEY

# 6

# THE *BRIAN BATES*
## 11 MAY 1885–NOVEMBER 1893

**Type:** *Self Righting*    **Propulsion:** *Pulling - Sailing*    **Oars:** *12*    **Crew:** *15*
**Length:** *37' 0"*    **Beam:** *8' 0"*    **Displacement:** *4T 2Cwt*
**Official number:** *43*    **Builder:** *Woolfe, Shadwell*
**Launches:** *3*    **Lives Saved:** *4*
**Coxswains:** *Charles Jackson (1885–93)*
*William J. Saunders (1893–94)*

The successor to the *City of Exeter* was the *Brian Bates*. Built by Messrs Woolfe and Son of Shadwell, London, she was three feet longer than her predecessor, although narrower in the beam. She was fitted with all the latest improvements, which included water ballast fittings, consisting of a series of tanks amidships:

*... one or more of which could be filled with water and emptied, at will, within one minute, the object being to increase the ballast and immersion of the boat and, consequently, her draught of water and stability without materially increasing her fixed weight for land carriage or her draught of water when launching or in very shallow water.*

As a result, the lifeboat had 'all the characteristics of the boats of the National Institution in the way of self-righting, self-ejecting water, etc.' The boat-house was lengthened to accommodate her increased length. Her added propulsion came from two additional oars and the provision of a sail.

The *Torquay Directory and South Devon Journal*, dated 20 May 1885, recorded:

*The National Lifeboat Institution has just sent a lifeboat to Brixham to take the place of the* City of Exeter, *which was brought down and launched on the 10th of November 1866, just 19 years ago. The new boat brought down last week possesses all modern appliances, and the cost has been defrayed by a legacy bequeathed by the late Mr. Brian Bates, of Buxton, and*

*bears his names. The old lifeboat, together with the small lifeboat,* Hans Busk, *belonging to the Orphan Home, were taken round to Dartmouth on Wednesday, and sent off by train to the depot of the Institution in London.*

The Brian Bates cost some £390.0s.0d. to build.

Following two lifeboat disasters, at St Annes and Southport, in December 1886, the RNLI appointed George Lennox Watson, a yacht designer of Glasgow, as the Consulting Naval Architect to the Institution. Watson was tasked with conducting an in-depth review of lifeboat designs. As the review progressed, the Chief Inspector of Lifeboats, Captain Hon. H.W. Chetwynd RN, and his assistants compiled a list of lifeboats, which required testing to a standard, far more exacting than that employed at the time. Details of some 290 lifeboats, which were allocated to operational stations, were listed together with between 20 and 30 relief boats. Upon being entered into the Official Register, each folio was allocated a unique number, this Official Number (ON) serving to identify an individual lifeboat throughout the vessel's service life.

The *Brian Bates* was the first Brixham lifeboat to be allocated an Official Number and was recorded as ON.43. In the eight years the *Brian Bates* was on station at Brixham she was launched for service on only three occasions, the first being on the evening of Sunday 6 December 1885, when she went to the assistance of the steamer *Bretton Hall*. The vessel, owned by the Bretton Hall Steamship Company of Liverpool, was 320 feet in length with a gross registered tonnage of 2,421 tonnes. She had left Antwerp on Monday 30 November in ballast, bound for Newport via the Isle of Wight.

The first indication that a ship was in distress came when signal rockets were sighted in the vicinity of Berry Head. The alarm was raised and the lifeboat set out, in fog, pulling against a south-easterly gale, to round Berry Head. On rounding the headland they found the Liverpool-registered steamer, *Bretton Hall*, aground by the bow, on Sharkham Point. A number of the crew members had managed to get ashore by placing a ladder across the rocks and using it as a makeshift bridge. Efforts made to refloat the *Bretton Hall* failed. Several small craft, however, put out from Brixham and, assisted by the lifeboat crew under the direction of the Ship's Master, were successful in saving valuable cargo from the steamer's hold. The *Brian Bates* stood by until morning but by this time the *Bretton Hall* had swung broadside on to the shore and been driven further onto the rocks of Sharkham.

It subsequently transpired that the Captain of the ship, T.H.S. Millard, was at the wheel when the steamer ran aground. The passage was being made in thick fog and, as the fog lifted, Captain Millard was confronted with Mudstone Bay. He put the helm hard to starboard but there was insufficient time for the *Bretton Hall* to respond. Chief Mate J.H. Blair explained that the vessel had been steaming at 11 knots, steering 'W (?) N from St Catherine Point, Isle of Wight'. At the time of the accident, the Captain believed his vessel to be in mid channel, 73 miles from St Catherine Point, when in fact he was 86 miles from the Point – 13 miles out on reckoning. It was claimed that the vessel's cargo of iron affected the ship's compass.

The *Bretton Hall* became a total wreck and lays at the position 50°23'.03"N, 03°29'.52"W.

Life was made more comfortable for the Brixham lifeboat crew during 1896 when water and gas were laid on to the boathouse.

On the evening of Monday 5 November 1888, the townsfolk of Brixham were in a festive mood celebrating the laying of the foundation stone of the monument, which was to commemorate the landing of William, Prince of Orange, in 1688. The town and ships at anchor in the harbour were ablaze with lights and a grand firework display was in progress. These illuminations unfortunately hid the distress beacons which were being shown by the schooner *Gwen Jones*, the vessel being at anchor in the bay. The Coastguard stated that the *Gwen Jones*, which was bound for Teignmouth and carrying a cargo of slate, was labouring heavily in the face of a south-easterly gale. At 21.30 hours the *Brian Bates* was launched and upon reaching the schooner took off the crew of four. The subsequent fate of the *Gwen Jones* is unclear.

The *Brian Bates* was launched for service, for the third and final occasion, during a severe easterly gale and great blizzard which swept the West Country on the night of Friday 9–Saturday 10 March 1891. The vessel in difficulty on this occasion was the Brixham smack *Pioneer*. The *Pioneer* had been moored in Brixham Harbour but, being subjected to heavy seas and strain, her moorings parted and she began to drift precariously close to the rocks of Fishcombe Point. The crew of the *Pioneer* dropped anchor in an attempt to stop her drift. Fortunately the anchor held and prevented the *Pioneer* from being swept onto the rocks and destroyed. The *Brian Bates* stood by until the gale had moderated and the smack could be safely re-moored.

The *Brian Bates* was condemned and withdrawn from service in November 1893; her initial replacement was a 'reserve' lifeboat that the RNLI placed on temporary duty. The reserve lifeboat was launched on one occasion only, that being on Tuesday 12 December 1893. Details of the launch are limited but it would appear that she went to the assistance of a ketch, which had been reported in difficulty. On this occasion the lifeboat again stood by.

*The* Brian Bates *(1885–93) heading out of Brixham Harbour.* RNLI

# 7

# THE JAMES AND ELIZA WOODALL
## 11 NOVEMBER 1889–6 MAY 1902

**Type:** *Self Righting*    **Propulsion:** *Pulling*    **Oars:** *12*    **Crew:** *15*
**Length:** *37' 0"*    **Beam:** *8' 0"*    **Displacement:** *4T 5Cwt*
**Official number:** *269*    **Builder:** *Watkins of Blackwall*
**Carriage Drawn**    **Launches:** *3*    **Lives Saved:** *0*
**Coxswains:** *William Henry Brown (1889–1900)*
*John Gill (1900–02)*

The second lifeboat to enter into service at Torquay did so on Monday 11 November 1889. The boat was built at a cost of £564 (defrayed by Mrs O'Connell of Manchester) by Messrs Watkins & Co., of Blackwall, London and 'possessed all the latest improvements'; two sliding keels, being a new adaptation, which materially increased her stability and handling qualities in deep water, without sacrificing the flat floor and light draught vital in shallow water. Each sliding keel could be lowered to its full extent at the after end or triced up or put in any desired position. If damaged, either keel could be slipped downwards and abandoned without impairing the stability or self-righting qualities of the lifeboat.

The naming ceremony was held at Torquay on Friday 15 November. Coxswain William Brown, in common with his crew of 12, was dressed in a blue jersey and scarlet cap. With her gear stowed in the boat, two hawsers were attached to the carriage and the boat was placed at the water edge. The lifeboat's flag was shipped and the crew donned their cork jackets. Eight Coastguardsmen, in full uniform, led by Chief Officer Nevin, took up their positions and the lifeboat was manoeuvred for the launch, the two Coxswains taking the yoke lines. Torre's vicar, Revd H.W. Majendie led the service of dedication assisted by the Revd B. Airy and the Revd Oswald Rigby. Mrs O'Connell formally handed the boat over to Captain Beddoes, who received it on the behalf of the RNLI. Mr Kitson (Chairman) thanked Mrs O'Connell on the behalf of the local branch of the

Institution, a bottle of champagne was broken across the bow of the boat and Mrs O'Connell named the lifeboat the *James and Eliza Woodall*. To the sound of the Post Office Fife and Drum Band, playing 'Sailing', the lifeboat was launched.

During her 13 years of service as the Torquay lifeboat, the *James and Eliza Woodall* was only launched for service on three occasions, on two of which she rendered service.

The first launch took place on Tuesday 13 October 1891 when she assisted the Plymouth fishing smack *Louie*, which had been fishing off the rock-strewn coastline below Daddy Hole Plain, adjacent to the Lifeboat Station at Beacon Cove. Whilst hauling in her nets, she began to drift perilously close to the rocks. The alarm was raised and the lifeboat launched at 12.20 hours, although the crew of the *Louie* successfully regained clear water prior to the arrival of the lifeboat and no useful service was rendered.

Shortly after this incident, the *Louie* was struck by a sudden squall as the result of which she sustained damage to, and lost, her sail. The *James and Eliza Woodall* returned to the stricken vessel and escorted her in to harbour.

The second service launch took place at 09.45 hours on Thursday 24 November 1898. At that time Torbay was being lashed by a south-easterly gale. Six seine-net fishing boats were caught out in the gale and, with the heavy seas running, were experiencing extreme difficulty in making port. The *James and Eliza Woodall* was launched and stood by the fleet until they gained the safety and shelter of Torquay Harbour.

Above: *The crew of the* James and Eliza Woodall *outside the Torquay Lifeboat Station, c.1900.* RNLI

Left: *The* James and Eliza Woodall *(1889–1902) on her arrival in the town, 11 November 1889. Note The Terrace dominating the skyline. See also pages 2–3.* RNLI

Right: *Brixham Harbour, c.1895. The picture shows the vessels,* left to right: *DH 517; DH 207* Harrier *(partially masked by DH 517), DH 36* Tartar *and DH 135* Dart.

# 8

# THE *BETSEY NEWBON*

## *5 FEBRUARY 1894–4 DECEMBER 1896*

*Type:* Self Righting    *Propulsion:* Pulling - Sailing    *Oars:* 12    *Crew:* 13
*Length:* 38' 0"    *Beam:* 9' 7"    *Displacement:* 4T 10Cwt
*Official number:* 361    *Builder:* Woolfe & Son, Shadwell
*Launches:* 2    *Lives Saved:* 0
*Coxswain:* J. Sanders

The new lifeboat which officially replaced the condemned *Brian Bates* arrived in Brixham on Monday 5 February 1894. She was a 38ft self-righter and had been built at a cost of £588, from the legacy of the late Mr Newbon of Islington. She was one of five lifeboats to be provided by the legacy. The boat was named *Betsey Newbon*.

The new boat was not well received by the lifeboat men of Brixham and at times difficulty was found in manning all 12 oars. She remained on station for 34 months, during which time she was launched for service on only two occasions.

The first launch took place on the afternoon of Wednesday 30 January 1895 when she went to the assistance of the ketch *Nellie* of Littlehampton, who was lying at anchor in Torbay in an easterly gale, when it was noticed that she was flying a distress signal of an inverted ensign. Lifeboat men were placed on board the ketch and the *Nellie* was successfully recovered to a safe anchorage in Brixham Harbour.

The *Betsey Newbon* was launched for the second time on Thursday 26 November 1896. With an east-south-easterly gale blowing, she stood by in heavy seas whilst the local fishing smack, *Laurel*, and the cutter *Hilda*, made port and were moored.

*The* Betsey Newbon *in Brixham Harbour.* RNLI

*William G. Sanders, Coxswain of the* Betsey Newbon *(1896–1922),*
*the* Alfred and Clara Heath *(1922–30),*
*and the* George Shee *(1930–32).*
RNLI

# 9

# THE *BETSEY NEWBON (II)*
## 4 DECEMBER 1896–JUNE 1922

**Type:** *Self Righting*    **Propulsion:** *Pulling - Sailing*    **Oars:** *10*    **Crew:** *13*
**Length:** *37' 0"*    **Beam:** *9' 7"*    **Displacement:** *4T 10Cwt*
**Official number:** *395*    **Builder:** *H. Roberts, Mevagissey*
**Launches:** *56*    **Lives Saved:** *46*
**Coxswain:** *William G. Sanders*

The RNLI commissioned H. Roberts of Mevagissey, Cornwall, to build the boat that was to replace the *Betsey Newbon*. The replacement boat was a 37ft self-righter, one foot shorter than its predecessor, and the pulling power had been reduced from 12 to 10 oars. The boat, which cost £495, was once again provided from the legacy of the late Mr Newbon, and also named the *Betsey Newbon*.

During the late 1890s and the early 1900s Brixham continued to flourish as a fishing port and Torbay in general continued to be busy with shipping. It is clear from the content of Institution correspondence that concern was being expressed regarding possible time delays that may have occurred in alerting the lifeboat crew at the time of call-out. Such concerns were the subject of a letter (*below*) received from the Secretary, RNLI, by the Brixham Station Secretary, Alfred Kendrick, on 24 March 1900.

The Local Committee did not let matters settle there, for on 28 March 1904 an application was made to the National Secretary at 20 Charing Cross Road, London, WC, for the installation of a telephone at the Coxswain's house. Charles Dibdin answered the application for 'the proposed telephonic connection', saying that he was 'at once writing to the General Post Office on the subject' and hopeful that the application would be successful, although he was careful to sound the note of caution in pointing out that this was 'by no means certain'.

The wheels of officialdom and bureaucracy ground on, the matter finally being resolved in a letter of 22 June 1904, in which Mr Dibdin had the sorry task of reporting that the application had in the end been turned down by the Post Office. Their reasoning for this being that it was only a distance of some 750 yards between the Coxswain's house and the Coastguard Station,

*My Dear Sir,*

*You will be glad to know that I have today received information from the General Post Office that the Postmaster General has ordered the necessary arrangements to be made, as recommended by my Committee, for connecting the Brixham Coast Guard Station with the Brixham Post Office.*

*The Secretary of the Post Office states that it would not seem desirable to provide a call bell at the Post Office for night communication as it would appear that it would take less time for a Coast Guard to deliver a telegram to the Life-Boat Coxswain at night than for a telegram to be sent to the Post Office and for the Postmaster to get up and dress and attend to the receipt and deliver the telegram.*

*Very faithfully yours, Charles Dibdin, Secretary.*

telegrams received at the latter in connection with a call for the Brixham lifeboat could be 'delivered by hand in a very few minutes'. The Post Office had also supported their refusal by pointing out that 'the previous communication was made as an altogether exceptional arrangement because the distance between the two points was nearly a mile.'

As the prevailing easterly gales continued to lash the South-Devon coastline each winter, it seems something of an enigma that the service records show that the *Betsey Newbon* had to wait seven years before making an effective service.

The first service is recorded on Tuesday 27 October 1903 and occurred whilst the lifeboat was engaged on her quarterly exercise. With a south-south-easterly gale blowing and a heavy sea running, many vessels had sought the shelter of Torbay to ride out the storm. Coxswain Sanders' attention was drawn to the French-registered schooner *Amiral L'Hermitte*, which was rolling heavily and was too close to the lee shore for the ship's safety. As the schooner was riding to only one anchor, at the Master's request Coxswain Sanders put three of his crew members aboard to assist in laying a second. The *Betsey Newbon* stood by for four hours until the wind veered and all danger passed. The lifeboat then returned to harbour.

On Saturday 28 November 1903, an estimated 150 steamers and smacks were anchored in the outer harbour at Brixham, sheltering from the strong winds, which had blown for much of that day. During the early hours of Sunday 29th the winds died away but by 04.00 hours had sprung up once again, from the north-east, causing a strong sea to run within a couple of hours. A gig, of the fishing smack *Insurance Society*, was manned and rendered assistance to fishing vessels that were labouring heavily and dragging their anchors. The majority of the steamers and smacks managed to get under way, seeking the relative safety of the open sea, the exceptions being the Brixham brigantine *Patra*, and a large barque (light). The *Patra*, which was on passage from Wicklow to Teignmouth with a cargo of manure, was riding heavily at anchor in the rough seas. She was under the command of Captain T. Bate and carried six hands. There was growing concern that in dragging her anchor the *Patra* would ultimately drift into the trots and decimate trawlers at their moorings.

At 10.00 hours the mortars were fired to summon the lifeboat. Coxswain W. Sanders and his crew made good progress under sail and reached the brig as the sea started to break completely over her. In extremely difficult conditions, the crew of six were taken from the *Patra* and

conveyed by the lifeboat to safety, the brigantine being left to weather the gale. The anchors of the *Patra* obviously found purchase as the next day, the gale having eased, the lifeboat returned the crew of the brigantine to their vessel. After much hard work and pumping, Captain Bate weighed anchor and the vessel was escorted, by the *Betsey Newbon*, to Torquay Harbour.

Within a fortnight, Torbay was again lashed by south-easterly gales. The lifeboat was launched at 11.15 hours on Saturday 12 December, following the sighting of a distress signal being flown by the three-masted schooner *Camborne*. Following the pattern of previous rescues, the *Betsey Newbon* negotiated the heavy seas and swell and succeeded in rescuing the crew of five from the schooner. The lifeboat immediately went to the assistance of the barque *Celtic* and rescued the crew of three. All eight persons were landed safely. The next day, the lifeboat returned the crews to their respective vessels. Assisted by members of the lifeboat crew, the *Camborne* was taken in to port.

During an extremely violent storm on the night of Wednesday 5–Thursday 6 December 1906, the Guernsey-registered ketch *Tyrant* was one of a number of vessels which sought the shelter of Torbay. It was a familiar service requirement, heavy seas were raging and the ketch was dragging her anchors. The *Betsey Newbon* was launched at 02.00 hours, located the casualty and initially stood by. The ship's anchors failed to find purchase in the seabed and the vessel started to drift dangerously close to rocks. After one hour the Captain of the *Tyrant* gave the order to 'abandon ship'; the crew of four were taken off by the lifeboat and landed safely. The *Betsey Newbon* returned to port at 05.30 hours but within the hour she was launched for a second time, as more vessels reported their anchors dragging. Without exception all crews remained with their vessels and the lifeboat returned to port without rendering effective service.

Later the same day, when the storm had abated, the *Betsey Newbon* was launched for a third time, on this occasion returning the crew to the *Tyrant*. Assisted by members of the lifeboat crew, the ketch was taken safely to harbour.

On Wednesday 16 October 1907 the crew of the ketch *J.B. Charcot* found themselves in serious trouble whilst attempting to manoeuvre the vessel away from a dangerous anchorage near Fishcombe Point, Brixham. During her manoeuvres the ketch fouled four trawlers, as the result of which she lost her bowsprit and spars and became totally unresponsive to the helm. As the *J.B. Charcot* continued to drift towards the rocks, the *Betsey Newbon* was launched and placed six of her crew onto the stricken vessel.

Eventually, the efforts of the lifeboat men saved the ketch and her crew of six.

An instance of a vessel dragging her anchor, in heavy seas and gale-force conditions, occurred yet again on Saturday 8 December 1907, the casualty in question being the ketch *Lily*, of Falmouth. On this occasion the lifeboat manoeuvred alongside the ketch, taking off and landing the crew of two. During the course of this service lifeboat man Robert Northway sustained an injury to his left arm. In 1908 a grant of £200 was made to Mr Northway, his arm being 'considered useless'.

The assistance provided to the ketch *John Rees*, on Friday 6 March 1908, was of a far more serious nature. The vessel was bound for Dublin when she sought shelter, from an extremely severe north-north-westerly gale, in Torbay. She had a cargo of explosives aboard. It was at 18.30 hours that distress signals were seen in Torbay. Great difficulty was experienced in launching the *Betsey Newbon* as the gale was blowing directly on to shore. Once launched into the teeth of the gale, further difficulty was experienced in clearing the head of the breakwater. The lifeboat located the casualty, by the light of flares, at about 20.00 hours. The Coxswain found that the *John Rees* had parted both cables and was relying solely on a small ancillary anchor. Members of the lifeboat's crew were placed aboard the ketch and assisted in setting sail. The vessel was being sailed seaward, to comparative safety, when her mainsheet parted and she lost headsail. Luckily, she was soon brought under control and sailed to the safety of Brixham Harbour.

The *Betsey Newbon* was launched on the morning of Monday 18 January 1909, supported by the Torquay lifeboat *Wighton*. Together they went to the assistance of the Dutch steamship SS *Heelsum*, the vessel having suffered mechanical failure five miles off Berry Head (see Chapter 10).

The crew of the 25-ton Brixham fishing smack-cutter *Gleaner* (BM 51) got into difficulties when caught in a sudden north-easterly gale whilst fishing the area of the Skerries Banks, Start Bay, at 21.00 hours on Monday 15 November 1909. The crew repeatedly put up distress flares from 21.00 hours until supplies were exhausted at about 03.00 hours the following day. The crew members James Tooley (owner/skipper), Abraham Bartlett (second hand) and Jack Salisbury, were unaware that their signals had been sighted until nearly 12 hours after disaster had struck the smack.

It was intended to send a Dartmouth tug to assist the *Gleaner* but, owing to the fact that none were available, assistance was sought from the Brixham lifeboat. The *Betsey Newbon* was launched at about 09.00 hours on Tuesday 16 November. Upon reaching Start Bay, the crew initially had difficulty in locating the stricken smack, which was now lying low in the water amongst breaking waves. The smack's mast had been carried away and she had lost all of her fishing gear. She was riding to two anchors. It was mid-morning before the lifeboat located the smack two and a half miles off Strete Gate. It was not until this time that the crew realised their distress signals had been acknowledged.

After assessing the conditions, the Coxswain decided not to enter the breakers but to anchor the lifeboat and veer down, on a cable, in order to reach the *Gleaner*. The attempt was successful and the crew of three, who were cold, wet and suffering from exposure, were rescued. The *Betsey Newbon* landed the fishermen at Dartmouth during the early afternoon.

Another instance of a ship dragging her anchors was that of the French schooner *Margaret*, of Paimpol; the incident occurred, in gale-force winds on Sunday 13 November 1910. Fortunately as the winds dropped the schooner's anchors bit securely and brought her to a halt only six feet away from another vessel. The *Betsey Newbon* stood by throughout the incident.

As west-north-westerly hurricane-force winds raged on Friday 16 December 1910, the 47-ton Brixham trawling ketch *Bia* (BM 132) collided in the Channel with another vessel. The *Bia* sustained extensive damage, her planking sprang leaks and she was partially dismasted. The *Betsey Newbon* accepted a tow from a local tug, the *Torbay Scout*, which had recently been placed at Brixham, and located the casualty off Berry Head. Whilst the tug took the trawler in tow, the lifeboat stood by and escorted the *Bia* to harbour.

The lifeboat was launched on Thursday 12 January 1911 to render assistance to the ketch *Vesta*, of Plymouth, which had parted a cable and was being driven perilously close to rocks. The *Betsey Newbon* rescued the crew of four minutes before the *Vesta's* second cable parted. Within 30 minutes the ketch was driven onto rocks and totally wrecked.

It was at 22.15 hours on Thursday 13 February 1913, that the *Betsey Newbon* was launched in response to a message that a steamship was aground at Strete Gate, Start Bay. In dense fog the lifeboat was taken in tow by a tug and rounded Berry Head, guided purely by the sound of the foghorn. The passage to Start Bay took nearly four hours and the tug anchored and cast off the lifeboat. The lifeboat crew searched the shoreline for three hours before finally locating the casualty, the Glasgow-registered steamer *Strathroy*, which was on passage from London to Buenos Aires. The Coxswain went aboard the *Strathroy* in order to give assistance and advice to the steamer's Captain, while the lifeboat, guided by the sound of a steam whistle, returned to the tug. At dawn the fog had lifted a little but it became all too obvious that any initial attempt that could be made to refloat the steamer would be inadequate. The *Betsey Newbon* therefore stood by until the *Strathroy* was refloated with the aid of tugs.

Further improvements were made to the lifeboat house during 1913, particularly with the provision of an electrical supply. There appears to have been a lull in the service requirement of the lifeboat during the First World War, during which time Torbay became a base for patrol craft. However, the *Betsey Newbon* was launched on Saturday 27 January 1917, under the command of Coxswain W.G. Mogridge, when the Greek steamship, *Eftichia Vergotti*, of Argostoli, became totally disabled in an east-south-easterly gale, which was accompanied by a bitterly cold wind and driving snow. The vessel, which was carrying food and clothing for the relief of Belgians, had lost both anchors and was drifting dangerously close to the Brixham breakwater. As the steamer entered inside the breakwater she became completely uncontrollable and the lifeboat crew attempted to stop her drift by securing wire ropes and hawsers to the breakwater bollards. Pilot J.K. Sanders, 2nd Coxswain of the lifeboat, together with other members of the crew, boarded the steamer and, following consultation, it was decided to beach the vessel abreast of the breakwater, at a point between the breakwater itself and the lifeboat slip. This manoeuvre was successfully achieved but difficulty then arose in securing the steamer in order to prevent it from swinging around and colliding with the moored smacks on the rising tide. Hawsers were used to secure the steamer to bollards but, unfortunately, the strain was such that the bollards collapsed. Warps and hawsers were then fastened to the wall on the Berry Head road but, by late evening, the wall had also collapsed. By midnight the steamer was safely beached and J.K. Sanders and his colleagues rejoined their crew. The lifeboat was stood down, the crew being ordered to return for duty at 06.00 hours.

At 05.00 hours the following day, the signal sounded to once more summon the lifeboat crew for duty. On arriving at the boathouse they were informed that the *Eftichia Vergotti* had broken loose. The *Betsey Newbon* was launched immediately and Coxswain Mogridge succeeded, once again, in placing J.K. Sanders on board the steamer. As daylight dawned the steamer was seen to be underway and with great skill Sanders manoeuvred her through the lines of moored fishing smacks, until she was abreast of the shipbuilding yards where, with the assistance of the

lifeboat crew, she was finally moored. The Service Boards record that on the Saturday evening the crew of the *Betsey Newbon* merely stood by, but following the service on the Sunday, they were credited as having saved the vessel.

During wartime, even the homely waters of the South-Devon coastline were not free from onslaught. In 1911 the liner *Medina*, of Greenock, was built for the P&O Navigational Co. Ltd., she weighed 12,358 tons and was driven by quadruple expansion engines, which gave her a top speed of 19 knots. She was 550 feet in length, had a beam of 63 feet and a draught of 35 feet. On Saturday 28 April 1917, the *Medina* left Plymouth for London, under Captain H.S. Bradshaw, this being the last leg of her voyage from India. She carried a cargo of copper ingots. At a point three miles east-north-east of Start Point, without prior warning, she was torpedoed by the German submarine *UB-31*. Although the torpedo caused extensive damage to the liner's starboard engine-room, the radio operator successfully transmitted a distress call. The *Medina* sank within 45 minutes of the attack. The Brixham lifeboat immediately responded to the distress call but, whilst en route to the scene of the tragedy, she was hailed by a patrol boat which had rescued a number of survivors. The *Betsey Newbon* went alongside the patrol boat and took off 33 survivors, landing them safely at Brixham. Various craft in the vicinity of the crippled liner went to her assistance, saving all but the Fourth Engineer, Mr Palmer, and five firemen. In total 411 lives were saved. The *Medina* now lies upright, north to south, with a 15° list to port, at 50°20'.15"N 03°32'.11"W, in 60 metres of water.

On the evening of Sunday 12 December 1920, the tug *Warrior* was on passage from Cherbourg to Teignmouth towing two former First-World-War German Torpedo Boats. (One contemporary newspaper account records the tow as being 'two destroyers' and the passage as being from Cherbourg to Tynemouth.) As far as steerage and power were concerned, the torpedo boats were 'dead tows' and totally helpless. A running crew manned each boat. The passage was being made in a full easterly gale. As the *Warrior* was unable to make headway the vessels anchored in Torbay.

Just after 23.00 hours, one of the torpedo boats, known simply as *T189*, broke her tow and, in the heavy seas and gale-force conditions, was driven ashore at Roundham Head, Paignton. The *Wighton* was launched from Torquay and, at 23.10 hours, the *Betsey Newbon* was launched. The Paignton Life-Saving Apparatus team, under the command of Chief Officer Parvin, were successful in taking off the crew of three and the *Betsey Newbon* returned to Brixham, having not rendered service.

*The German Torpedo Destroyer, T189, aground on Roundham Head, Paignton, 12 December 1920.*
**Courtesy Torquay Museum**

The lifeboat was launched for a second time at 04.20 hours the following morning, when the second torpedo boat, *S24*, broke adrift and ran aground at Preston Beach, Paignton. Coxswain W.G. Sanders headed the *Betsey Newbon* towards Preston Beach and entered a sea of seething white foam. The lifeboat was sailed to within 50 or 60 yards of the stranded vessel, in order that the torpedo boat would be clearly visible to the lifeboat crew. Sanders instructed the crew to keep a lookout for survivors as, if any were seen, he fully intended to take the lifeboat in for the rescue. What followed next is portrayed in Coxswain Sanders' own words, which he recounted immediately following the incident. Referring to the lifeboat, he said:

*I was just in the act of staying her when an unfortunate sea hit her right under the starboard bilge, the sea filled the lug and jib and forced her bows down under the water. She nearly capsized keel upwards. I should say she turned quite 60 degrees beneath the surface of the water. She had gone keel upward, the mast must have struck the sandy bottom, as the water appeared as thick as soup through the breakers stirring up the sand. But the* Betsey Newbon *did exactly what I expected her to do. She righted herself handsomely and it was fortunate that she answered her helm so readily and smartly, as she could not have been many lengths off the shore then. I sang out 'Are you*

*all right?' and getting the reply 'All right', we stayed the boat and got her about. Through one of the tholls getting unrove and the tackle for working the aft drop-keel getting out of order, the crew got the drop-keel up smartly through sheer main strength. I then asked the crew if, in their opinion, another venture ought to be made by going still closer to the wreck to see if there was anyone aboard. The men replied, to a man, 'If you think there is life to be saved, we'll go wherever you'll take us.'*

*It is not possible to describe the accident. It happened so quickly and it was a case of every man for himself almost before any of us realised such a thing could happen. I estimate that the* Betsey Newbon *was down for over ten seconds... In my opinion, if it had not been for the excellent discipline and prompt attention to my orders by the whole of my crew, the boat could never have been brought out safely from such a dangerous position in seas all of a white turmoil through breaking in such shallow water.*

*All things sinkable were lost out of the boat, the greatest mystery to us all being how the compass and binnacle went astray. It was a good job that* Betsey Newbon *was under full mizzen and main. That undoubtedly saved her. Her lug was double-reefed. All the men but three were washed out of the boat. Young Dalley had the presence of mind to pull himself up the weather side when he realised what was going to happen. Second-Coxswain T. Blackmore was washed under the mizzen sail. When I saw him, he had hold of the mizzen-shroud with one leg over the lee quarter. I pulled him aboard.*

Fred Tucker said that he was stationed two-seats aft, tending to the drop-keel. He was watching the wreck and recalls the accident happening suddenly:

*When I looked up above the water I saw the peak of the mizzen just coming up clear of the water with Ted Blackmore hanging on to it. I shouted out as soon as I felt myself safe 'Is every man in the boats safely?' I saw Second Blackmore hanging on to a line to leeward. For a man of his age Coxswain Sanders was a brick. I had to congratulate him on his coolness. He appeared to take no notice of the whole affair, and took it as though nothing had happened. He was as cool as cool could be. When the boats was in stays, he said 'What about it men, shall we go further in to see if there is life?' We answered, 'What's good enough for you Coxswain is good enough for us.' He then up tiller and away the* Betsey Newbon *goes in off the wind. Yes, Coxswain Sanders was a wonder. He gave us orders with authority.*

W.H. Mogridge, the Bowman, had a miraculous escape. He owed his life to the main mast coming right under his life jacket and lifting him bodily out of the water. He had to clamber down the mast to get into the boat.

Another crewman, William Coleman, spoke in the highest terms of the manner in which Coxswain Sanders commanded the situation. He said:

*He never lost his nerve and none of the crew lost heart. No sooner had the boat recovered herself than the Coxswain had her under way, and that proved the salvation of the whole crew.*

As in the previous service that night, the Paignton Rocket Apparatus Team rescued the crew of the torpedo boat and the lifeboat did not render service. The *Betsey Newbon* returned safely to Brixham with her crew, cold and wet but safe. The crew of the *S24*, five from Deal and the other from Southampton, were taken to Brixham Harbour where they rejoined the *Warrior*.

Within days of this incident Commander Hale of the RNLI conducted an inquiry into the capsizing of the lifeboat. Coxswain W.G. Sanders, Deputy Coxswain T. Blackmore and Bowman W.H. Mogridge gave evidence. In a

report to the RNLI, comment was made of 'the splendid conduct of the boat in fulfilling all that was ever expected of a lifeboat on righting herself in so short a time.'

The two German vessels were subsequently sold by public auction, the sale being conducted on Preston Beach by Mr R.S. Dugdall, Auctioneer, of Brixham. The first lot to come under the hammer was the *S24*, which was considered to be in a 'fairly safe position' on the beach. She was described as weighing 555 tons, and being 220 feet long, having a 22-feet beam and 6'6" mean draught. She was built in 1910–11, and was fitted with turbine engines of 15,000hp. Bidding started at £200 and rose slowly to £545, at which figure she was 'knocked down' to Mr H.W. Shaw of Brixham. The second boat, which was in a 'much more precarious position', was then offered. This vessel was described as 225 feet in length, having a beam of 23 feet and a draught of 7 feet. She was fitted with 16,000hp turbine engines and carried an armament of two small guns. The *T189* was sold for £100, the purchaser again being Mr Shaw. It was rumoured that the vessels each cost £40,000 to build.

The wreck of the *T189* remained on the rocks below Roundham Head and over the years salvers stripped her of her valuables. Local diver and salver, Jimmy Thorpe, who dived, using a surface pump with air supplied via a line to a traditional diving helmet, brought most of her brass and bronze ashore in the 1930s. In the 1950s her boilers were raised but her ribs and some sheet metal remained on the seabed to mark her passing.

In conditions of fog, driving rain, heavy seas and a south-westerly gale, just after midnight on Sunday 2 January 1921 the oil tank steamship *Broadmayne*, of Swansea, ran aground at Newfoundland Cove near Kingswear (50° 20'.15N 03°33'.02W). She was a tanker, under the command of Captain Forth, and owned by John J. Jacobs & Co., bound from London to Newport News. Upon the report of the incident being received from the Dartmouth Coastguard, Frederick C. Sanders, the Brixham Lifeboat Station's messenger, and R. Northway, the Station's shore-signal man, made their way to Newfoundland Cove, by road, to inform the crew of the steamship that help and assistance were at hand. Due to the atrocious weather conditions, they initially made their way to a farmhouse to summon assistance. They eventually located the wreck and found that some members of the crew had climbed off the ship, onto the rocks at Warren Point, and made their way to the cliff top. In pitch darkness, Frederick Sanders climbed down the cliff face and boarded the vessel to personally reassure the crew.

**This image and left:** *The SS* **Broadmayne** *aground on Warren Point, Kingswear, 2 January 1921.* RNLI

In atrocious weather conditions, the *Betsey Newbon* was launched at 02.00 hours, but was unable to locate the grounded steamship until dawn. Other vessels including the tug *Dencade* accompanied her. At about 05.30 hours, with the fog lifting and the gale abating, a rocket was fired, thus allowing Coxswain W.G. Sanders to locate the steamer. The lifeboat approached the *Broadmayne* and, manoeuvring to the lee side of the vessel, took off 22 persons including three women and a child.

Members of the Brixham section of the Board of Trade Life-Saving Apparatus Team, under Chief Officer Burmstead, hauled their wagon containing heavy equipment from Berry Head to Mr John Brock's Mews, Bolton Cross, where they requisitioned three horses to pull the wagon up the climb of Hill Head to Nethway. On reaching Brownston Farm, Chief Officer Burmstead detailed his men to search the coastline and locate the stricken vessel, an almost impossible task in the prevailing weather conditions. A local man, Mr Buller, who was more than 70 years of age, guided the team down the cliffs to Newfoundland Cove. Upon their arrival at the cove they spotted the flare, which had been fired from the *Broadmayne*, and realised that the lifeboat was already in attendance. The team had no alternative but to carry their heavy rescue gear back up the cliff to the road, a distance of nearly one mile.

A tug, which had assisted in locating the *Broadmayne*, towed the lifeboat to Dartmouth where those who had been rescued were landed.

In recognition of his actions that day, Mr Sanders was awarded the RNLI's Certificate of Thanks on Vellum.

The last service provided by the *Betsey Newbon* took place on Friday 2 March 1922 when she was launched, at 18.00 hours, to assist the steamship *Eider*, of London. The steamer, which was owned by J. and N. Wyndham of Cardiff and under the command of Captain Atkinson, was under passage from Antwerp to Penarth with a cargo of bog ore, when she was observed by the Berry Head Coastguard flying the International Code signal 'NC', indicating 'Not Under Control'; the vessel appeared to be taking in water and sinking. The *Eider* had left Weymouth on Thursday morning, having sheltered from the weather for some ten days. All had gone well until 16.00 hours, on 2 March, when she started to settle heavy by the head, and it was established that she was indeed rapidly taking in water. Captain Atkinson made a bold effort to beach her but unfortunately she grounded, in an exposed position, at the base of cliffs between Berry Head and Durl Rock. At this point the cliffs rose some 150 to 200 feet vertically above her. The intake of seawater flooded the *Eider's* engine-room and extinguished her fires. The ship's cook, Mr Bibby, narrowly escaped drowning as, whilst in the forecastle he fell. Fortunately the Chief Engineer rescued him. The Brixham trawler *Amy* attempted to help but could only stand by the steamer, her crew being unable to get aboard.

The Denaby tug *Dencade* set out for the scene, as did the *Betsey Newbon* with Coxswain W.G. Sanders in command. At the end of the breakwater, the lifeboat was taken in tow by a motor pilot boat under the command of Capt. J.N. Scoble and Mr J.B. Tucker. As the boats made their way to the casualty the Brixham Life-Saving Apparatus Team, under Chief Officer Burmstead, hauled their heavy cart to Berry Head, from the house at Berry Head Farm. At Berry Head, bystanders watched in horror as the steamer floundered on rocks. She was so low in the water that her decks were awash and she was in danger of sinking. By this time, thanks to a speedy tow, the lifeboat was standing by, the sea state was good and the crew of ten were quickly and efficiently taken aboard the lifeboat.

The *Eider* was floated on the rising tide and taken in tow, by the *Dencade*, to Elberry Cove where she was pumped out overnight. The following morning she was taken in to Brixham inner harbour.

At the end of her career as an RNLI lifeboat, the *Betsey Newbon* was sold for the sum of £40.

*It drives on with a mercy, which is stronger than the storm. It drives on with a mercy, which does not quail in the presence of death. It drives on as a proof, a symbol, a testimony that man is created in the image of God and that valour and virtue have not perished in the British Race.*

Winston Churchill,
speaking of the Lifeboat Service during the RNLI's Centenary in 1924.

# 10

# THE *WIGHTON*

## *1 MAY 1902–MARCH 1923*

*Type:* Watson Class    *Propulsion:* Pulling    *Oars:* 12    *Crew:* 15
*Length:* 38' 0"    *Beam:* 9' 4"    *Displacement:* 6T 1Cwt
*Official number:* 487    *Builder:* Thomas Ironworks, Blackwall
*Carriage Drawn*    *Launches:* 11    *Lives Saved:* 0
*Coxswains:* William Brown
Thomas Martin

The third, and last, lifeboat to be placed at Torquay took up station on Thursday 1 May 1902; she replaced the *James and Eliza Woodall*, which had been declared 'unfit for further service'. The 38ft non-self-righting boat had been built at a cost of £900, defrayed by the legacy of Mrs Mary Ann Wighton of Hornsey. The lifeboat was conveyed by rail from London to Teignmouth where, with the aid of a travelling crane, she was placed in the water. She was sailed over from Teignmouth to Torquay by the Coxswain, Second Coxswain and four of the crew, and moored in the harbour alongside the old boat. It was acknowledged that the former boat had made a very conspicuous feature at its launch on Charter Day. It was proposed that the new boat might form a feature in the procession in honour of the Coronation. It was pointed out that a carriage was not provided for the *Wighton* and difficulty would be experienced in launching the boat on that day. A sub-committee of the local branch of the Institution was set up to arrange a public christening on a suitable day!

Although launched 11 times, the *Wighton* is not credited with saving lives. The first launch took place late in the evening of Friday 30 January 1903, when she responded to distress signals shown by the schooner *Silvia*, of Beaumaris, at anchor in Torbay. Riding to just one anchor, she had lost spars and sail in a southerly gale which had whipped up very heavy seas. At the request of the *Silvia's* Captain, the lifeboat stood by for five and a half hours until the wind subsided and danger had passed.

The *Wighton* was not launched again until Monday 2 May 1904 when she went to the assistance of the 3,000-ton, four-masted barque, *Howth*, of Dublin. She had left America, bound for Liverpool, and had sought shelter in Torbay having been blown far off a course whilst running before the gale. The lifeboat went to her aid and, at the request of the Captain, stood by until the gale abated. The Coxswain then carried a message, from the Captain of the *Howth*, to the Lloyds Agent in Brixham. Her services no longer being required, the *Wighton* returned to Torquay.

It was in rough seas and south-westerly winds, of near gale-force strength, that on Monday 18 January 1909 the SS *Heelsum*, of Amsterdam, suffered engine failure five miles north-east of Berry Head. Drifting slowly, but helplessly towards the shore, her crew signalled for assistance. The *Betsey Newbon* was launched at 11.35 hours, and shortly afterwards the *Wighton* was launched in her support. Both lifeboats stood by for four hours whilst running repairs were made to the vessel; these being successfully carried out, the SS *Heelsum* continued her passage.

The crew of the 32-ton ketch *Girl Edith* (BM 311), owned by Mr Alfred Arnold of Brixham, found themselves in difficulty as they attempted to make their home port on the evening of Thursday 26 October 1916. The crew comprised Samuel Arnold, 26 (skipper and son of owner), William Mogridge, 25 (Mate and brother-in-law of skipper) and Charles Williams, 19 (third hand). Being unable to make headway, the skipper decided to drop anchor and ride out the storm. During the night, however, the weather deteriorated; exceptionally high seas carried stones, sand and general debris across Torbay Road and deposited it on Torre Abbey Meadow, Torquay. Debris blocked the Torquay to Paignton tramlines, which ran along Torbay Road. The *Girl Edith* lost her anchor; a second anchor failed to hold and the vessel began to drift.

At about 03.30 hours on Friday, Mr S.H. Easterbrook, of Seaway Lane, Torquay, heard distress signals and saw flares from the ketch. He rushed to Corbyns Head where he saw the vessel laying at the western extremity of the sands and being buffeted mercilessly by the waves. At this time the crew did not appear to be in imminent danger and Mr Easterbrook went to the Grand Hotel to summon assistance. Torquay Police Officers attended the scene together with Lt Adams and C/O Sleep of Torquay Coastguard. In the prevailing weather conditions, it was deemed useless to launch the Torquay lifeboat, the *Wighton*, but assistance of the Brixham boat, *Betsey Newbon,* and the tug *Dencade* was sought.

Coxswain William Sanders received an order to launch the lifeboat from a Brixham Customs Official at 04.45 hours. His crew assembled and launched at 05.20 hours, immediately making for Torquay. When approximately one mile from the scene of the incident, Sanders burnt white lights, to indicate his position, but received no response from the *Girl Edith*. Unknown to Sanders, as he and his crew battled their way across Torbay, the crew of the fishing vessel had launched a small boat in an attempt to reach the shore, and safety. Unfortunately, the small boat was immediately swamped by huge waves and the crew were thrown into the sea. Without consideration for his personal safety, Mr Easterbrook entered the raging sea and dragged William Mogridge to safety. Sadly Samuel Arnold and Charles Williams were lost. Having received a signal from Corbyns Head, that the services of the lifeboat were no longer required, Sanders took the *Betsey Newbon* back to Brixham. Later that same morning the body of Charles Williams, dressed in sea-boots and heavy black oilskins, was washed ashore on the sands below Abbey Crescent. The distinctive yellow sails of the *Girl Edith* and a small boat were also washed ashore.

This frightful incident occurred on the day that, having launched to assist the Plymouth fishing vessel, *Western Lass*, the Salcombe lifeboat, the *William and Emma*, was capsized by heavy seas running over Salcombe Bar. Some 13 brave lifeboat men, out of a crew of 15, lost their lives.

At the subsequent inquest into the loss of the *Girl Edith*, the Foreman posed the question, to Coxswain Sanders, 'Do you think any assistance could have been rendered by a lifeboat?' Sanders replied, 'In any ordinary time a lifeboat could not get there, but owing to the direction of the wind, there was four feet more water there.' He admitted: 'It would have been risky but I should have tried it.' William Edward Gill, son of the late Torquay lifeboat Coxswain, deposed 'that it would have been absolutely impossible to launch the lifeboat on the morning in question on account of the weather.' 'When the lifeboat was not wanted', he explained 'in the summer months, it was kept in the boat-house, and at other times in the outer harbour.' The Secretary of the Torbay Lifeboat Association gave evidence that the 1st and 2nd Coxswains had both retired on grounds of ill health and that difficulty was being experienced in finding suitable replacements. Under normal circumstances the lifeboat would have been on its mooring from 1 October.

Feelings ran high within the local fishing community that, had the lifeboat been at a mooring in the harbour when *Girl Edith* was driven ashore, it would have been extremely perilous to have attempted to place a crew on her, by any boat available in the harbour. It was noted that three ships' lifeboats were currently for sale, within the harbour, and enquiries were to be made as to their suitability. At a meeting of the Institution held at Torquay, under the Chair of Captain Philpotts in early January 1917, it was announced that the local ship-owners, 'Whiteway and Ball', had purchased the best of the three craft and generously donated the vessel to the RNLI. This vessel, which was initially kept on Beacon Quay and latterly on a mooring within the harbour, was known as the *Torquay Harbour Life-Saving Boat*. It remained in service until 1928.

The only record of service found in respect of this vessel took place on Tuesday 7 January 1919. The previous evening, as Torbay had been subjected to a south-easterly gale accompanied by heavy seas, the iron schooner, the *Skell*, owned by Messrs Stephenson and Davis of Plymouth, on passage from Harve to Hull, had anchored in the Brixham Roads. During the late evening sea conditions worsened, and the *Skell* moved to Torquay, mooring close to Haldon Pier. In the heavy seas, she started to drag her anchor and, when her warps parted, she drifted into vessels moored by the Princess Pier.

Heavy seas and a severe south-westerly gale again savaged Torbay on Thursday 15 April 1920. At this time the 39-ton Brixham fishing ketch, *Renown* (BM 259), found herself in extreme difficulty east of Hopes Nose, Torquay. The Coastguard at Babbacombe first noticed the plight of the vessel, which carried a crew of four, at about 15.00 hours. She had lost her mainmast, which was hanging over her side, and was riding out the gale with little or no steerage. The vessel was in peril of being carried further out into the bay. The *Wighton* was launched at 16.00 hours and at first, in the heavy seas, navigation was extremely difficult. After clearing surrounding rocks, she made good headway and reached the *Renown*. By this time the tug *Dencade* was approaching from Brixham; the lifeboat stood by the casualty until she was taken under tow by the tug. Both vessels received a severe buffeting, but the *Dencade* returned the *Renown* safely to her home port. The *Betsey Newbon* had been launched from Brixham, in support of the *Wighton*, but, as adequate assistance was at hand, she returned to her station.

The Torquay boat experienced even greater difficulty in returning to port as she headed directly into the teeth of the south-westerly gale. Several hundred people anxiously awaited her return and cheered heartily as she sailed into Torquay Harbour at 20.30 hours. During this operation the *Wighton* had been under the command of committee member Oliver Toms, during the temporary absence of Coxswain Martin. Mr Toms received a Letter of Thanks from the RNLI for his assistance.

During a north-easterly gale and snowstorm, at 22.00 hours on Sunday 12 December 1920, the call-out guns sounded and the Torquay boat was launched to go to the assistance of an ex-German torpedo boat. She was one of two in the tow of the tug *Warrior*, which was bound from Cherbourg to Teignmouth, where the torpedo boats were to be scrapped. The *Warrior*, being unable to make headway in the gale, had put in to Torbay for shelter. The vessels anchored one mile from Torquay in what local seamen considered 'not too favourable a position'. The vessel, with three hands on board, had dragged her anchor and run aground at Roundham Head, Paignton.

Initially, difficulty was experienced in mustering a crew to man the *Wighton*, but despite being more than 79, William Brown, a former Coxswain, offered his services and proudly took his place in the boat. Upon arrival at Roundham Head, the lifeboat crew found that the heavy seas were crashing directly onto the headland making it impossible to render assistance to the crew of the torpedo boat. Men of the Paignton L.S.A. Rocket Apparatus Team, under the charge of Chief Officer Parvin, having failed to secure a rocket line, managed with some difficulty to rescue the crew by means of lifelines. The *Wighton* subsequently returned to Torquay having stood by. The Brixham lifeboat, *Betsey Newbon*, was also launched to complement the *Wighton* (see Chapter 9).

The *Wighton* was launched on Saturday 8 July 1922 in answer to distress flares being fired by the yacht *Amaryllis*. Contemporary reports record that 'fully 1,000 people witnessed the launch.' Due to the prevailing wind direction, the sea within the inner harbour was running very high and the task of the lifeboat crew was 'watched with anxiety'. Waves crashed furiously against the piers and the crew of the *Wighton* had to call upon all their skills and expertise to pass through the harbour entrance into the open sea and face yet rougher waters. The *Wighton* had to thread her way out between a number of destroyers which were at anchor in the bay. Upon her arrival the Coxswain found the new Brixham motor lifeboat, the *Alfred and Clara Heath*, to be in attendance. The services of the *Wighton* were not required and she stood by throughout the operation.

The *Flaondi*, a 25-ton steam trawler with 14 hands, left Boulogne on Monday 16 October 1922 and, having battled through an east-south-easterly gale, sought the refuge of Torbay on the afternoon of 17 October. At about 17.40 hours on 18 October, in heavy seas and a continuing easterly gale, her Captain found his vessel to be in a dangerous position, off Hollicombe Beach, below the Paignton Gas Works. At this time, the Honorary Secretary of the Torquay Branch of the RNLI was on Beacon Quay watching the vessel, and gave instruction to alert the Paignton Coastguard Rocket Apparatus Team. Several members of the lifeboat crew accompanied him. The trawler, which was dragging her anchor, continued to drift perilously close to the entrance to Torquay Harbour and at 19.45 hours on Wednesday 18 October the lifeboat was launched, following the sighting of a flare. Fortunately the lifeboat had been moored in Torquay's outer harbour and was immediately launched, under the command of Coxswain Thomas Martin. The lifeboat overcame the heavy, running sea and Second Coxswain J. Holden was placed aboard the French vessel. The *Flaondi's* Captain asked the lifeboat to pilot his vessel into harbour and handed over command of the trawler to Second Coxswain Holden, who, with the assistance of lifeboat men G. Douch, J. Brown and J. Pym, successfully manoeuvred the *Flaondi* into Torquay Harbour.

This was the last launch undertaken by a Torquay lifeboat. With problems constantly being experienced in launching the boat due to the shifting beach and the introduction at Brixham of the motor lifeboat, the *Alfred and Clara Heath*, the Torquay Lifeboat Station was closed on Thursday 31 March 1923. The *Wighton* was sold to a local boat builder, for conversion to a yacht.

In their combined 47 years of service, the Torquay lifeboats recorded 26 services and saved 19 lives.

*The crew of the* Alfred and Clara Heath *(1922–30).* Left to right: *Ted Gardner,
Tom Gardner, Mr Ivy (Coastguard), Bill Mogridge, William George Sanders, William Babb
(boy), Fred Walsh, Jack Lovell, Alf Babb, Jack Babb, Bill Pillar, Archie Friend.* RNLI

*The crew of the* Alfred and Clara Heath, *1928.* Left to right, back: *Jack Gempton, Ernest
Friend, Alf Babb, Fred Tucker, Bill Mogridge, Fred Welsh (Mechanic), Archie Friend, Bill Pillar;*
front: *T. Blackmore, Bill Edhouse, William George Sanders (Coxswain).* RNLI

# 11

# THE *ALFRED AND CLARA HEATH*
## 18 MARCH 1922–6 OCTOBER 1930

*Type:* Watson Self Righting    *Propulsion:* 40bhp Taylor Petrol    *Speed:* 7.27 knots
*Crew:* 9    *Length:* 40' 0"    *Beam:* 10' 6"    *Displacement:* 11T 6Cwt
*Official number:* 672    *Builder:* J.S. White, Cowes
*Launches:* 39    *Lives Saved:* 37
*Coxswains:* Robert Chivers (1922); Charles Phillips (1922–23);
F. Welsh (1923–30)

The first motor-lifeboat to be placed at Brixham arrived on station on 18 March 1922, although the *Betsey Newbon* also remained in Brixham until June 1922. The boat was provided from the legacy of the late Mr Alfred J. Heath of Putney, London; whilst the engine was purchased from a legacy left by the late Mrs Augusta H. Tozer of Oxford. The lifeboat was one of five self-righting sister-boats fitted with a petrol engine giving her a top speed of just over seven knots. The boat was built at a cost of £8,302.0s.0d. Robert Chivers was appointed Motor Mechanic of the new boat.

The new lifeboat was first launched for service on Saturday 8 July 1922, the casualty requiring assistance being the auxiliary twin-screw schooner yacht *Amaryllis*, owned by Mr Herbert Sullivan of Brightlingsea. South-westerly gales and heavy seas had dominated the weather that day and the schooner had entered Torbay and anchored in an exposed position, about one and a half miles north-north-east of Berry Head. Shortly after the schooner had reached an anchorage, at about 18.00 hours, distress flares were seen to be fired from the yacht. The lifeboat was launched at about 18.20 hours, to assist the vessel. The tug *Dencade*, under the command of Captain Washer, also proceeded to render assistance.

Having reached the casualty, two of the lifeboat's crew, W. Pillar and W. Northway, boarded the *Amaryllis*, accompanied by the Trinity Pilots, Capt. J.N. Scoble and J.B. Tucker. It was then discovered that the schooner's petrol supply had been exhausted and that the Captain,

J.W. French, had thus been forced to anchor the vessel in the exposed position. Petrol was supplied by the lifeboat, which enabled the crew of the schooner to set their heaving machinery in motion for saving the anchors, instead of slipping them. Attempts to restart the yacht's engine failed, and a tow was established, but the steel jib boom stays cut through the towrope twice. In manoeuvring for the tow, the lifeboat had her mizzenmast carried away and sustained damage to her port bow cork belt batten. The tow being ineffective, the lifeboat men on board the *Amaryllis* hoisted mainsail, foresail and staysail and, some seven hours later, the yacht, together with the crew of ten, were taken in to Brixham Harbour.

At 19.00 hours the Torquay boat, the *Wighton*, had also been launched in response to the distress signals fired by the *Amaryllis*. Her services were not required and she stood by throughout the operation. It subsequently transpired, in an incident report made by Captain French, that the vessel's voyage from Gibraltar had taken in excess of a month. At Gibraltar the Italian crew had refused to carry out their duties until the Captain threatened to hand them over to a British Man-of-War. At Lisbon two of the Italian crew were landed and two Portuguese hands were taken on. At Cezembo Bay, Captain French was compelled to go down to the forecastle to 'tame them down'. The *Amaryllis* encountered a series of gales during the voyage and, whilst off Ushant, a strong gale buffeted the yacht continuously for two days. This storm was followed by

12 hours of calm and then a further south-westerly gale, off Start Bay. When the fuel ran out off Berry Head, the crew, who claimed to be worn out by the experiences of the past month, rebelled and flatly refused to hoist sail. It is perhaps surprising that the *Amaryllis* made Torbay.

The naming ceremony of the new lifeboat took place on Saturday 9 September 1922; two months after she had answered her first call. Uniquely, both the boat and the engine were subject of the naming ceremony. Following the service of dedication, Lady Churston named the boat *Alfred and Clara Heath*, in memory of the donor and his wife, and the engine *Mary and Catherine*, in memory of the sister and niece of Mrs Tozer.

Drifting helplessly in a north-westerly gale, on Wednesday 20 December 1922, the schooner *Alroy*, of Falmouth, fouled two Brixham trawlers, the 49-ton ketch *Terminist* (BM 321) and the 48-ton ketch *Resolute* (BM 261). The schooner was undamaged but it was necessary for the lifeboat to convey crews out to the two trawlers and assist in finding both vessels safe moorings.

Later the same day the *Alfred and Clara Heath* was launched to assist in bringing ashore an injured seaman from the ketch *Hosianna* of Truro.

It was on Wednesday 3 October 1923 that the *Alfred and Clara Heath* became involved in a series of rescues, which would see Coxswain William Sanders and his crew battle against gale-force winds and appalling sea conditions for some six and a half hours.

In the teeth of a north-north-westerly gale and heavy seas, the SS *Tuscarora* of Sunderland, which was not under command, had collided with a Swedish steamer, *Torvald*, of Landskrona. As a consequence of that collision, the *Tuscarora* was drifting towards a number of the local trawler fleet that were either returning to harbour or at anchor. The lifeboat was launched at midday and ferried additional crew members out to assist the trawler fleet.

Upon the lifeboat approaching the fleet, the crew of the 47-ton ketch, *Osprey* (BM 148), requested that they be taken off and landed. Having landed the crew safely, Coxswain Sanders immediately put to sea again, this time going to the assistance of the 34-ton fishing ketch *Espero* (BM 319). The crew of two were landed in a fashion similar to the former. More crewmen

*Coxswain William G. Sanders.*
RNLI

were shipped out to the floundering trawler fleet and Coxswain Sanders was successful in placing pilots on board both the *Tuscarora* and the *Torvald*. Coxswain Sanders and his crew also gave assistance to the 24-ton ketch *Guess* (BM 80), which had sustained damage amounting to £37.17s.6d, to the 34-ton ketch *Leonaro Minnie* (BM 339), which had sustained damage amounting to £53.12s.6d. and to the 24-ton ketch *Lizzie* (BM 55), which had sustained damage amounting to £42.10s.6d. That day the lifeboat also assisted another five trawlers.

Without returning to shore and continuing to fight against the gale-force winds and a heavy sea, Coxswain Sanders set the *Alfred and Clara Heath* on a course to assist a ketch, which had been reported in difficulty, approximately eight miles south-south-east of Berry Head. Upon locating the ketch it was found that she needed help; the lifeboat returned to harbour, arriving in port at 18.30 hours. For his prolonged, excellent service, Coxswain William Sanders was awarded the RNLI's Thanks on Vellum.

At 05.00 hours, on Wednesday 9 January 1924, the *Alfred and Clara Heath* was launched into a full south-easterly gale and accompanying heavy sea, her destination being Goodrington Sands, Paignton, where the steamship *River Lagan*, of Glasgow, had run aground. The *River Lagan*, a collier of 950 tons, under the command of Captain John Sutherland, had recently left dry dock in Portsmouth, with a crew of 12, bound for Barry Docks. Throughout Tuesday she made her way down the Channel in gale-force conditions and extremely heavy seas. The Captain made a futile attempt to put into Brixham and subsequently anchored in Torbay. She rode to one anchor but her cable parted in the storm and she started to drift towards the lee shore. The gale raged all night and just before 03.00 hours, a vessel was seen in the bay burning flares. The crew attempted to lay another anchor but this failed to hold and the vessel continued to drift. Captain Sutherland made attempts to steer the *River Lagan* towards the open sea but, with the waves frequently lifting her propeller clear of the water, her engines had insufficient power to battle directly into the teeth of the gale. The collier was driven further and further towards the beach until finally, broadside on, she was driven ashore.

*The 950-ton collier* **River Lagan** *driven ashore during a south-easterly gale, at Goodrington Beach, Paignton, 9 January 1924.*
COURTESY TORQUAY MUSEUM

A Life-Saving Apparatus Team, under Commander Royal, of Torquay, was soon at the scene and attempted to establish contact with the ship. This proved extremely difficult as a snow-storm was now blowing and the vessel continued to shift position. The first rocket was fired successfully but the crew of the *River Lagan* were unable to locate the rope in the darkness and blinding snow. It was extremely dark and the vessel could only be seen by the illumination provided by the exploding rockets. A second rocket struck the collier amidships, but the third rocket proved a success and a line was established at the bow of the vessel. By 06.30 hours the crew of 13 had been taken off safely. The *Alfred and Clara Heath* was unable to approach the steamship, due to the shallow water, but stood by the vessel until a signal was given indicating that her services were no longer required.

The *Alfred and Clara Heath* recorded only two services during 1924; that described above and one in December. A Paignton fisherman, Mr Endicott, found himself in difficulty as a storm swept across Torbay on Thursday 4 December 1924. Mr Endicott was fishing off Livermead when his seine boat became swamped by waves. An onlooker, noticing his predicament, summoned assistance from the Torbay lifeboat and, under the command of Coxswain W.G. Sanders, the *Alfred and Clara Heath* was launched.

A Torquay motorboat, the *Sunbeam*, approached the seine boat and the crew of the motorboat threw a line, but the fisherman refused the offer of a tow. Mr Endicott was concentrating his efforts on saving his catch of sprats and in throwing the towline into the sea, it became entangled in the propeller of the motorboat. Both vessels were facing potential danger when a Brixham tugboat managed to get a towline to the *Sunbeam* and towed her to the safety of Torquay Harbour. On reaching the seine boat, the lifeboat took the vessel, with the crew of four, in tow to Torquay Harbour. Coxswain Sanders remarked 'there was little doubt the Paignton seine boat was in considerable danger when the lifeboat arrived.'

Surprisingly, no launches whatsoever are recorded on the Service Boards for 1925, although that it not to say that none took place.

The Salcombe Lifeboat Station was closed in 1925, leaving the Hope Cove 'pulling/sail' lifeboat, *Alexandra*, as the only lifeboat in the immediate vicinity. It was during the night of Sunday 14–Monday 15 February 1926 that the Italian steamer *Liberta*, of Genoa, found herself in difficulties off the Salcombe Estuary. Being tossed around in heavy seas in a south-south-westerly gale, the 4,073-ton vessel ran aground on the Mew Stone, off Bolt Head. She was 376 feet in length, with a beam of 48 feet. The *Alexandra* was launched, as was the *Alfred and Clara Heath*. The Torbay boat put to sea at 01.10 hours, locating the casualty at 04.00 hours. Gale-force winds continued to enrage the sea off Bolt Head, turning the area into a cauldron, with waves breaking on the mass of rocks that litter the area. It is reported that some waves were breaking and completely engulfing the stranded vessel.

Conditions were such that Coxswain Sanders would have endangered the lifeboat and the lives of his crew had he approached the casualty during the hours of darkness; he therefore stood by until dawn. At first light, with great skill and dexterity, Coxswain Sanders manoeuvred the lifeboat into a position as close as possible to the casualty. Whilst the *Alexandra* stood by, a line was fired from the *Alfred and Clara Heath* to the *Liberta*, and three crew members were rescued. A breeches buoy was rigged between the shore and the steamer, by which means the remaining crew members were taken off. Having landed the three rescued crewmen at Salcombe, both lifeboats returned to their respective stations.

The courage and skill shown that night was subsequently acknowledged by the Italian Government when, in a letter dated 15 February the following year, the Ambasciata d'Italia forwarded letters of thanks to each member of the Torbay and Hope Cove lifeboats:

*Dear Sirs,*

*The Italian Ministry of Communications to whom was reported the wreck of the s.s. LIBERTA and the rescue of her crew, have charged me to convey to the Torbay Lifeboat the warm thanks and the highest praise of the Italian Government for the gallant efforts they made in saving the lives of Italian sailors and for their great courage and endurance in standing by for so many hours in order to render all possible assistance.*

*TORRETTA, Italian Ambassador.*

The wreck of the *Liberta* now lies, broken in two, between the Great and Little Mew Stones (50° 12'.31N 03° 47'.05"W).

The service provided to the *Liberta* had entailed the longest passage to have been undertaken to date by a Torbay lifeboat, although the *Alfred and Clara Heath* was to return to Start Bay within 48 hours, on Wednesday 17 February, when reports were received of a boat being on fire in the area of Start Point. Following a very arduous passage, in heavy seas and a west-south-westerly gale, the lifeboat rendezvoused with the steamship *Izvor*, of Dubrovnik. The steamer had a crew of 30 and was on passage for Casablanca. Communication proved difficult, due to language problems, but it transpired that the vessel was not on fire but that she was 'in ballast', her weight being such than her propeller frequently cleared the water.

Upon receiving the alert, the Royal Navy dispatched HMS *Champion*, a light cruiser, to the scene. The lifeboat stood by until the arrival of the warship, following which HMS *Champion* escorted the *Izvor* to the safety of Torbay.

The Falmouth ketch *Ivy* required the services of the lifeboat twice within a nine-day period. The initial instance was on Thursday 18 October 1928, when she was seen to be dragging her anchors. The vessel, which had been anchored close under Fishcombe, had drifted nearly two miles in the strong south-westerly gale. Her crew were not on board, having landed at Brixham earlier in the morning, during fairly fine weather. When the crew saw their ketch drifting, they set off pursuing her in a small rowing boat. The rate of drift of the ketch was such that the crew appeared to be making little headway in reaching their quarry. In the end they were successful in the chase, reaching the ketch at the same time as the lifeboat and the tug *Dencade*. The *Alfred and Clara Heath* escorted the *Ivy* as her crew sailed her to a safe anchorage in the harbour at Brixham.

The second service was provided on Saturday 27 October, when the *Ivy's* position became precarious in a north-easterly gale. The lifeboat placed a member of the *Ivy's* crew on board the vessel, together with the skipper of another ketch. The two men were successful in laying a second anchor thus securing the vessel.

On the afternoon of Thursday 15 November 1928, Mr Henry Thomas and Mr G. Doulton set out from Brixham on a fishing trip in the small open motor trawler *Test*. They left port at 16.00 hours, in fine weather, and made the five-mile journey, eastwards, to the Great Rock (Thatcher) where they shot their fishing lines. Concern for the crew and vessel grew the next day when the trawler failed to return to port. The Coastguard were put on alert, as were local fishermen who realised that in the prevailing weather conditions, a boat such as *Test* would be in considerable danger.

With an expected deterioration in the weather the Torbay boat was launched, running before the wind to commence a search in the assumed locality of the trawler. At about noon, the lifeboat located *Test* sheltering under the lee shore, on the eastern side of Hopes Nose. The vessel was taken in tow and the crew safely landed at Babbacombe. Following their rescue, Mr Thomas explained that they had tried to make for Brixham, using a small sail and an auxiliary motor, but against a strong wind and heavy sea this was impossible. The wind had veered, from south-west to west, and they were driven towards Ansteys Cove. The *Test* shipped a considerable amount of water and pumps had to be used. Following heavy rains, the wind often changes to northward, and this would inevitably have driven the small vessel onto the rocks. Fortunately the trawler made Ansteys Cove by 20.00 hours, before the wind again increased in severity, and by setting her anchor she safely weathered the gale. A larger Brixham trawler, the *Dawn*, captained by Harry Stockman, was also unable to make Brixham that night and likewise sheltered in Ansteys Cove.

Monday 31 December 1928 saw several vessels at anchor in Torbay, sheltering in heavy seas and an easterly gale. At 13.25 hours the *Alfred and Clara Heath* was launched following distress signals being made by one of the sheltering vessels. Before the lifeboat could reach the casualty it was taken in tow by a tug. Whilst at sea, the lifeboat crew saw distress signals coming from a second vessel, the schooner *Jane Banks*, of Fowey. The schooner was dragging her anchors in the surging sea. The lifeboat rescued and safely landed the crew of five, leaving the schooner to successfully ride out the gale. The following day the lifeboat returned the crew to the *Jane Banks*, and she continued on to Teignmouth.

The *Alfred and Clara Heath* was launched twice on the afternoon of Sunday 12 January 1930 and succeeded in rescuing the crews of two vessels in distress. The first call-out was at 17.00 hours when the schooner *Katie*, of Padstow, which had been on passage from Par to Rochester with a cargo of china clay, was seen being driven by gale-force winds from her berth in Brixham Outer Harbour. Storm conditions had forced the schooner to seek the shelter of Torbay. Commanded by Coxswain Sanders, the lifeboat was launched and stood by the schooner. Whilst so engaged, the lifeboat crew observed a green light being displayed from the shore; to the Coxswain this indicated a recall. The lifeboat returned to the inner harbour and, having established that no such signal had been made, headed back towards the schooner. The *Alfred and Clara Heath* had barely rounded the breakwater when red distress flares were fired from the *Katie*. Upon reaching the vessel, Coxswain Sanders found that she had dragged her anchors and was riding about a ship's length from the end of the breakwater. Coxswain Sanders manoeuvred the lifeboat alongside the *Katie* and successfully took off Captain Edward Curry, of Newquay, and his crew of three.

The lifeboat had just succeeded in taking off the crew, when further distress signals were seen, these being from the French ketch *Reine des Cieux*, of Paimpol, which had been riding out the storm with three cables down. One of her cables had parted and the remaining two failed to hold, allowing the ketch to be swept rapidly out of Brixham Harbour. For the second time that afternoon, Coxswain Sanders manoeuvred the lifeboat alongside a stricken vessel and took off the crew. On this occasion however one crew member was nearly left behind. The Captain of the ketch, Captain Nedlec, of Paimpol, thought that the crewman had been washed overboard and drowned, and the lifeboat crew also thought that they had seen a body drifting astern of the boat. In actual fact, the crewman was in the forecastle where he had gone to pack his kit bag. When last seen the *Reine des Cieux* was drifting rapidly seaward, she eventually drove ashore near Bridport, Dorset. The crew of both vessels were landed safely at Brixham.

During this period at sea, three other vessels, the yacht *Westward*, the 23-ton ketch *Hermes* (BM 58), and the 34-ton ketch *We'll Try* (BM 338), were also saved with the assistance of lifeboat men who were placed aboard the vessels.

To crew members of the RNLI, Christmas Day is like any other day when lives are in danger and the services of the lifeboat are required. Such was the case on Christmas morning, 1930, when the Torbay lifeboat responded to two separate distress calls. The first launch was in response to an SOS call received from the SS *Cantanac* which had radioed that she had lost her propeller some 30 miles south-south-east of Berry Head. The call for assistance came via Ventnor and Seaton, to the lifeboat, shortly before 05.00 hours. Following consultation with Coxswain Sanders, the Honorary Secretary, Mr H.M. Smardon, authorised the launch of the *Alfred and Clara Heath*. At 06.30 hours a message was received, via Torquay Coastguard, that the SS *Irene* had located the *Cantanac* and was standing by. Recall signals were fired, and acknowledged. The lifeboat, having travelled some seven miles, returned to her station within the hour. The Torbay and Brixham Coaling Company's tug, *Dencade*, under the command of Captain Z.T.

Durham, also proceeded to render assistance. After steaming for several hours and not locating the *Cantanac*, she also returned to Brixham.

The waters of Brixham Inner Harbour were a dead calm, at 06.00 hours, when local fisherman George Shipley left the harbour to make his way across to Goodrington, in the boat *Pollywake*, to haul his herring nets. At dawn a rather strong south-easterly wind sprang up creating a nasty lop in the more exposed areas of Torbay. In his small open boat, Shipley soon found himself in difficulties and with one paddle broken was unable to row towards Brixham. He noticed a herring net set close by and succeeded in securing a rope, from his vessel, to the anchor rope. Mr Shipley remained standing in the bow of his boat for several hours, holding on to the mooring rope.

The *Alfred and Clara Heath* was launched for the second time at 10.30 hours when Coxswain Sanders received notification, from the Torquay Coastguard, that an open boat 'with a lad as occupant' was drifting ashore at Goodrington. Mr Shipley was fortunate to be spotted by a member of the public, as his only method of attracting attention was by waving his hat. On arriving at Goodrington, Coxswain Sanders had to navigate the lifeboat through lines of moored herring nets. When the *Pollywake* was reached, lifeboat man Soper jumped aboard, assisted Mr Shipley on to the lifeboat and established a tow. Both Mr Shipley and the *Pollywake* were returned safely to harbour.

With the re-opening of the Lifeboat Station, the *Alfred and Clara Heath* was relocated to Salcombe, where she remained on station from 1930 to 1938. She was subsequently stationed in Guernsey and undertook duties in the role of a reserve lifeboat. In 1940 she was commandeered by the German Forces and totally neglected. It was a sad and unbefitting end for a proud and noble vessel.

*Having drifted through the moorings of Brixham Harbour, the SS* Sebastian, *of Bilbao, was escorted to a mooring by the* Alfred and Clara Heath, *7 December 1929.*

*Crowds congregate at Brixham Harbour for the dedication of the George Shee.*

The
Royal National Life-boat Institution
(Supported solely by Voluntary Contributions)

TORBAY BRANCH.

INAUGURAL CEREMONY

OF THE

MOTOR LIFE-BOAT

"GEORGE SHEE"

The Outer Basin, Brixham Inner Harbour,
On WEDNESDAY, JULY 27th, 1932, at 2 p.m.

The Life-boat will be named by
H.R.H. THE PRINCE OF WALES, K.G.,
President of the Institution.

The Right Hon. THE LORD MILDMAY OF FLETE, P.C., J.P.,
Lord Lieutenant of Devon, in the Chair.

PRICE THREEPENCE

*HRH The Prince of Wales at the naming and dedication ceremony of the George Shee,
27 July 1932.* A. CURNOW

# 12

# THE *George Shee*

## 27 SEPTEMBER 1930–25 JULY 1958

*Type:* Barnett   *Propulsion:* 2 x 60bhp, CE6 engines   *Crew:* 15

*Length:* 37' 0"   *Beam:* 8' 0"   *Displacement:* 24 ton   *Speed:* 9 knots

*Official number:* 734   *Builder:* Saunders-Roe, Cowes (S56)

*Launches:* 245   *Lives Saved:* 190

*Coxswains:* William G. Sanders (1930–32); William H. Mogridge (1932–42); Frederick C. Sanders (1942–51); Henry O. Thomas (1951–58). **Mechanics:** F. Welsh (1930–39); R.T. Harris (1939–58).

The *Alfred and Clara Heath* was replaced in September 1930, but Brixham had to wait until July 1932 for HRH the Prince of Wales, K.G., the President of the Institution, to visit Brixham and name the new Torbay offshore lifeboat. The new boat was a 'Barnett Class' non-self-righter, built at a cost of £9,614, which was defrayed by RNLI funds. She was divided into eight watertight compartments and was fitted with 160 air-cases. The engine-room was a self-contained watertight compartment and each engine, in turn, was itself watertight, which permitted the engine to continue running even if the engine-room became flooded. The lifeboat was fitted with a solid cork 15' x 7' wale, a staysail and trysail. She had a fuel capacity that allowed her to travel for up to 16 hours at a top speed of nearly 9 knots, without refuelling. She had seating accommodation in her cabin for ten people and in rough weather was capable of carrying up to 100 persons. The lifeboat was equipped with a powerful searchlight, a line-throwing gun, oil spray, and was also fitted with electricity throughout. Because of her size, the *George Shee* became the first Torbay lifeboat to be permanently moored on a deep-water mooring, in Brixham's outer harbour, adjacent to the boat-house. The boat-house was retained by the RNLI for use as a workshop and store.

The lifeboat was launched on three occasions prior to the naming ceremony, the Service Records showing that on each occasion she stood by. The first launch was on Tuesday 10 November 1931 when the Spanish steamer, SS *Cilurnum*, of Bilbao, was reported to be dragging her anchors in heavy seas to the north of Torbay. In a full south-westerly gale the lifeboat located the steamer approximately half a mile from the Orestone, this distance in the prevailing conditions being dangerously close. The lifeboat stood by while the anchor was raised and the vessel moved to a sheltered anchorage.

On Wednesday 6 January 1932 the tramp steamer *Trevaylor*, of St Ives, got into difficulties off the Eddystone, Plymouth; her propeller became loose and was finally lost. The *Trevaylor* transmitted an SOS and tugs out of Falmouth responded to her call. The Royal Navy dispatched HMS *Exeter* to the incident. As the casualty was drifting eastwards, the lifeboat was launched in the hope of intercepting the vessel. It was not until morning that she was located off Prawle Point. The tugs successfully attached hawsers to the *Trevaylor* and took her in tow. The lifeboat returned to Brixham having been at sea for 15 hours.

The dedication and naming ceremony for the new lifeboat took place on Wednesday 27 July 1932. The Royal party travelled by aeroplane to Haldon and then progressed to Brixham by road via Torquay and Paignton. HRH the Prince of Wales took lunch at Lupton (now Gramercy Hall School) with Lord Churston. The Bishop of Exeter (Lord William Gascoyne Cecil), the Lord Lieutenant of Devon (Lord Mildmay of Flete), Sir Godfrey Baring and Sir George Shee, after whom the lifeboat was to be named, also took lunch at Lupton.

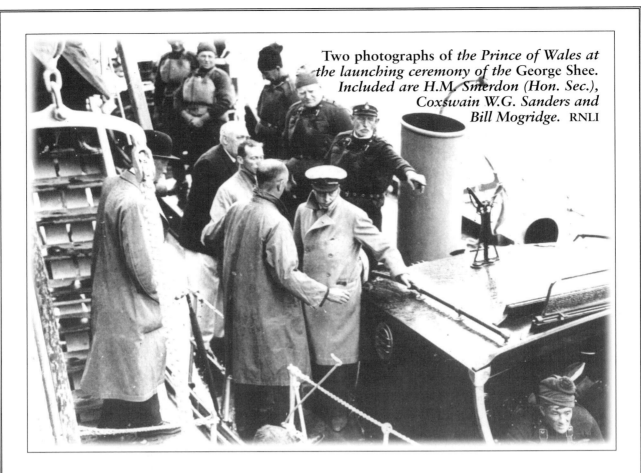

Two photographs of *the Prince of Wales at the launching ceremony of the* George Shee. *Included are H.M. Smerdon (Hon. Sec.), Coxswain W.G. Sanders and Bill Mogridge.* RNLI

*HRH the Prince of Wales at the launching ceremony of the*
George Shee. RNLI

Having lunched, the Royal procession moved on to Brixham. The car in which the Prince travelled stopped at Bolton Cross where he inspected the guard of honour, comprising Coxswains of the Devon lifeboats and local Legionnaires, before going down to the harbour for the naming ceremony.

The first speaker was Sir Harold Clayton, Bt., Chairman of the Torbay Branch of the RNLI, who introduced Colonel C.R. Satterthwaite, OBE, Secretary of the Institution and successor to Sir George Shee. The Chairman of the Urban District Council, Frank Lee, gave the following loyal address:

*To His Royal Highness, The Prince of Wales, K.G., Master of the Merchant Navy and Fishing Fleets.*

*May it please your Royal Highness, we, the Chairman and Members of the Urban District Council of Brixham, in the County of Devon, acting on behalf of the inhabitants of Brixham, beg leave to humbly approach your Royal Highness and desire to convey to you our heartiest congratulations and loyal welcome on your visit to this ancient and historic town of Brixham, better known as 'The Mother of Deep Sea Fisheries' and also our thanks for your so kindly undertaking to perform the naming ceremony of the Torbay lifeboat George Shee.*

*We rejoice to see the heir and representative of royalty so actively engaged in promoting the interests of such a worthy Institution, and we sincerely pray that life and health may long be given to your Royal Highness for the completion of the important objects you have in hand.*

*It gives us added pleasure that Your Royal Highness, the President of this great National Institution, has so graciously consented to journey specially to Brixham for this important ceremony, and to make this day one that will ever be remembered in the history of our town.*

*We offer to Your Royal Highness, on behalf of the inhabitants of our town their liveliest thanks and appreciation at your presence here today.*

*Given under the Common Seal of the Urban District Council of Brixham this 27th day of July, 1932.*

*Frank P. Lee, Chairman of the Brixham U.D. Council,*

*Sanders Lear, Clerk of the Brixham U.D. Council.*

The Prince of Wales responded. Lord Mildmay opened the naming ceremony and called upon Sir George Shee to present the lifeboat. Sir Godfrey

Baring, Chairman of the Committee of Management, accepted the lifeboat on behalf of the Institution. The boat was then presented to the Branch and accepted by Lord Churston, the local President.

Following the service of dedication, which was conducted by the Right Reverend Lord Bishop of Exeter, Lord William Gascoyne-Cecil, and the singing of the hymn 'Eternal Father, Strong to Save', the Prince of Wales, K.G., named the lifeboat *George Shee*, in honour of Sir George Shee and in recognition of his 21 years of service as Secretary of the RNLI (1910–31). In appreciation of his great services, the Management Committee of the RNLI defrayed the cost of the boat, requesting Sir George to nominate a location, from six given places, at which the lifeboat would be stationed. He chose Torbay.

As an alternative to the traditional bottle of champagne, HRH was to break a bottle of Symons' Devonshire cider over the vessel. The bottle proved somewhat more substantial than anticipated and it required a crew member to strike the bottle with an iron bar to complete the ceremony. A maroon that was described as 'music to the ears of a shipwrecked mariner' sounded as the lifeboat steamed out for a short cruise.

The *George Shee* was launched for service only two days after the naming ceremony, the Coastguard having reported a motorboat, the *Commodore*, of Paignton, in distress off Ivy Cove. The motorboat was crewed by seven very inexperienced holidaymakers. Upon her arrival the *George Shee* found that the boat had been taken in tow by another vessel. Both were escorted into harbour by the lifeboat.

On the morning of Monday 30 December 1935 the French trawler *Satanicle* lost all power when she suffered engine failure. She drifted all day in the English Channel, in a full south-south-westerly gale and heavy seas, without being able to attract assistance. It was not until early evening that she was located by the American steamer *Black Hawk*. The steamer failed in her attempts to take the trawler in tow and summoned further assistance by wireless. The German steamer *Westernland* answered the request for assistance and initially succeeded in taking the trawler in tow, although this subsequently failed.

The *George Shee* cast off her mooring at 18.50 hours and commenced the long, arduous 25-mile haul to the scene of the incident. Given the appalling weather conditions, Coxswain Mogridge had reservations about locating the casualty. However, *Black Hawk* had remained with the stricken vessel and her Captain was requested to indicate their position with the use of the vessel's searchlights. Coxswain Mogridge spotted the searchlights, when he was about 30 minutes steaming time from the scene, at 20.45 hours.

Prior to the arrival of the lifeboat, in confused seas, the *Westernland* had closed alongside the *Satanicle*, secured a line, and taken off three crew members by breeches buoy. In making a further approach she made heavy contact with the trawler and had to withdraw. The *George Shee* then approached the trawler, which was sinking, in an attempt to rescue the skipper, who was the sole person remaining on the vessel. At times the height of the waves obliterated the *Satanicle* from

view, but Coxswain Mogridge placed the lifeboat to the lee side of the trawler and a line was thrown to the skipper, who made it fast. The crew, coordinating their actions with the rise and fall of the waves, managed to pull the lifeboat in closer to the trawler. Again, on two occasions, the vessels collided. Coxswain Mogridge held the *George Shee* steady and as she was lifted by a wave, to the level of the *Satanicle's* rail, the skipper jumped for the lifeboat, crew members grabbed him and the securing line was immediately cut allowing the lifeboat to pull clear. Five hours later the lifeboat reached her mooring at

*RNLI's 'Certificate of Thanks' awarded to Harold Soper in recognition of the service to the* Satanicle, *30 December 1935.*

Patrons, Their Majesties The King & Queen

ROYAL NATIONAL LIFE BOAT INSTITUTION

FOR THE

Preservation of Life from Shipwreck

(INCORPORATED BY ROYAL CHARTER.)

ESTABLISHED 1824.

SUPPORTED BY VOLUNTARY CONTRIBUTIONS.

President

*His Royal Highness the Duke of York, K.G.*

Chairman.                                         Deputy Chairman.

*Sir Godfrey Baring, Bt.*                *The Hon. George Colville.*

*At a Meeting of the Committee of Management of the Royal National Life-Boat Institution for the Preservation of Life from Shipwreck, held at their Offices, London, on the 13th day of February, 1936, the following Minute was ordered to be recorded on the Books of the Society.*

*That the Best Thanks of the Royal National Life-boat Institution be accorded to*

## Harold P. Soper,

*in recognition of his endurance and meritorious conduct in the Torbay motor life-boat when she rescued the master of the motor trawler "Satanicle," of Cherbourg, which was in distress about fifteen miles South West of Portland Bill, in a whole S.W. gale with a very heavy sea, on the night of the 30th December, 1935.*

President

Secretary.                                         Chairman.

Brixham. In horrendous weather conditions the *George Shee* had covered some 60 miles, the complete service having taken a full ten hours.

In recognition of the rescue, Coxswain George Mogridge was awarded the RNLI's Bronze Medal and each crew member received formal Thanks on Vellum. The French Government later awarded Silver Medals to Coxswain Mogridge and Second Coxswain Pillar and Bronze Medals to each other member of the crew.

Although not recorded in the Service Records, an incident worthy of note occurred on the evening of Thursday 9 January 1936 when extremely heavy seas and a strong south-westerly gale were pounding the coastline. Information was received, through the Coastguard, that distress signals had been sighted south-west of Bolt Head. The signals emanated from the Dutch motor vessel *Zeehond*, of Groningen, which had experienced engine failure. The vessel was on passage from Southampton to Plymouth with a cargo of timber. She carried a crew of six. The Salcombe lifeboat, the *Alfred and Clara Heath* (formerly of Torbay), was launched at 16.15 hours, but could not make headway against the wind and tide. As she was unable to cross the Salcombe Bar, the launch of larger lifeboats was requested. Both the 60ft Barnett Class Plymouth lifeboat *Robert and Marcella Beck* (Official Number 696), and the *George Shee* were launched at 17.25 hours, the Plymouth boat reaching the *Zeehond* at 19.35 hours. On the arrival of the *George Shee* the Plymouth lifeboat was already in attendance and her services were not required. She returned to Brixham arriving shortly after midnight. The *Robert and Marcella Beck* stood by the *Zeehond* until the repairs to the engine had been completed. She then escorted the vessel in to Salcombe. This demanding service lasted for 16½ hours. The Netherlands Government sent a Letter of Thanks to the crews of both the Plymouth and Torbay lifeboats, as did the Motor Coastal Owners at their Annual General Meeting in Groningen.

Another excellent service was provided on Saturday 23 January 1937 by the lifeboat men of the *George Shee*. The day saw extremely rough seas accompanied by a strong southerly wind. In these conditions, the steamer *English Trader*, under the command of Captain Edmund Howe, a native of Brixham, was bound from Argentina to the Baltic, with a cargo of grain. The 3,953-ton steamer was 374 feet in length and had a beam of 57 feet. She carried a crew of 32. In the early hours, the *English Trader* developed steering-gear problems, which lead to her being driven aground on Checkstone Ledge, at the entrance of Dartmouth Harbour and the River Dart. The Coastguard contacted the RNLI's Torbay Secretary and Launch Authority, Mr H.M. Smardon, and the *George Shee* cast off her mooring at 05.25 hours, reaching the casualty within the hour. Coxswain William H. Mogridge, being aware that a Royal Naval destroyer, HMS *Witch*, the Admiralty tug, *Retort*, and the Dutch salvage tugs *Witte Zee* and *Zwarte Zee*, had also been deployed to the scene, stood by the stricken vessel.

Throughout the day the tugs made repeated efforts to free and re-float the steamer, but she remained fast. With a forecast of worsening weather conditions, the Captain of the steamer requested that the lifeboat should stand by his vessel though the night. With a southerly gale imminent, the *George Shee* put in to Kingswear to refuel.

Weather conditions deteriorated to a full south-south-easterly gale with heavy seas, as the lifeboat took up her stand-by position to the *English Trader*; she remained 'on station' throughout the night. Further attempts were made to salvage the craft, on the high tide of Sunday morning, but these attempts were also made in vain. High, heavy seas continued to pound the vessel, smashing the port side of the bridge, breaking clean over the top of the boat, and flooding two holds. The tremendous buffeting that the steamer received on her weather side was probably responsible for her sudden shift in position, causing her to lie across the entrance to the harbour on the Dartmouth side of the fairway near the Checkstone Buoy. Fearing that his ship could take no further punishment, at 06.00 hours on Monday 25 January, Captain Howe fired three distress flares.

Coxswain Mogridge immediately answered the distress signals and, in a strong ebb tide and seas that were rising and falling between 10 and 15 feet, with great skill and determination, in total darkness, brought the 51ft lifeboat in beneath the stern of the stranded steamer. This manoeuvre was an extremely anxious undertaking, through fear of contacting the wire hawsers attached to the ocean-going tugs and the destroyer. With the heavy sea and swell, there was a constant threat that the lifeboat would be crushed beneath the rising and falling stern of the *English Trader*. It took Coxswain Mogridge 20 minutes to manoeuvre the *George Shee* into a position, aft of the bridge, on the starboard side, thus gaining the full advantage of the steamer's lee. This positioning placed the lifeboat perilously close to the very rocks upon which their casualty had foundered. Once alongside the steamer, ropes were thrown aboard and were made fast, fore and aft.

The lifeboat continued to rise and fall on the 15ft waves and at one point, two of the lifeboat men, Fred Tucker and George Mogridge, who were on the open fore-deck, had to throw themselves flat on the deck to avoid being crushed beneath one of the steamer's lifeboats, which was hanging above their heads in davits. A rope-ladder was lowered from the *English Trader* to the *George Shee*, and in a period of 15 minutes a total of 52 persons had been taken aboard the lifeboat, this number comprising the steamer's crew of 32, 15 stevedores, the pilot, a Royal Naval Signalman, and three salvage officers who had boarded the steamer from the rescue tugs in an attempt to refloat her.

With all hands rescued, Coxswain Mogridge again had to call upon all his skills of seamanship to take the lifeboat clear of the ship. In surging seas and ebbing tide he had to steer the lifeboat, stern first, clear of the surrounding rocks and once more pass beneath the steamer's heaving stern. Judging his timing to the split second, the lines securing the vessels were cut and with the engine 'full astern' the lifeboat pulled clear. This process in itself was not without incident. As huge waves broke over her stern, threatening to flood the lifeboat, the *George Shee* sustained minor damage to belting on her fore quarter. After landing the rescued crew at Dartmouth, at 11.00 hours, Coxswain Mogridge commenced the return journey to Brixham. The *George Shee* regained her mooring at 12.15 hours. This exacting and extraordinary service had lasted for just under 31 hours.

Subsequent efforts made by the tugs and HMS *Witch* failed to refloat the *English Trader*. Finally a decision was made to cut away the bow section of the vessel, an operation that reportedly took 19 days. A new bulkhead having been fitted in Dartmouth, the vessel was towed to Southampton where the Middle Docks and Engineering Co., of South Shields, fitted a new bow section.

For his courage and outstanding seamanship, Coxswain William Mogridge was awarded a Bronze Medal by the RNLI. The presentation took place at the Annual Meeting of the Institution, which was held at Central Hall, Westminster, on Friday 9 April 1937, when Coxswain Mogridge was presented to the Duke of Kent. Also present at the ceremony was Mr Ernest Brown, Minister of Labour, whose father had been the Coxswain of the Torquay lifeboat, the *Wighton*. The *Herald Express*, of 10 April 1937, reported Mr Brown as saying:

*This is a wonderful piece of organisation, for the men who man our lifeboats are not like men in the Navy or mercantile marine; they are volunteers, awarded by the institution for work done. I recall being held at the window while a gale of wind was blowing, and rain beating on the panes and knowing afterwards that my own father was in the lifeboat, and to be here with the Torbay lifeboat men is to me a particular pleasure.*

The meeting was also addressed by the French Ambassador, M. Charles Corbin, who said:

*I also express my warm thanks to Coxswain Mogridge and the crew of the Torbay lifeboat who on the night of December 30, 1935, went out in particularly heavy seas to the rescue of the trawler* Satanicle, *of Cherbourg. In recognition of these splendid achievements the French Government has awarded Silver and Bronze Medals to the coxswain and crew to which I have referred. In the name of the French families who but for this might be mourning today I offer my profound gratitude.*

Thanks on Vellum were awarded to each other member of that brave crew, Second Coxswain William Pillar, Bowman Frederick Sanders, Motor Mechanic Frederick Welsh, Assistant Mechanic Edwin Lamswood and lifeboat men Frederick Tucker, John Glanville and George Mogridge. The Station Honorary Secretary, Mr H.M. Smardon, received a Letter of Thanks for the assistance which he had given on that occasion. Mr Smardon in turn paid tribute to the oil companies who assisted in the replenishment of the petrol supply, which kept the lifeboat in active service.

During the summer of 1937, the *George Shee* was taken 'off station' for routine maintenance and an overhaul. During her temporary absence, the reserve lifeboat *City of Bradford I*, a 45ft, single-engine, Watson Class lifeboat replaced her. The *City of Bradford I* was called on to provide only one service, that being to the yacht *Iona*, on Thursday 12 August. The lifeboat was launched at 21.00 hours and located the disabled yacht. The yacht, with a crew of four men on board, was taken in tow by the lifeboat and assisted in to Dartmouth Harbour. The lifeboat returned to her mooring at 01.35 hours.

A Dartmouth wife's anxious vigil, at Baynards Cove Pilot Station, ended on the afternoon of Friday 9 December 1938, when, at 17.30 hours, a call was received from Compass Coastguard, that the Brixham lifeboat had located the *Channel Pride*, a 36ft crabber, owned by the Channel Fishing Company, Dartmouth. The crabber had left Dartmouth at 08.00 hours to drop her pots off Coombe Point, near the entrance to the River Dart. Early in the afternoon the crew of two, Alec Tucker, of Dartmouth, and Cyril Courtenay, of Beesands, had been busily engaged in examining the pots when, without warning, a southerly gale sprang up. Being close to the lee shore, the skipper of the crabber decided to return to port but in so doing, fouled his propeller with a crab pot, stalling the boat's motor. From 13.00 hours the boat had been under observation by the Dartmouth Coastguard who saw that it was heading back towards Dartmouth Harbour, but noted that the vessel stopped about one mile off Coombe Point. The *Channel Pride* started to drift towards the cliffs but luckily a local man, Mr F.P. Ingham of Oversea, Stoke Flemming, noted the plight in which the vessel found herself and immediately notified the Coastguard, who in turn alerted the Torbay Lifeboat Station. Coxswain William Mogridge, having mustered his crew, Second Coxswain William Pillar, Bowman Frederick Sanders, Motor Mechanic Richard Harris, Assistant Mechanic Edwin Lamswood and lifeboat men Frederick Tucker, C. Bickford and F. Lamswood, slipped the *George Shee* from her mooring at 14.20 hours. The lifeboat then commenced a ten-mile journey, directly into the teeth of the gale, the crew having to contend with heavy and unpredictable seas, very heavy rain and extremely limited visibility. The Coastguard also contacted the pilot's office at Baynards Cove. At 14.45 hours, pilot R. Gatzias, accompanied by W. Bellamy and Charles Drew, put to sea in the pilot cutter. The heavy seas, rain and fog impeded their progress, the visibility being so poor that the cutter actually passed by the *Channel Pride* without sighting her. The pilot cutter turned, and returned to port. Gatzias, Bellamy and Drew were subsequently joined by pilot G. Riddalls, and the party proceeded, on foot, to Redlap Cliffs, where they attempted to guide the lifeboat to the crippled crabber.

In an attempt to slow down their rate of drift, Alec Tucker lashed his oilskin to a mop handle in an attempt to provide a makeshift sail; this being ineffectual, the crew of the crabber dropped anchor, which finally held when they were less than 200 yards from shore. They flew a large brown paper bag, attached to a mop handle, as a distress signal. The crew were all too aware of the ferocity of the waves as they continued to crash against Redlap Cliff. Fearing for their lives the two men took off their sea boots and tied rubber crab pot markers around their waist in an attempt to provide some element of buoyancy, should the need arise.

The light was fading as the *George Shee* approached the mouth of the River Dart and conditions were such that the lifeboat crew had extreme difficulty in locating the disabled crabber. The lifeboat proceeded along the cliffs of Start Bay before turning and retracing her course. In circumstances such as those in which the *Channel Pride* found herself, a lifeboat Coxswain would consider dropping anchor and veering down on to the stricken vessel, but on this occasion the lifeboat was almost on top of the crabber before the Bowman, Frederick Sanders, spotted her. With the fishing boat in such close proximity, the lifeboat was committed to her course. Using his great skill and seamanship Coxswain Mogridge manoeuvred his 51ft craft until he protected the *Channel Pride* in the lee of the port bow of the lifeboat, allowing the two fishermen to jump to safety. At that very moment the *George Shee* was hit by an enormous wave that swung her bow around towards the shore. Coxswain Mogridge was unable to go astern for fear of fouling the lifeboat's propellers with the crabber's cable. He chose to go full ahead towards the shore, throwing his helm hard over, and bringing her round when only 15–18 feet from the base of the cliffs. Her head turned, the lifeboat crashed through the oncoming breakers and regained the comparative safety of the open sea. The lifeboat then made the signal 'ALL SAVED. HEAVY SEAS. RUNNING FOR BRIXHAM.' The *George Shee* returned to her mooring in Brixham Harbour at 19.45 hours.

Having witnessed the rescue from the top of Redlap Cliff, the pilot Riddalls told a local news reporter 'It was the cleverest piece of work I've ever seen.'

For his outstanding courage, skill and seamanship, Coxswain William Mogridge was awarded a Silver Medal by the RNLI. Each member of his crew was awarded the RNLI's Thanks on Vellum.

Services provided by the Torbay lifeboat, between September 1939 and May 1945, were under war conditions; records and newspaper accounts of these launches were very sketchy and, in most cases, they were not reported upon at all. During the wartime period, the Torbay lifeboat was launched on 16 occasions, when varying degrees of service were provided; additionally there were some 17 launches which proved to be false alarms. The Service Boards at Brixham do not detail launches carried out between January 1942 and January 1944. The RNLI Headquarters at Poole, Dorset, and the Brixham Museum and History Society, by virtue of the records of the late Arthur C. Ellis, have been able to provide some information in respect of a number of the wartime services.

The *George Shee* was launched on Wednesday 18 October 1939, together with the Exmouth lifeboat, in response to reports that two RAF launches had broken down 12 miles southwest of Beer Head. Fortunately both launches were able to make slow progress to their home base at Lyme Regis and both lifeboats were recalled to station at approximately 23.39 hours.

The *Henrietta* was a 60-year-old schooner, built on the River Fal, which originally plied the copper ore trade between Cornwall and Wales, before working in the general coasting trade. On the afternoon of Saturday 16 December 1939 she was crossing Start Bay when she was blown off course by an east-north-easterly gale, onto the Skerries, a series of sandbanks to the south of Dartmouth. She rolled dangerously, her gunwales being frequently submerged in the heavy, shallow seas. The alarm was raised and the *George Shee* was launched at 13.40 hours, reaching the casualty some 90 minutes later. A tug and a trawler also responded to her distress signals but were unable to make an approach or offer assistance. Both vessels stood by.

Upon the arrival of the lifeboat, the Coxswain, William Mogridge, quickly assessed the scene and deemed conditions to be far too excessive for the use of a breeches buoy; he feared for the safety of the *Henrietta's* crew should they be dragged into that icy, raging surf. The only option open to Coxswain Mogridge was to steer the lifeboat directly into the breakers in order to reach the schooner. The *Henrietta* rolled violently, continuing to submerge her gunwales. The yardarm on the foremast was swinging freely over the side and the starboard anchor, which had fouled the hawser, also hung dangerously over the side, impairing any approach. Coxswain Mogridge slowly and cautiously approached the casualty and, seeing a window of opportunity, took the *George Shee* straight in to lie along the starboard side of the stranded schooner. Ropes were made fast between the two vessels and, in just three minutes, the schooner's crew of seven had jumped and gained the safety of the lifeboat. Before the securing ropes could be cut, the *Henrietta* rolled, sending her foreyard crashing onto the lifeboat and inflicting a 12ft split in her gunwale. The ropes were severed and the lifeboat pulled clear into open water, returning to station at 17.40 hours. The *Henrietta* was lost.

For this service, on 26 July 1940, on behalf of the RNLI, Mrs Hay Mattey, President of the Ladies Lifeboat Guild, presented Coxswain William Mogridge with his second Silver Medal. Second Coxswain William Pillar, Bowman Frederick C. Sanders and Motor Mechanic Richard Harris were each awarded Bronze Medals. The other members of the crew, Assistant Mechanic Edwin Lamswood, A. Disney, W. Rogers, W. Coleman and E. Cronin received the RNLI's Thanks on Vellum together with a reward of £2.0s.0d.

During the period of the Second World War, through necessity, several foreign-registered trawlers found themselves fishing out of British ports. Brixham was no exception in receiving what became known as 'refugee trawlers'. One such trawler was the Belgian vessel *Jan Denye*, of Ostend. On the bitterly cold evening of Monday 29 January 1940 she was seen to be dragging her anchors in a position uncomfortably close to the cliffs below Daddy Hole Plain, Torquay. The lifeboat was launched at 22.50 hours into rough seas and an east-south-easterly gale-force wind. Great difficulty was experienced in locating the casualty as this was the first night of the wartime 'black-out', and when she was located she was less than 200 yards from the shore. The *Jan Denye's* anchor was slipped and in total darkness the *George Shee* escorted the vessel to the safety of Brixham Harbour. Unfortunately, during this service, lifeboat man Frederick Tucker suffered severe exposure and hypothermia.

The lifeboat was launched only two nights later to go to the assistance of the Greek steamer, *Avra* of Andros, which was reportedly aground near Start Point, at Sour Mill Cove. Following the launch of the *George Shee*, a further signal was received updating the position of the stranded steamer and placing her outside the Torbay operational area. The lifeboat was recalled.

During the night of Monday 11 March 1940 the English Channel was shrouded in fog when the steamship *Clan Stuart* was in collision with a destroyer, 22 miles south-east of Berry Head. As a result of the collision the steamship was cut in two. Both the *George Shee* and the Salcombe lifeboat, the Watson Class *Samuel and Marie Parkhouse*, were launched but were recalled when confirmation was received from Plymouth that the *Clan Stuart's* crew of 75 had been successfully picked up by local shipping.

In June 1940 the Admiralty requisitioned the *George Shee*. On Saturday 15 June, together with other boats, she was ordered to Dartmouth, where she was placed under direct Admiralty Orders. The crew were ordered to take on board sufficient fuel for 350 miles and provisions for four days, the object being to return Allied troops from Brest. The proposed voyage was not undertaken.

On the evening of Tuesday 9 July 1940 the Torbay boat was launched in order to assist two Allied vessels that had reportedly been under attack by enemy aircraft, off Start Point. When the lifeboat was off Dartmouth, she was met by the Dutch vessel *Jola*, which had been strafed with machine-gun fire whilst attempting to rescue the crew of the Latvian steamer, *Talvaldis*. The *Jola* was flying the International Code Flag 'W', which denoted 'I am in need of medical assistance.' Being satisfied that she could make port safely, the lifeboat continued on and located the steamer that had foundered some four miles south-east of Start Point. It was established that

*Lifeboat crew of June 1936.* Left to right: *Fred Tucker, Fred Welsh (Mechanic), William Pillar, William Mogridge (Cox'n), Fred Sanders, H.M. Smardon (Hon. Sec.).*
COURTESY BRIXHAM MUSEUM

the crew of the *Talvaldis* had been located in a life-raft by Lannacombe fishermen then transferred to the Salcombe lifeboat and taken to safety.

The French Navy training yawl, *Mutin*, which was under Admiralty Orders, found herself in difficulty off Berry Head on Friday 6 December 1940. The vessel's engine had been swamped and she was unable to raise her anchor. The lifeboat was called out to assist, the crew slipped the anchors and the yawl was towed into Brixham.

A south-south-easterly gale was blowing at midnight on Monday 31 March 1941, when the Resident Naval Officer at Brixham reported that a boat from HM Tanker *Pomerol* was adrift outside Brixham Harbour. The *George Shee* was launched and put out for the boat, accompanied by the former Lowestoft trawler, *Flag Jack*, now in the role of a Naval examination vessel. The lifeboat located the ship's boat about two miles off the breakwater, HM Tanker *Pomerol* having highlighted the boat with her searchlight. As shore lights were not visible, due to the wartime blackout, the lifeboat guided the ship's boat into harbour.

Allied shipping came under attack some five miles south-south-east of Berry Head on the night of Wednesday 9 April 1941, when a Norwegian oil tanker and a British steamer became the victims of an aerial torpedo raid. The lifeboat was launched and on arriving at the scene, at 23.10 hours, found the SS *Benston* with her bow projecting above the water and her stern submerged. Oil had spread 500 yards from the vessel setting the sea around her ablaze, the flames reaching a height of 60 to 70 feet. The lifeboat approached the leeward side of the fire zone and came within 150 yards of the stricken tanker. Twice she circled the fire zone but failed to locate any member of the vessel's crew. Five critically injured crewmen were in fact landed at Dartmouth by a Royal

Navy motor launch; all subsequently died from their injuries. A further three bodies were landed at Brixham.

The British vessel that was attacked was the steamer *Dudley Rose*; she was sunk as a result of the attack, her crew being successfully taken off by escorting vessels. A second Norwegian vessel made port at Dartmouth, nursing an unexploded bomb in her hold. The bomb exploded the following day as the vessel lay on the mud of the River Dart. The lifeboat was only one of many craft at the scene of the disaster, the other vessels being taken to be British patrol boats and motor launches. It was later reported that German craft actually mingled with the rescue vessels but the confusion at the scene of the disaster was so great that they did not fire on the British vessels.

Coxswain William Henry Haywood Mogridge died suddenly on Tuesday 6 January 1942; he had served as Coxswain of the Torbay lifeboat for ten years. He was succeeded, as Coxswain, by his nephew, Frederick Collier Sanders.

In October 1942, the Admiralty requisitioned the Brixham boat-house. One third of the building's length was demolished to provide space for the construction of a hard standing. On Wednesday 5 January 1944 the lifeboat was placed at the disposal of the Resident Naval Officer, Brixham, to take mail and supplies to minesweepers, which were sheltering in the bay. During one such trip, in gale conditions, the lifeboat encountered a small Naval launch that had broken down. The lifeboat took the launch in tow returning it and the crew of three to the mother ship.

Numerous Army, Naval and RAF units were established in Torbay and the surrounding area during the war. The waters of Torbay became extremely busy with a constant stream of Allied Naval craft using the bay as a rendezvous point and seeking shelter during inclement weather. In an east-north-easterly wind and heavy seas on Saturday 19 February 1944, four landing craft were driven ashore at Paignton. The craft, belonging to the American Infantry, were the *LCI.493*, *LCI.498*, *LCI.502* and the *LCI.506*.

The *George Shee* was launched at 17.00 hours to assist American salvage officers in recovering the vessels. Having worked throughout the night, the lifeboat returned to her mooring at 04.30 hours. At 10.00 hours the same day, the lifeboat conveyed the Coastguard's rocket apparatus to Paignton, in order that towing hawsers could be established between the craft and tugs. As sea conditions were not conducive to using the rocket apparatus, the lifeboat anchored and veered down towards the landing craft. Although the lifeboat was being buffeted by waves, a line was successfully fired to one of the craft. The American servicemen, being unfamiliar with the apparatus, heaved upon the line until it broke, therefore being unable to pull in the heavier towing hawser. Having missed the tide and the opportunity to refloat the landing craft, operations were suspended for the day. The *George Shee* again returned to the landing craft, on the afternoon of 21 February and stood by. The vessels remained stranded for over 50 hours, the operation to refloat the craft being concluded at 19.00 hours.

At about noon on Friday 13 October 1944 the Belgian trawler *H.68 De Meeuw*, of Heyst, developed engine trouble while fishing between Berry Head and Hopes Nose. Oscar Vantorre, the owner/skipper, and Albert Bogaert anchored *De Meeuw* in order to effect a repair. The weather at the time was a strong breeze, freshening to gale force, with exceptionally strong gusts accompanying rain squalls and deteriorating visibility.

At 14.26 hours the Resident Naval Officer at Brixham informed the Coxswain of the Torbay lifeboat that a trawler had reportedly broken down off Hopes Nose. Coxswain F.C. Sanders was requested to muster his crew and await confirmation of the report. The crew were together by 14.47 hours and at 14.48 hours Sanders was instructed to launch the lifeboat and proceed to a position one mile east-south-east of Hopes Nose. As the lifeboat made her way across Torbay to the stricken trawler, the visibility worsened due to blinding rainstorms. The crew of the *De Meeuw* observed the *George Shee*'s approach and hoisted a flag to attract attention. The lifeboat crew saw the flag but did in fact lose sight of the boat temporarily during heavy rain.

Having located the trawler the lifeboat established herself to starboard of the *De Meeuw*, Coxswain Sanders being very aware of the possible danger of fouling the lifeboat's propeller with

Left: *Coxswain Frederick C. Sanders, Coxswain of the* George Shee *(1942–51).*

Below: *Henry O. Thomas, Coxswain of the* George Shee *(1951–58) and of the* Princess Alexandra of Kent *(1958–60).*
BOTH RNLI

the trawler's anchor wire. The Second Coxswain called to the crew of the trawler to keep their vessel riding at the anchor until the tow had been secured, but the Belgians misunderstood the instructions and chopped the anchor wire away. This caused the trawler to immediately come broadside on into the troughs of the very steep, white, breaking sea – the gale at this time being at its zenith. With the *De Meeuw* now totally at the mercy of the elements, Coxswain Sanders had to reposition the *George Shee* in order to establish towage. When closing to take the rope from the Bowman, the belting of the lifeboat came into contact with the trawler's forestay, which instantly parted, throwing 19-year-old Albert Bogaert, who was clutching the stay, into the heavy sea. The youth was now in imminent danger of being crushed between *De Meeuw* and the lifeboat. He failed to catch the first rope, which was thrown to him from the *H.68* and also the second, which was thrown from the lifeboat.

Coxswain Sanders manoeuvred the *George Shee* into a position, under the port quarter of the *De Meeuw* and put a crewman on board the trawler to assist in the rescue of Bogaert. The gale had now reached F9 and it was in these conditions that Coxswain Sanders excelled in his application of seamanship and motive power. It is estimated that in the following quarter of an hour, the engines of the lifeboat were manipulated on well in excess of 20 occasions, each manipulation being perfect both in timing and speed. Seas broached incessantly over both craft as the trawler continued on a lee drift, varying in both speed and direction, rendering a connective service between the lifeboat and the casualty exceptionally hazardous. During each manoeuvre there was the ever-present danger of Bogaert being crushed between the bluff of the bow of the lifeboat and the *De Meeuw*. It was at this point that the trawler's skipper Oscar Vantorre, a non-swimmer, made a super-human bid to save his crew mate. It was reported thus:

*Clutching the port bulwark with both hands directly abreast of where Bogaert was splashing the flat of his hands to keep himself afloat, Vantorre poised both feet in mid-air and then dropped full length over the ship's side into the surging elements. Bogaert gripped onto his skipper's heels. With super-human strength he hauled his ship mate close to the ship's side. Bogaert firmly gripped the* De Meeuw's *bulwarks.*

*Bogaert wore rubber thigh sea boots, and thigh sea stockings. The boots filled with water and the sea stockings completely saturated, adding weight to the task of Vantorre getting his mate safe aboard the ship. Attempt after attempt failed. Bogaert, adroitly using his feet, forced each sea boot and each sea stocking off his legs. His physical strength well nigh spent to exhaustion point, Vantorre succeeded in establishing a grip of his ship mate's trousers, and with a super-human heave hauled Bogaert inboard, a daring feat of rescue from drowning.*

Just as this feat was accomplished, Coxswain Sanders manoeuvred the *George Shee* sufficiently close to *De Meeuw's* port quarter which allowed lifeboat man Soper to make a perilous leap to board the trawler in order to assist the two exhausted crew. Towage was established and Soper took the trawler's wheel. The *De Meeuw* was birthed at Brixham at 16.00 hours. The Service Report contains the following paragraph:

*I have been requested by Coxswain Sanders to express his sincerest admiration of Motor Mechanic R.T. Harris for his prompt response to commands and smart efficiency in handling*

*William George Sanders, the oldest Coxswain in the RNLI, retired aged 73 after 36 years as Coxswain of the Torbay lifeboat.*

*the engine controls, single handed, during the crucial stages of the Service, it being mutually agreed that Assistant motor Mechanic H.O. Thomas would through deck experience prove a greater asset to assist the Lifeboatmen one short of the boat's complement: of Bowman S.B. Glanville, who deputised as Second Coxswain, for his watchfulness and ready judgment in handling the Lifeboat under such severe weather disabilities, the Coxswain being so stationed at his post that he had no view of the man overboard: to the Lifeboatmen for the most exemplary way each co-operated to accomplish such a worthy Service.*

It is of note that *De Meeuw* had previously been recorded in the annals of the RNLI, through a service that took place on Friday 9 December 1938. At the time of that service she sailed under the name *Channel Pride*!

On the night of Saturday 16–Sunday 17 December 1944, the tug *Empire Alfred*, with a hopper barge (*Yard Craft 345*) in tow, was at anchor and sheltering in the roads off Brixham Harbour. A full south-easterly gale was blowing, which brought with it torrential rain and heavy, confused seas. The conditions were such, that unnoticed by her crew, the tug dragged her two anchors and the vessel started a lee drift in excess of three miles, towards the shoreline of Paignton.

At 23.30 hours, on Saturday evening, the cast-off lead showed three fathoms of water and almost immediately the tug bumped heavily. Her sirens sounded SOS and distress rockets were fired. The *Empire Alfred*, carrying a crew of 14, and her tow carrying a crew of five, was stranded off Hollicombe Point, close to the Torquay and Paignton Gasworks. At 00.43 hours, in atrocious weather conditions, the lifeboat, manned by a crew of six, slipped her mooring. Visibility was poor in the extreme and shore lights were obliterated. Coxswain Fred Sanders steered the *George Shee* in the general direction of the reported incident but it was not until 01.05 hours that the lifeboat crew, using their searchlight, spotted the white masthead light and green deck light of the stricken vessel. Coxswain

Sanders manoeuvred the lifeboat towards the *Empire Alfred* but in torrential, blinding rain the tug was not easily discernible. It was impossible to work out exactly how the tug was lying. Worryingly for the Coxswain the casting of the lead revealed that the lifeboat was entering very shallow water. What followed was described in the Service Launch Record:

*The Coxswain backed the lifeboat out, full speed astern, still in shallow water, consulted the Bowman, who had vacated the Second Coxswain's chair, over the exceptionally hazardous task that confronted them to achieve a rescue. Bowman Glanville, replying to the Coxswain's 'Could you see which way the ship was laying on the beach?' said, 'I think she is laying half slued across the beach.'*

A second attempt to ascertain the correct way in which the vessel lay, again brought the lifeboat into very shallow water, ranging from two fathoms on the crest of the breakers to one and a half fathoms in the troughs of the sea. Again, in torrential rain, Sanders was forced to engage 'full astern' and back out into the raging surf.

The third attempt to establish the lay of the vessel also failed. Coxswain Sanders shouted to the crew of the tug to show a stern light for guidance. Receiving a signal that this would be done, he backed the lifeboat out of the shallow breakers for a third time. The *George Shee* made a sweep of the outer shallow breakers. Due to the manner in which the tug was slewed across the beach, and through lack of depth of water, it was impossible to seek the lee side of the vessel but, guided by the stern lights on the ship and the depths sounded by the lead, with great skill and seamanship Coxswain Sanders berthed the lifeboat abeam the engine-room on the starboard, weather side of the *Empire Alfred*. Ropes were used to secure the lifeboat fore and aft, as heavy breaking seas breached clean over both ship and lifeboat, causing them to roll and bump heavily. The ship's lifeboat had been swung out on the weather side, and was moving uncontrollably. Bowman Glanville shouted a warning to Harry Soper and undoubtedly averted a serious accident as the lifeboat swung perilously close to his head.

The two craft were rolling wildly in the raging surf and the lifeboat touched the seabed in the troughs. As the lifeboat dropped into a trough, one of her fend-offs caught in something on the side of the ship and hung the lifeboat up, until the holding rope parted. Coxswain Sanders and his crew stuck resolutely to their job, ready at any moment to cast off the ropes if both craft failed to synchronise their rolling, each being at the mercy of the sea. It took nearly 30 minutes to take the crew of 14 off the *Empire Alfred*. The Captain of the tug was deeply concerned regarding the safety of the crew of the *Yard Craft*, which was lying further inshore, in shallower water. He made the following appeal to Coxswain Sanders to rescue them:

**Coxswain:** 'We're going to get them off the ship at all cost, if it is possible.'
**Captain:** 'We'll get a line in over the ship with our line-throwing gun.'
**Coxswain:** 'What depth of water is she drawing?'
**Captain:** 'Eleven feet.'
**Coxswain:** 'If she's drawing eleven feet, our boat can go there all right. We're going into a very dangerous hole. I want every attention to my orders. Is everything right with you Dick?'
**Dick Harris:** 'Cox'sun I'm ready'
**Coxswain:** 'Standby everyone. We're going in.'

As the lifeboat approached the *Yard Craft*, which was much further inshore, the lead sounding averaged two fathoms. Inching his way forward, Coxswain Sanders became very suspicious of the depth of water the *Yard Craft* was drawing. The following conversation is again taken from the Service Record:

**Coxswain:** 'Dick. Be ready to come astern hard, when I shout full astern.'
**Soper:** 'Still getting two fathoms.'

Then came the shock:

**Soper:** 'Just over a fathom.'
**Coxswain:** 'Come astern full.'

Simultaneously the lifeboat hit the bottom, every man on board being lifted off his feet and Coxswain Sanders being thrown upwards in his steering chair.

**Soper:** 'Two fathoms again.'

Motor Mechanic Harris manipulated the controls instantly, crying 'Come astern full'. The *George Shee* went back into the tumultuous breakers. It was estimated that for over 120 yards, the lead sounding remained at two fathoms. In the pitch darkness, the grey side of the *Yard Craft* suddenly loomed into view. The lifeboat crew judged her to be no more than 40 yards ahead when a terrific bumping occurred. It was immediately evident that there was still an insufficient depth of water to approach.

By this time the Paignton Life-Saving Association had fired three rockets and established a line connection with the barge, although

*Making for the boat!* Left to right: *Blake Glanville, 'Ratio' Stone, Harry Thomas, ?,*
*Charlie Coram.* Note the old boat-house in the background. KEN THOMAS

*Cox'n F.C. Sanders and crew of the* George Shee, *in the boarding boat, 1945.* RNLI

any attempt of rescue by breeches buoy in the prevailing conditions was ruled out. In consultation with the Tugmaster, A. Warder, of West Hartlepool, it was agreed that as a precaution against hypothermia, the crew of the *Empire Alfred*, who were cold and wet, should be landed at Brixham before any further attempt to reach the barge be made. At 04.18 hours the Brixham Coastguard received a R/T message, via Dartmouth: 'Have taken off tug crew. Have made an attempt for salvage ship but not enough water yet. Will try again later.' At 04.34 hours the Hon. Secretary received the R/T message: 'Am returning to Station with 14 survivors. Please arrange accommodation.' This request was attended to and the *George Shee* returned to the second casualty, carrying the Captain of the tug who had volunteered to assist the lifeboat crew with the rescue.

On approaching the wreck of the *Yard Craft*, the Torbay lifeboat sent a Morse-code signal to the LSA at Paignton, 'Have you taken crew out?' The reply was: 'No. Our whip has caught foul. You carry on and get in to take them out.' The lifeboat responded: 'We'll do our best.'

As the shallow waters continued to prevent the lifeboat approaching the barge on the lee side, Coxswain Sanders attempted to approach the craft from the Paignton end of the beach. Again the water depth dropped drastically from two to one and a half fathoms. Once more the lifeboat pulled out, full astern, but on this occasion Coxswain Sanders took the *George Shee* to a position where he could drop a cable and veer the lifeboat down onto the weather side of the tug. Bowman Glanville reported that he had veered out 80 fathoms of cable, and then the lead sounding gave one and a half fathoms. The craft continued to roll violently in the breakers but eventually, with great skill and determination and with waves breaking over the aft cockpit of the lifeboat, Coxswain Sanders reached the casualty berthing the port quarter of the lifeboat against the *Yard Craft's* weather quarter. Due to a shortage of crew on the lifeboat, they had launched with six instead of eight, the Assistant Mechanic had to leave his post at the controls and assist his crew mates on the open deck. Motor Mechanic Harris was left to control both engines from the flooded cockpit. Two men were taken on board but the rebound of the waves, caused by the vicious undercurrent, parted the lifeboat from the casualty. Skilful manipulation of the engines reunited lifeboat and casualty and a further two men were taken off before the rebound once more parted the vessels. The *George Shee* approached the *Yard Craft* for a third time. In extremely difficult and deteriorating conditions it took 20 minutes to rescue the fifth man. The

rescue being achieved, the securing ropes were severed and Coxswain Sanders put his helm hard to starboard. The *George Shee* responded to the helm and hearing the Bowman call 'two fathoms', he knew that the lifeboat was clear. At 07.00 hours the Torbay Lifeboat Station Honorary Secretary received the signal 'lifeboat have got the crew.'

For outstanding skill and bravery that night, Coxswain Frederick C. Sanders was awarded the RNLI's Silver Medal, with a Clasp to his Bronze Medal being awarded to Mechanic Richard Harris. Crewmen Samuel Glanville (Bowman), Henry Thomas (Assistant Mechanic), Harold Soper and Abraham Bartlett each received the Institution's Thanks on Vellum in acknowledgement of the role that they had played in the rescue.

The RNLI awarded £24.0s.0d. to the crews of the Torbay and Salcombe lifeboats following their launch on Monday 7 May 1945. An explosion had been heard and it was believed that the Norwegian minesweeper, *No.382*, had hit a mine approximately 15 miles off Berry Head. Together with the Salcombe lifeboat, the 46ft Watson Class *Samuel and Marie Parkhouse*, the *George Shee* carried out a search for survivors but, despite finding two cushions, tragically none were found. The *Samuel and Marie Parkhouse* in fact launched at 23.59 hours on 7 May, VE Day, just one minute before the end of the war in Europe.

The *George Shee* and the *Samuel and Marie Parkhouse* were the last RNLI lifeboats to be launched during the war years.

A launch which must rank amongst the quickest call-outs achieved by a crew, took place on the afternoon of Friday 20 July 1945. The crew of the *George Shee* had assembled at the Brixham station, in preparation for a visit to Dartmouth in connection with a Dartmouth Ladies' Lifeboat Guild Flag Day, when a report was received of a boat drifting out to sea in Babbacombe Bay. Coxswain F.C. Sanders immediately cancelled the visit to Dartmouth and proceeded, at full speed, to Babbacombe. Upon their arrival, the lifeboat crew found four rowing boats drifting seawards on a fresh westerly breeze.

A Polish Air Squadron, enjoying a spot of leave, had hired out a number of rowing boats. Mr and Mrs Gadeke, of Chingford, who were also drifting out to sea, gained the attention of the Officer in Charge, Captain L.J. Pagozalski. Capt. Pagozalski rowed to their assistance and took Mrs Gadeke on board his boat, leaving Mr Gadeke to row back to shore. Four young women had also observed the plight of the Gadekes and rowed to their assistance. Mr Badcock, a local boat owner, also went to assist. Upon reaching Mr Gadeke, Mr Badcock took him into his rowing boat and together they attempted to row for shore but were unable to make headway into the stiff headwind. The lifeboat, having rescued the Polish officer and Mrs Gadeke, and subsequently Mr Badcock and Mr Gadeke, then went to the assistance of the four women who were drifting seawards. They then recovered the empty craft, taking all four craft in tow, in a short loppy sea, back in to Babbacombe Bay where the occupants were landed safely.

A Torquay motor boat, the *West Coast*, caught fire off Roundham Head, Paignton, shortly before 22.00 hours on the evening of Thursday 11 October 1945. The fire started when heat from a hurricane lamp ignited fumes as petrol was being poured into the fuel tank. The crew attempted to get the craft as close to shore as possible, but she was enveloped in flames and sank off Goodrington. A local resident reported the incident to the Paignton Police, they in turn contacted Coxswain F.C. Sanders, and the lifeboat was soon launched. As the lifeboat approached Goodrington Beach she entered dense fog, and only found the stricken vessel by homing in on the shouts for help. Coxswain Sanders found that the motor boat was in fact one of a fleet of three vessels, the other two being Torquay punts in which were four men and two boys. It transpired that the boats were prawning, with baited drop nests, with the *West Coast* being used as the 'parent craft'. The lifeboat crew rendered first-aid to one of the fishermen, who had received burns to his hands. The men and the punts were landed at Torquay Harbour. Due to the dense fog, it was 02.00 hours before the *George Shee* regained her mooring at Brixham.

The 999 emergency telephone service was responsible for the speedy and efficient service given to the motor boat *Miss Ann* off Paignton Beach, at just after 23.00 hours on Thursday 18 July 1946. Mr H.J. Terry, a visitor, was taking a late-evening stroll, when he heard continuous whistling coming from a boat, approximately half a mile offshore. He reported his concerns to a local hotelier, Mr F.W. Baker, of the Sefton Hotel, Paignton, who telephoned the Torquay Police. The lifeboat was launched, under the command of Coxswain F.C. Sanders and, upon seeing the approaching navigation lights of the lifeboat, the occupants of the motorboat lit a flare. The motorboat had lost the use of its engine due to a pinion stripping. The crew of four were taken aboard the lifeboat and the motorboat taken in tow and landed at Brixham.

Although the service provided that night was somewhat routine, it was unique as it is believed to be the first occasion on which the 999 service was used in the launch of a Torbay lifeboat.

The *George Shee* was launched at 05.45 hours on Friday 24 November 1946 for what was to be a long, exacting and demanding service. The launch was made to assist the steamer *Ayrshire Coast*, of Liverpool, and her crew of 12, who were reported in difficulty approximately ten miles south-east of Start Point. To reach the steamer, the lifeboat had to head directly into heavy seas, resulting from south-westerly gale-force winds. The exact location of the casualty was unknown and restricted visibility severely hampered the search. All that morning, and well in to the afternoon, the lifeboat continued the search for the *Ayrshire Coast*, but their efforts were to no avail. Predictably, after so long at sea, the *George Shee* had to return to Brixham to refuel, this break giving the crew a chance to have a hot meal and a change of clothes.

The lifeboat left Brixham to recommence the search at 16.30 hours. After about two hours, the *Ayrshire Coast* was located in Lyme Bay, where the Admiralty tug *Enforcer* was attempting to take her in tow. A tow-rope was attached and at 19.20 hours, escorted by the lifeboat, the long tow to Portland was commenced. The gale continued to blow and the sea state remained rough and confused. At 21.00 hours the tow-rope parted but was re-established and the tow continued. When the vessels had rounded Portland Bill and entered the comparative safety of calmer waters, the lifeboat went on ahead to Weymouth, where she arrived at 10.50 hours on 25 November. The lifeboat was refuelled for a second time and once again the crew welcomed a hot meal and a brief rest, after which they immediately set out for Brixham, returning to their mooring at 19.45 hours. The service time for the *George Shee* totalled 36 hours during which, in atrocious conditions, they covered in excess of 200 miles.

On Thursday 16 October 1947, a NAAFI supply boat was bound from Plymouth to Torquay when she suffered engine failure three miles off Dartmouth Harbour. She floated helplessly throughout the night on a flood tide, but without distress flares was unable to attract the attention of small fishing vessels. With the coming of daylight, on 17 October, the vessel was spotted by the Coastguard at Compass Point, Dartmouth. On raising the alarm, pilot G.H. Riddalls, of Dartmouth, put to sea in his ex-RAF rescue launch and towed the stricken vessel in to Dartmouth. The Berry Head Coastguard had also spotted distress signals from the vessel, which was crewed by Captain Baker and Captain Harris, and had immediately called out the Torbay boat. The services of the lifeboat were not directly required but she stood by as the craft was towed to safety.

During a period in 1948, when the *George*

*Shee* was 'off station' for an overhaul, she was temporarily replaced by the relief lifeboat, *Hearts of Oak*. The relief boat was launched on Tuesday 4 May to go to the assistance of the 600-ton Dutch Motor Vessel *Cowen*. The exact plight of the *Cowen* is not known but, when 14¹/₂ miles off Berry Head, she flashed SOS to a passing aircraft. Upon receipt of the 'SOS', Plymouth Naval Headquarters diverted the submarine HMS *Alcide*, en route from Scotland to Plymouth, to the area, together with the Devonport Destroyer, HMS *Burghead Bay*. The lifeboat, under the command of Coxswain F.C. Sanders, was launched immediately upon the receipt of a telephone message from the Harbour-master, Plymouth, via Hope Cove and Berry Head Coastguards.

The submarine was the first rescue vessel to reach the *Cowen* and stood by until the arrival of the other vessels. On Tuesday night a message was received from the *Hearts of Oak* to the effect that she had contacted the Dutch vessel and, as her services were not required, she was returning to Brixham. HMS *Burghead Bay* arrived in Torbay, with the *Cowen* in tow, at midnight on Tuesday; she then handed over the towage to two tugs, which towed the Dutchman to Dartmouth.

Brixham was in the grip of a severe south-south-westerly gale on the evening of Wednesday 30 January 1952 when, at 21.20 hours, the Coastguard saw flashing signals coming from a vessel which they estimated to be about four miles north-east of Berry Head. At this time violent squalls of rain and sleet were lashing the bay and the sea state was extremely heavy and confused. These conditions made the reading of the light signals impossible. The alarm was raised and the *George Shee* was launched at 21.45 hours, under the command of Coxswain Henry Thomas.

Coxswain Thomas engaged in a search pattern for one and a half hours before locating the casualty, approximately one mile off Straight Point, at the mouth of the River

Exe. This location was eight miles north-east of the vessel's estimated position when the signal was first spotted. The vessel was very close to the shore and Coxswain Thomas had to make his approach through very heavy, breaking seas, which shallowed alarmingly as he neared the casualty. The crippled vessel was the Royal Engineers' tug *Trieste*, which had become disabled when her main steam pipe ruptured. The tug was rolling violently in the breaking waves and heavy sea as Coxswain Thomas attempted to go alongside on her lee starboard side. As he did so, the tug yawed violently and swung around, forcing the lifeboat to back off immediately. The lifeboat's action caused the sea to flood over her stern and into the aft cockpit. Coxswain Thomas then made his second approach to the *Trieste*, this time on her port side, which was now in her lee. Four men were quickly taken off the *Trieste* and the lifeboat backed off. Coxswain Thomas approached the tug for a second time and saw two men appear on deck, assisting a further five men who were suffering badly from seasickness. All seven men were rescued, making 11 in total. The *George Shee* then turned to face the full force of the gale and set a course for her home station, arriving in Brixham at 02.00 hours.

For this first-class service, Coxswain Henry Thomas was awarded a Bronze Medal by the RNLI, with Thanks on Vellum being awarded to his son, David Thomas, for his skilful navigation throughout the service.

After 28 years of service, the *George Shee* was replaced as the Torbay lifeboat on Friday 25 July 1958, having recorded 245 launches and having saved 190 lives. She was subsequently sold by the RNLI to the Guatemala Rescue Service where she was to continue to serve as a lifeboat.

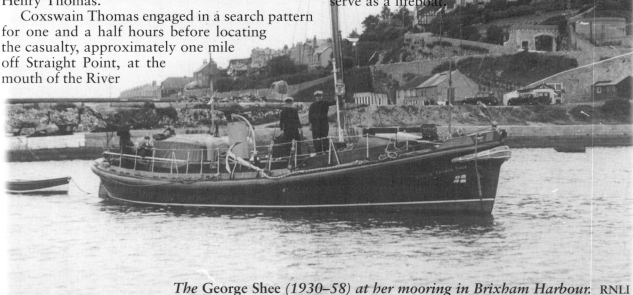

*The* **George Shee** *(1930–58) at her mooring in Brixham Harbour.* RNLI

*Lifeboat man Ken Thomas is introduced to HRH Princess Alexandra, 25 July 1958.*
Left to right: *Peter Easton, Doris Burridge, Ken Thomas, Joy Thomas.*  KEN THOMAS

*Crew of the* Princess Alexandra of Kent, *1958.*  Left to right: *?, Mike Lawrence, Ron Bradford,*
*Ken Gibbs, George Dyer, ?, Francis Janssens, Owen Macinally, Albert Janssens, Alistair McKay,*
*Dud Stone, Barry Pike (Mechanic), Harold Coyde (Coxswain).*  THE DEVONSHIRE PRESS

# 13

# THE *PRINCESS ALEXANDRA OF KENT*
## 25 JULY 1958–16 APRIL 1975

**Type:** *Barnett*  **Propulsion:** *2 x 72bhp, Gardener 6LW Diesel*  **Crew:** *8*
**Length:** *52' 0"*  **Beam:** *14' 0"*  **Displacement:** *28T 7Cwt*  **Speed:** *9 knots*
**Official number:** *945*  **Builder:** *J.S. White, Cowes*
**Launches:** *157*  **Lives Saved:** *69*

**Coxswains:** *Henry O. Thomas (1958–60); Abraham Bartlett (1960–61); Harold Coyde (1961–70); John D. Stone (1970–72); Kenneth Gibbs (1972–75).* **Mechanics:** *Richard Harris; Barry Pike.*

The streets of Brixham were decked with flags, flowers and bunting on Friday 25 July 1958, when HRH Princess Alexandra of Kent paid her first visit to Torbay. She primarily visited Brixham where she was the guest of honour at the dedication and naming ceremony of the new Torbay lifeboat. The Princess arrived at Torquay by train and was driven to Torre Abbey where a luncheon was served. The Princess' route to Brixham took her via Torquay Seafront, Preston and Paignton Greens, Goodrington, Churston and on to Brixham Harbour. To mark the occasion she was presented with a glass tankard which was inscribed with the signatures of the lifeboat crew and Sea Ranger E.M. Park, daughter of the Hon. Sec. of the Torbay lifeboat. Alderman T.F. Adams, President of the Torquay Branch of the RNLI, opened the proceedings. Comdr S.W.F. Bennetts, Chief Inspector of Lifeboats, gave a detailed description of the boat.

The Chairman of the Committee of Management of the RNLI, Earl Howe, had the pleasure of handing the new boat over to Mr F.W.H. Park, the Honorary Secretary of the Torbay Branch. The Bishop of Plymouth, the Right Revd N.H. Clarke, assisted by the Vicar of Brixham, Revd H. Yeomans, and the Minister of Brixham Congregational Church, Revd H.M. Westall, dedicated the boat, with the singing of Henry Francis Lyte's hymn 'Abide with me'.

Following the dedication and the singing of the traditional hymn 'Eternal Father, strong to save', Her Royal Highness formally named the new lifeboat *Princess Alexandra of Kent*.

For Mr F.P. Lee, Chairman of Brixham Urban Council, the ceremony was particularly memorable, for when he was Chairman of the Brixham Council for the first time he had been present when the Prince of Wales named the *George Shee*.

The new lifeboat, which replaced the *George Shee*, was built at the yard of J. Samuel White, of Cowes, Isle of Wight, and was one of the first boats to be built with a steering position amidships and enclosed. Visibility was gained through all-round perspex windows, the two front windows being fitted with Kent clear-view screens capable of being hinged forward to give a completely clear opening. All engine manoeuvring and operating controls were arranged for working from within the steering position thus alleviating the need for any member of the crew to be in the engine-room with the boat under way. She was divided into ten watertight compartments, which were fitted with 303 air-cases. Below, the engine-room floor had a double skin to ensure even greater protection against flooding. The lifeboat carried enough fuel to allow her to travel 350 miles at a full speed of 9 knots, without refuelling. In rough weather she was capable of carrying 100 people on board.

The *Princess Alexandra of Kent* was the first lifeboat in which fluorescent lighting was installed in the cabins and engine room. She had a comprehensive electrical installation, including radiotelephony, which was housed in a separate compartment within the deck cabin. Very High Frequency (VHF) radiotelephony was fitted for direct communication with aircraft. She also carried a loud-hailer, a searchlight, a signalling lamp and direction-finding equipment. A line-throwing pistol and oil spray, for smoothing the water around a wreck, were also carried. The cost of the new boat, £38,500, was met from the Institution's funds.

The *Princess Alexandra of Kent* was called to the assistance of the Dutch tug, *Cycloop*, on the evening of Monday 7 December 1959. The tug, which had three barges in tow, *Cosray 9*, *Cosray 10* and *Cosray 11*, had sought the shelter of Torbay from heavy seas and a full south-easterly gale. The tow-rope from one barge fouled the tug's propeller, which necessitated the Tugmaster cutting the tow and casting the barge adrift. The barge, *Cosray 10*, which had a 'running crew' of two, was 120 feet long and was carrying a cargo of 12" diameter steel pipes. The crew attempted to set their own anchors but failed and she ran aground, approximately half a mile south-east of Torquay Harbour. The lifeboat was launched at 12.35 hours, into driving rain and frequent violent squalls, which greatly reduced visibility.

The lifeboat found the barge aground beneath Natural Arch. As heavy seas were breaking over the barge, preventing a direct approach by the lifeboat, Coxswain Thomas anchored the *Princess Alexandra of Kent* and, running out her line, allowed the lifeboat to veer down on to the stranded barge, until rocks prevented further approach. As the lifeboat came up to the stern of the barge, one of the crew jumped to safety, but the second crew member hesitated and waves forced the vessels apart.

Coxswain Thomas made seven further attempts to rescue the second crew member. With the force of each wave the barge was being driven further on to the rocks and becoming more inaccessible. Coxswain Thomas took the lifeboat in as close as possible to the barge and, with the rescued crewman giving instructions to his stranded colleague, a line was thrown to him. Unfortunately instead of securing himself to the rope and allowing the lifeboat crew to pull him to safety, he secured the rope to the vessel and lowered himself into the surging sea. Using the rope, he attempted to pull himself across to the lifeboat. In the crashing seas and heavy squalls, Coxswain Thomas manoeuvred the lifeboat into a position from which the man could be pulled from the sea. Unfortunately the man was unconscious and despite the valiant efforts of the lifeboat crew he was unable to be revived.

It is always a bonus to be able to locate contemporary notes made by an eyewitness or indeed someone closely connected with an incident. Such notes exist in respect of the *Cosray 10* service, although they are unsigned and cannot be attributed to an individual, albeit the tenure of the document tends to suggests that the author was possibly either Coxswain Harry Thomas or the Station Honorary Secretary Fred Park. The notes are reproduced as follows:

*The weather had been very wild all day. There were about a dozen coastal craft sheltering in Torbay & Brixham Harbour among which was a Dutch Ocean going tug with three dumb barges in tow, anchored over the Torquay side of Torbay off Daddy Hole Plain. During the morning with gale force Southerly wind the tug and barges had some difficulty in holding to anchor. L/B crew was alerted & so tug got under weigh & managed to tow barges ahead to windward. CG had watchers over Torquay side of Bay keeping observation & reported that the tug had the barges under control & did not require any assistance & weather moderated. Nevertheless Hon. Sec. instructed M/M to endeavour to contact the tug by RT & ask whether they would like us to come out & take the men off their barges.*

*The M/M tried to contact the tug during several occasions during the morning & as weather was moderating no further action was taken. We were not surprised however when at a quarter past nine in the evening the Coast Guard phoned to say that the tug had sent a R.T. message to Niton Radio asking that the Brixham lifeboat be informed that he was drifting towards the shore & asking for the lifeboat to come out & take the two men off his barges. He gave his exact location as 2 mile South of Torquay. It transpired later the Hon. Sec. immediately phoned Coxswain to launch immediately. Then M/M & Asst M/M were phoned while Coxswain was informing other members of crew. Maroons were fired & as soon as all the crew had arrived Coxn quickly left moorings at full speed.*

*Coxn knew the approx position at time of distress call & allowing that the tug & barges would still be drifting to leeward & towards the rocky shore decided to come up to the position some distance to leeward & then search to windward. The wind was of whole gale force veering South to SSE with misty rain & driving rain during the squalls.*

*On approaching the shore & working up to windward Coxn observed one barge which was lying to its anchor which was not holding & was almost ashore under the rocky cliffs. Coxn knew... that there were several sunken rocks in this vicinity & he would have to exercise the greatest caution in going in closer. The position was fully exposed to the heavy gale force winds & terrific seas & he decided that the only way he could get the men off was to go ahead direct to windward & drop anchor & veer down abreast the lighter on his anchor warp. He took the L/B up clear of the barge & dropped anchor close to some sunken rocks marked... as The Magwintons. Dropping anchor & paying out anchor cable & with both engines running slow ahead Coxn coaxed L/B down towards the lighter which by now had gone ashore by the stern although bow was still rising to each wave which then crashed over the after part of the L/B. Altogether 80 fathoms of anchor cable were let out before the Coxn decided that he could attempt to get alongside. He knew that just astern were more rocks & that he had little room to spare.*

*Judging that the time had arrived to go in Coxn swung rudder to Port & went ahead on both engines. This manoeuvre succeeded & L/B went alongside the lighter about midships. The waves were so high however that Coxn knew he could not stay alongside a second more than necessary. At one time the members of the crew who were aft called out that the L/B was going to come down on the deck of the lighter but mercifully she dropped clear. Two men were at the side of the barge & one man taking his chance threw a small dog aboard and jumped to the L/B where he was grabbed by the L/B crew. The other man on the barge did not jump before the seas carried L/B too far away from the lighter. Coxswain made no fewer than 5 more attempts to manoeuvre alongside the barge again but the heavy seas & backwash from the rocks defeated him. On the sixth occasion he was successful in contacting barge & although the man was shouted to both by the L/B crew & in Dutch by his companion now in the L/B they failed to persuade him to jump when the opportunity arose. Coxn knew he would be unable to keep L/B alongside told Bowman to throw him a rope with a bowline on the end. This they did it being their intention that he should fasten it around his body & they would pull him to the L/B. This was explained to him also in Dutch by his companion but despite this he dropped the bowline over a Bollard on the barge & dropped off the barge holding on to the rope & swung across hand over hand. L/B was now being washed away from the Barge, the motion & his weight, caused the line to drop & he went into the water the waves washing him under the stern of the barge. He came out again however & continued hand over hand but when he was about 10ft off the L/B & about halfway between he suddenly stopped & let go the rope. Coxn ordered L/B to be thrown to him. He seemed to be floating without any movement & made*

*no attempt to touch it. Coxn thereupon told Bowman to make fast the rope & by going slow astern on both engine brought stern of L/B closer to the man whereupon he was reached with the long gaff, pulled to the L/B pulled up over the side & aboard. He was so heavy with clothing & sea boots that it took the combined strength & efforts of 5 L/B men to get him aboard.*

*He appeared to be unconscious & so it was assumed that he must have taken in a lot of water & needed A.R. He was carried down into the cabin & the First Aiders Tony & DWO Thomas got to work on him immediately (carrying on without let up until Dr. & Ambulance man took over).*

*The rope was then cast off & engines were put slow ahead to enable anchor to be recovered with the power winch. This operation took about 12 minutes. When the Anchor was hove up high all the crew returned aft and Coxn headed for Brixham. It was later found that the anchor stock was bent & it is assumed the anchor, when it was dropped, must have caught foul in some of the rocks.*

*The man appeared to be bleeding from the neck & so RT message was immediately sent asking for a Dr. & Ambulance to be waiting their arrival at BXM.*

*The A.R. was kept up continuously by the two first aiders & two of the crew the whole time but unfortunately without success & after Ambulance men had continued for about 2 hours the Doctor decided it was hopeless. The Dr. & Ambulance men came out in the outer harbour in a fishing boat to meet L/B as L/B Anchor had slipped from its securing & had caught in a lot of wire hawsers which had been dumped into the outer harbour & some delay in returning to the landing steps while the entangled wires were being cleared from flukes of the anchor.*

*At the inquest it was stated that the P.M. revealed that the man had died from a severe shock stopping the heart action & that it was not a proper case of drowning.*

*The Coxswain desires to put forward for commendation the courage & cooperation of each member of his crew & especially to the M/M R T Harris for his quick reaction to all his orders for his instinctive control of the engines without which this rescue attempt could have ended in disaster.*

*The tug had had to let the barge go as its tow rope was fouling the propeller of the tug.*

The Honorary Secretary of the Torbay lifeboat subsequently received the letter of appreciation shown overleaf:

Above: *A member of the crew from the* Cycloop *is reunited with his pet dog.* MURIEL FRY

Right: *The Duchess of Kent presents Harry Thomas with the RNLI's Silver Medal for service to the* Cycloop, *7 December 1959.* KEN THOMAS

*ROYAL NETHERLANDS EMBASSY*
*LONDON*
*16 DECEMBER 1959*
*The Ambassador*
*No. 24779*

*Dear Sir,*
*From the Netherlands Consul at Plymouth and from reports in the newspapers, I heard about the excellent work done by you and the crew of the Brixham lifeboat 'Princess Alexandra of Kent' in the evening of 7th December, 1959, when a barge with two men on board ran ashore near Torquay and was being pounded by 30 feet high waves.*

*You and your crew saved the life of my countryman Leen Wassel and would have saved Jacob Visser, had he not died before of shock.*

*I heartily associate myself with the words of praise on your conduct and that of your crew spoken by the Coroner Mr. E.F. Windeatt and with Dr. H.S. Cunningham Smith's admiration for the, unfortunately, futile efforts to restore the life of Jacob Visser.*

*Yours sincerely*
*Baron Adolph Bentinck*

For this service, Coxswain Henry Thomas was awarded a Silver Medal by the RNLI and Motor Mechanic Richard Harris received his third Bronze Medal. The RNLI's Thanks on Vellum were awarded to Second Coxswain Abraham Bartlett, Bowman John Fry, Assistant Mechanic James Harris and crew members D.W.O. Thomas, K. Thomas and P. Easton. Queen Juliana of the Netherlands later awarded the 'Silver Medal of Humane Assistance' to Coxswain H. Thomas and a Bronze Medal to every other member of the crew.

But the story of the *Cosray 10* does not end there, albeit there was no further lifeboat involvement. The barge broke up and, having deposited her cargo on the seabed, one section of her sank. The remaining section of the upturned hull began a precarious drift towards Torquay Harbour; luckily it was washed clear of the harbour entrance but continued to drift on to Torre Abbey Sands. A new problem now arose with the possibility, given the prevailing weather conditions, of the hull causing major damage as the sea continuously dashed it against the sea wall.

As the attempts by local salvage man Ernie Lister, of Brixham, failed to secure a tow-line to the barge, the Local Authority took the unprecedented action of calling for assistance from the Royal Marines. Seated on the Torre Abbey sea wall, the Royal Marines strafed the hull of the barge with machine-gun fire and anti-tank rockets, in an attempt to puncture the buoyancy. The *Cosray 10* withstood this onslaught and it fell to a Royal Navy Bomb Disposal Unit to place an explosive charge and blow a hole in the hull. The hull sank and remained on Torre Abbey Sands for a considerable time before being removed by salver Ernie Lister. A contemporary note, held at the Torbay Lifeboat Station, records:

*His attempt to right it failed until a Furzeham Scholar told him to release the trapped air until the barge was just buoyant. He would then find it easy to roll it over.*

The classification of a service as 'saved', 'rescued', 'landed', 'helped' or 'stood by' is designated by the RNLI, following the receipt of the service launch report of the Coxswain and Honorary Secretary. The classification is based upon several factors, including the weather conditions, the state of the casualty, and the complexity of the rescue.

The entry on the Torbay Lifeboat Service Board against the *Princess Alexandra of Kent* for 22 December 1964 reads simply: 'Motor Vessel *Northwind*, of Copenhagen, stood-by while crew were saved from shore.' It was early on the morning of Tuesday 22 December when the Brixham Coastguard received a report that the Danish motor vessel, *Northwind*, was dragging her anchor. She had been lying at anchor in Torbay, sheltering from an east-north-easterly

gale. The Honorary Secretary, being the duty Launch Authority, was contacted and the lifeboat launched. The Coxswain was Harold Coyde; his crew was John (Dud) Stone (Second Coxswain), Richard Harris (Mechanic), Albert Janssens (Bowman), and crew members Owen Macinally, Anthony Rea, George Dyer, Martin Payne, Ernest Cudd, Alistair McKay and Francis Janssens.

The *Princess Alexandra of Kent* reached the casualty at approximately 03.45 hours and found the vessel, in heavy breaking seas, aground on Hollicombe Beach, a small beach situated between two sandstone headlands directly beneath the Paignton Gas Works. The lifeboat crew launched parachute flares by which Coxswain Coyde could see that the *Northwind* was bow-on to the shore. It was also evident that the Coastguard had managed to secure a line to the vessel and that a breeches buoy had been rigged between the vessel and the shore. Assessing the circumstances, Coxswain Coyde decided to stand by just outside the line of breaking waves. At about 04.30 hours the lifeboat was requested, by way of radio communication from the coaster, to come alongside as the rope securing the breeches buoy had parted. It was also requested that the lifeboat take off the remaining crew. Coxswain Coyde was also informed that, in coming alongside the *Northwind*, not only

Main: *A representative of Queen Juliana of the Netherlands presents Cox'n Harry Thomas with the 'Silver Medal of Humane Assistance' for service to the Cycloop, 7 December 1959. Left to right: Abe Bartlett, Bill Stokes (Chairman of Brixham UDC), F.R. Dunstan (Vice Consul for the Netherlands), David Thomas, Coxswain Harry Thomas, Ken Thomas, Peter Easton, Jack Fry, Jim Harris, Dick Harris. The ceremony was held at Brixham Town Hall on 20 February 1961.* KEN THOMAS
Left: *The Bronze Medal of Humane Assistance presented to Bowman John Fry following the Cycloop rescue.* MURIEL FRY

This image and right: *Waves pound the MV* Northwind, *of Copenhagen,
firmly aground at Hollicombe Beach, Paignton, 22 December 1964.*
RNLI (INSET); *HERALD EXPRESS* (OVERLEAF).

would he have to contend with the vast breaking sea, but that he would have a maximum depth of 5ft of water in which to manoeuvre the lifeboat.

Using all his skills of seamanship, Coxswain Coyde decided to drop the anchor and veer down on to the stricken vessel. His first attempt failed but undaunted by the worsening conditions he made a second attempt. It was then that the lifeboat received a message that all but the Captain and Chief Officer had been rescued.

A further attempt was made to reach the *Northwind* with the lifeboat grounding on several occasions. The lifeboat was hauled back out to her anchor whilst her crew prepared to launch and rig a breeches buoy between the lifeboat and the coaster. Motor Mechanic Richard Harris was on deck, waiting to fire the line, when a further radio message was received to the effect that both the Captain and Chief Officer had been taken off by the Coastguard and that the full crew were accounted for. Coxswain Coyde set course for Brixham and the lifeboat was back on station by 07.20 hours.

For his excellent seamanship and great courage, Coxswain Harold Coyde was awarded the RNLI Silver Medal and Motor Mechanic Richard Harris was awarded his fourth service

clasp to his Bronze Medal. Each member of the crew was awarded the Institution's Thanks on Vellum. The designation 'stood by', as recorded, was a totally understated record of service.

Flags were flown on trawlers moored in Brixham Harbour at half-mast as a sign of respect, in memory of Francois Janssens and Brian Easton who were lost on the evening of Thursday 15 June 1967, together with the Brixham trawler, *Casita*, BM 188. The owner of the *Casita*, Mr Bunce, had bought the vessel, which had been built in 1934, at Ostend, Belgium, the previous April. The 18-ton trawler had put out from Brixham Harbour at 06.30 hours on that Thursday morning, bound for the fishing grounds of Start Bay. Shortly afterwards Mr Janssens' father, Albert Janssens, put to sea in his boat and the two vessels kept in contact throughout the day. At about 16.30 hours Albert Janssens returned to port leaving the *Casita* to carry out night fishing. At 19.44 hours that evening the motor vessel *Echo*, on course from the Continent to Plymouth, picked up a distress signal, in which a male person said that there had been an explosion and the vessel was sinking. Due to thunderstorms, which caused considerable radio interference, the message was indistinct. It was unclear as to whether the explosion had occurred on the vessel or overboard. The signal did not state the name of the distressed boat or give her position. Niton Radio, on the Isle of Wight, monitored the call and sought to identify the name and location of the distressed vessel, but there was no answer. Shortly after the 'MAYDAY' signals were lost, a German ship in the Channel reported losing a man overboard.

The Honorary Secretary of the Torbay lifeboat, who thought that the name of the distressed vessel was *Capella*, also heard the 'MAYDAY' signals and immediately liaised with the duty Coastguard but a record of such a vessel could not be found. After further discussion with the District Officer of the Coastguard it was decided that, as it was impossible to identify the position of the distressed vessel, a search and rescue service could not be put into operation.

All shipping off the South-Devon coast was alerted to the disaster and at about 10.25 hours on Friday 16 June, a body, initially believed to be that of the missing German seaman, was located by the Dartmouth trawler, *Annie Jones*, five miles south-east of Start Point. Tragically the deceased was identified as Francois Janssens. Later that same day, the body of Brian Easton was recovered on the Brixham side of Start Point, by the Torbay lifeboat, near the Skerries Buoy.

At a subsequent inquiry, held by the Wrecks Commissioner, Mr David Sheen QC, sitting with three Assessors, it was stated that the lifeboat took the correct and appropriate action.

This tragic loss was particularly hard felt by the crew of the Torbay lifeboat as Francois Janssens was a regular and well-respected member of that crew; his father Albert Janssens was the lifeboat's Bowman.

The *Princess Alexandra of Kent* made local history on Friday 12 April 1968, when she became the first Torbay lifeboat to use radar to assist in locating a casualty. During a recent refit she had been fitted with the latest 'DECCA 101', 6-volt, radar system. On this occasion it was the 19-ton MFV *Cluaran* that required help. The vessel was bound from Dartmouth to Cowes, Isle of Wight, when her engines seized up off the Blackstone. The boat, with a crew of six, was approximately three-quarters of a mile north-east of Blackstone Rock when they sent up a distress flare. Brixham Coastguard, Mr Charles Dunn, spotted the flare and alerted the Torbay lifeboat. The 987-ton motor vessel *Yewdale*, which had monitored the Coastguard's radio broadcast, answered the distress call. The *Yewdale* located the *Cluaran* and stood by until the arrival of the lifeboat. Despite strong winds and a heavy swell, the crew managed to get a line to the fishing

vessel and establish a tow. It was then towed back to Brixham Harbour without incident.

On Saturday 13 April 1968, the Torbay lifeboat went to the assistance of the crippled motor yacht *Victoria*, of Dartmouth, which had got into difficulties in a heavy swell, following engine failure, off Beesands. The craft was being used as a dive-boat and carried a crew of two and ten skin-divers. The *Victoria* anchored and awaited the arrival of the *Princess Alexandra of Kent*, which, in difficult towing conditions, towed the vessel and occupants safely to Dartmouth.

Including this rescue, during the first four months of the year the lifeboat had saved more lives than the combined number saved by the offshore and inshore boats during the whole of 1967.

One of the most familiar sights for anyone looking out across Torbay during the summer months must surely be that of the Western Lady ferries, which ply between Torquay and Brixham. Thousands of holidaymakers each year board the ferries to view the beautiful coastlines and beaches of Torquay, Paignton and Brixham. It was on 9 July 1968, whilst making such a trip, that the *Western Lady I* had to call upon the services of the Torbay lifeboat. The Western Lady fleet comprises converted Royal Navy 'Fairmile B' Class Rescue Motor Launches, the vessel requiring the assistance of the lifeboat being the former *RML 535*, built by William Weatherhead & Son of Cockenzie, East Lothian, Scotland in 1941. During the Second World War, between 1942 and 1944, she was attached to the 63rd ML Flotilla, Plymouth Command, carrying out mine-clearance work out of Dartmouth and Appledore, latterly returning to Dartmouth. For a period of time she was under the command of Lt F. Blewett of Penzance, whose father was the Coxswain of the Penlee lifeboat.

The ferry left Torquay at 10.30 hours in sunshine but, in many localised parts, mist and fog blanketed Torbay. Such were the conditions near Elberry Cove, an area where the normal route would take the ferry close to the shore to allow passengers to view the coves and cliffs. On approaching Elberry Cove the ferry entered a bank of fog and holidaymakers, who were enjoying the tranquillity of the cove, were suddenly confronted with the sight of the dark shape of the blue-painted *Western Lady I* looming out of the fog towards them. At 11.15 hours, the ferry ran aground, approximately 40 yards from the beach. Fortunately, the ferry came to rest on a sandy bottom, and there was no real threat to either the vessel or its passengers, although the boat was reported to be listing. The ferry was so close to the beach that one of the passengers shouted to a girl on the sands to raise the alarm. Tom Sowerbutts of the Berry Head Coastguard

*The* Western Lady I *under tow by the tug* Penlee, *after having run aground in fog at Elberry Cove, Paignton, 9 July 1968. The* Princess Alexandra of Kent, *in the background, carrying 126 persons, and a dog, gained a place in the* Guinness Book of Records *for the most 'casualties' to be carried on a British lifeboat at one time. HERALD EXPRESS*

Station, upon receiving notification of the incident, contacted Mr Fred Park, the Lifeboat Secretary and Launch Authority, who ordered the immediate launch of the *Princess Alexandra of Kent* to disembark the ferry passengers. Using her radar system, Coxswain Coyde quickly found the stranded ferry. Mr Ernie Lister's salvage boat, *Penlee*, of Brixham, also attended the scene.

The passengers were taken off and landed at New Pier, the normal landing berth for the Western Lady fleet. The rescue was carried out in one operation; the deck of the *Princess Alexandra of Kent* was crammed full to capacity, with some ferry passengers being obliged to stand on the roof of the aft cabin. The landing of the 122 ferry passengers, four crew members and a dog constituted the highest number of 'casualties' to be carried by a British lifeboat at any one time, gaining the *Princess Alexandra of Kent* a place in the *Guinness Book of Records*. The *Western Lady* was successfully refloated and the *Penlee* towed her and her crew to Brixham Harbour, arriving at 12.45 hours.

Jersey Radio received a MAYDAY call at 16.57 hours on Thursday 9 July 1970 from the yacht *Lady Candy*. The yacht, which was adrift with engine trouble, gave her position as about three miles east of the Orestone, Torquay. The *Princess Alexandra of Kent* slipped her moorings at 17.05 hours into a strong north-westerly wind and a choppy sea. It was one hour before low water. The hatch boat, *18.03*, was launched at 17.20 hours. The exact location of the yacht was unknown but following a search the ILB made contact with the *Lady Candy* at 17.43 hours and directed the lifeboat to her location. The ILB returned to station, arriving at 18.22 hours. The lifeboat established a tow and landed the yacht, together with her two occupants, safely at Torquay. The *Princess Alexandra of Kent* returned to her moorings at 18.48 hours.

Saturday 9 June 1973 proved an extremely busy day for the Coxswain and crew of the Torbay lifeboat. Their first call of the afternoon saw the *Princess Alexandra of Kent*, assisted by the frigate, HMS *Mermaid*, the Customs launch, *Vigilant*, the coaster *Bristol Trader*, the Babbacombe Corinthian Sailing Club's safety boat and numerous other small craft, lead the search for a missing dinghy sailor. It was whilst taking part in local club racing that the 'Sprog' dinghy, *Scotch Mist*, capsized off Oddicombe Beach in a calm sea and light winds, throwing the two occupants into the sea. The Club safety boat conveyed Police Sergeant John Quantick to the scene. Sergeant Quantick spotted one of the men and dived into the sea in a bid to rescue him. The helmsman of the safety boat later recounted that the man was 'submerged in a perpendicular position with only his hair showing above the water.' Due to the murkiness of the water the Sergeant was unable to locate the man. The rescue boat helmsman also dived in but tragically the casualty sank without trace. The second crew member of *Scotch Mist* was able to right his dinghy and, with the aid of another craft, reached the shore safely.

Whilst the search for the missing yachtsman continued, the *Princess Alexandra of Kent* was diverted, at 17.45 hours, to a report of a woman and two children clinging to a buoy off Corbyn Head, Torquay. The 'casualties' were in fact two children who were drifting seaward in a rubber dinghy. The children, aged eight and six, were located and picked up by a passing motorboat prior to the arrival of the lifeboat.

The lifeboat was then diverted to take 53 passengers off the ferry *Western Lady II* which had suffered partial engine failure in Torbay. There were no casualties and the ferry eventually returned to Brixham under her own power. Numerically, this was the largest number of persons to be carried by the lifeboat since the *Princess Alexandra of Kent* rescued 126 persons and a dog from *Western Lady I*.

Finally, late on Saturday night the *Princess Alexandra of Kent* landed a male casualty who had fallen down cliffs at Walls Hill, Torquay. Members of the Coastguard rescue team carried the man on a stretcher to a small boat; he was then transferred to the lifeboat, which conveyed him to a waiting ambulance at Babbacombe.

A skin diver who, due to failing light, could not locate his support boat swam for three hours to raise an alarm and paradoxically save his three friends. The incident occurred off Torquay on Sunday 11 November 1973, when the diver surfaced from his dive and, not being able to see his friends, struck out for the shore, some one mile distant. In the failing light, the diver's colleagues

*The crew of the* Princess Alexandra of Kent, *c.1959.*Left to right, back: *Ken Thomas, Peter Easton, Dave Thomas, Jack Fry, Jim Harris;* front: *Harry Thomas (Coxswain), Fred Park (Hon. Sec.), Dick Harris (Engineer), Abe Bartlett (2nd Coxswain).*
PHOTOGRAPH BY THE DEVONSHIRE PRESS

*Coxswain Abraham Bartlett (1960–61).* RNLI

*Coxswain Harold Coyde (1961–70).* RNLI

*Coxswain J. Dudley Stone (1970–72).* RNLI

shouted to attract his attention and in their hurry to start the outboard motor on their 14ft craft, broke the starter cord; leaving themselves no option but to ride out the night in a fierce offshore wind.

The diver swam for a full three hours before he reached the shore and alerted the Coastguard. The *Princess Alexandra of Kent* was launched and, acting upon the information supplied, located the open boat after a short search. The occupants suffered no lasting effects from their ordeal, although it was thought unlikely that the diver would have reached the shore had he not been wearing a wetsuit.

The Secretary of the Torbay Lifeboat Station, Mr Fred Park, strongly criticised the action of the young people who had gone to sea without carrying flares or any other emergency equipment. He commented:

*They are extremely lucky that they did not drift right out to sea. It was foolhardy to chance being caught at sea after dark, especially at this time of the year, without taking stringent safety precautions.*

In keeping with an international flavour of rescues, the *Princess Alexandra of Kent* was launched at 19.50 hours on Monday 16 December 1973, in answer to a MAYDAY from the Norwegian vessel *Buenavista*. Some 38 miles south-east of Brixham in rough seas and a stiffening wind, it was standing by the fishing vessel, *Petite Michele*, and her crewman.

The nightmare journey for skipper John Jude, of Plymouth, had commenced some 30 hours earlier when, on Saturday, in the company of a second trawler, he had left Guernsey to bring the newly acquired trawler/queens dredger back to Plymouth. The two trawlers had become separated when the *Petite Michele* suffered engine failure. The skipper attempted to attract the attention of his escort vessel by firing a flare but was unsuccessful. The alarm was not raised until the escort vessel reached Plymouth on Sunday. In the meantime John Jude had managed to restart the trawler's engine but encountered further mechanical troubles. Whilst riding out the heavy seas, a particularly heavy wave swept the vessel's life-raft overboard. Coxswain Ken Gibbs recalls the situation as told to him by Skipper Jude:

*He kept his boat up into the wind to avoid being blown back to the Channel Island coasts. He ended up in Lyme Bay. He shipped a heavy sea which filled his boat. He drifted and went alongside, I understand, a Russian ship and they helped him to pump out. Although there was a language difficulty, they were most helpful. The only thing he could not communicate was his desire to get help from the shore. He started off again and his engine stopped once more, but he got it going again and then lost his steering. Until we picked him up, he drifted. He sent up all sorts of flares. The 38th and last was seen by the* Buenavista, *a good 40 miles offshore.*

Coxswain Gibbs further explained that *Petite Michele's* position was initially given to him as 35 miles east of Berry Head, but the flood tide and westerly wind were pushing the trawler away and for a time the lifeboat was chasing her. The *Princess Alexandra of Kent* was joined temporarily in the search by the frigate HMS *Ajax* and Sea King helicopter from RNAS Culdrose.

The *Buenavista* had attempted to rescue the fisherman by launching one of her own lifeboats but due to the sea conditions was unsuccessful. The vessel stood by the trawler, her Captain relaying her changing position to the lifeboat. The *Princess Alexandra of Kent* reached the scene, approximately 20 miles from the Casquets Lighthouse, at 00.45 hours in weather conditions that had reached a west-north-west severe gale F9, with wind speeds of 41 to 47 knots, and 28ft waves. The conditions became so severe that the lifeboat lost the use of her radar scanner that could not rotate against the force of the wind. The *Buenavista* provided lee shelter for the lifeboat while she manoeuvred to take off Mr Jude. From the time of his initial trouble until the time of his rescue by the lifeboat, Mr Jude had spent 32 hours alone at sea. Coxswain Gibbs summed up the trawler skipper: 'He was in very good shape but he had had enough. We offered him food but he was past eating. He is a quiet man.' The *Petite Michele*, which remained adrift, was recovered two days later off Alderney.

For this outstanding rescue, Coxswain Ken Gibbs was awarded the RNLI's Bronze Medal. Certificates were awarded to Motor Mechanic Barry Pike, Assistant Mechanic Michael Bower, and crewmembers Mike Kingston, Nick Davies, Phil Burridge (who sustained a badly gashed hand in the rescue) and John Hunkin.

The crew of the Torbay boat were at sea in a severe gale for nearly nine hours on Sunday 4 August 1974 when they rescued four people from the luxury cabin cruiser *Sagarol*. The 32ft cruiser had left Guernsey bound for Plymouth, the skipper having been informed that he would encounter favourable weather conditions. When she was approximately 25 miles off Start Point, the *Sagarol* encountered gale conditions. The sea state had deteriorated drastically with waves reaching an estimated 15 to 20 feet in height. One particularly heavy wave smashed the

*A Royal Navy Wessex helicopter over the* Princess Alexandra of Kent. RNLI

cruiser's forward saloon starboard window and she began to take in water. The cruiser then suffered bilge pump failure and partial engine failure. At this point the skipper transmitted a MAYDAY. This was monitored by the 57,135-ton ore carrier *Dunstanburgh Castle* and the 10,952-ton *Athelcrown*. These two vessels located the cruiser and provided lee shelter, allowing the crew of the *Sagarol* to bale out their craft, and awaited the arrival of the lifeboat.

The relief lifeboat, *Princess Royal* (Civil Service No.7), was launched under the command of Coxswain Ken Gibbs and in severe gale conditions proceeded to a location 20 miles south-east of Start Point. Coxswain Gibbs located the *Sagarol* and attempted to secure a line between the two vessels. In so doing the lifeboat was lifted by a wave and dashed against the hull of the *Sagarol* making a hole in the bow of the cruiser. The crew of four men were taken off the cruiser, a tow line was established and the *Sagarol*, towed by the lifeboat, reached the safety of Torquay Harbour at 22.45 hours. The *Dunstanburgh Castle* stood by throughout the rescue operation.

Coxswain Gibbs was once more in command of the *Princess Alexandra of Kent* when she went to the aid of the MFV *Thalassa* on Monday 20 January 1975. The trawler had set out from Brixham at 11.00 hours the previous morning for the fishing grounds off Start Bay. The weather subsequently worsened and in gale-force winds and heavy seas the trawler went in close to the shore to lift her gear. The skipper was unsure of his exact position and it was then that the *Thalassa* ran into trouble. Shortly after 01.45 hours the Berry Head Coastguard Lookout received a radio message, from the *Thalassa*, stating that she was wedged between two rocks on the Shoe Ledge Reef, Start Point. The lifeboat was launched at 02.00 hours manned by Coxswain Ken Gibbs, Motor Mechanic Barry Pike, Mike Bower, Steve Bower, Mike Hingston, John Hunkin and Richard Brown. The Prawle Point Coastguard cliff-rescue team was also tasked to the scene and were preparing to take the crew off by line, should it have become necessary. On arriving at the scene the lifeboat crew found the trawler to be well and truly stuck fast. 'We could not go up to her for fear of being smashed against the rocks ourselves,' explained Coxswain Gibbs. In high winds and a heavy swell he exercised all his seamanship skills and, going astern, manoeuvred the lifeboat through a narrow, foaming gap in the rocks. Having placed

*Coxswain Harold Coyde and Motor Mechanic Dick Harris.*
RNLI

the *Princess Alexandra of Kent* in a position as close to the stranded trawler as possible without endangering the lifeboat, he dropped anchor. The lifeboat crew fired a rocket with a line attached, which was secured to the trawler. All that the lifeboat could do then was to wait for the tide to rise. As the tide rose Coxswain Gibbs nursed the lifeboat's engines and gradually took up the strain. Slowly and gently the trawler slid off the rocks. The whole process took about one and a half hours. In going aground the *Thalassa* had sustained damage to her propeller and was unable to proceed unaided. The *Princess Alexandra of Kent* took the trawler in tow and by 08.30 hours had moored the vessel in the Brixham Inner Harbour. The *Thalassa's* skipper, Tony Armstrong, and his crew Michael Moor, Doug Peplow and Brian Snell, remained onboard the trawler throughout the rescue.

Lifeboat Mechanic Barry Pike, holder of the RNLI Silver Medal for bravery, was a crew member on this service and paid tribute to Coxswain Gibbs' seamanship. He was quoted in the *Herald Express* as saying: 'There were rocks all around us and it was Ken's great handling of the boat which saved the day.'

Some 12 days later the Mayor and Mayoress of Torbay, Mr and Mrs Stewart Finch, gave the lifeboat crew and their wives a civic reception at Torre Abbey, Torquay. During his address, in which he paid tribute to the crew for their rescue of the *Thalassa*, the Mayor said, 'I am not surprised that you are known as the magnificent seven.' The local press thereafter readily applied this term of phrase to the crew.

One of the last services to be undertaken by the *Princess Alexandra of Kent* was to the cabin cruiser *Antiope*. The craft, with a husband-and-wife crew, was on passage from Christchurch, Dorset to Torquay on Wednesday 12 March 1975 when the vessel suffered engine failure. The *Antiope* fired a distress flare, which was spotted by a Coastguard patrol. The lifeboat was launched at 06.25 hours and quickly located the vessel drifting helplessly, approximately four miles off Berry Head. The lifeboat established a tow and the cabin cruiser was moored in Brixham Harbour at about 08.15 hours. The owners stated their intention to stay in Torquay a while before crossing the Channel in the *Antiope*.

On the completion of service in Torbay, the *Princess Alexandra of Kent* spent several years in the RNLI Reserve Fleet before being sold, later to become a fishing boat.

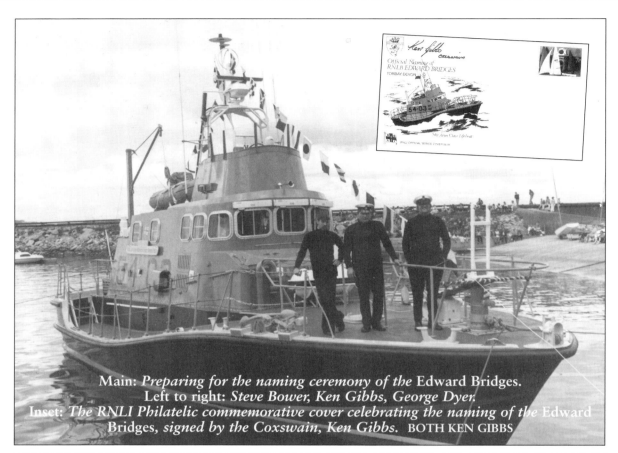

Main: *Preparing for the naming ceremony of the* Edward Bridges.
*Left to right:* Steve Bower, Ken Gibbs, George Dyer.
Inset: *The RNLI Philatelic commemorative cover celebrating the naming of the* Edward
Bridges, *signed by the Coxswain, Ken Gibbs.* BOTH KEN GIBBS

*A crew of the* Edward Bridges. *Left to right, back:* Captain Anderson, Derek Winning,
George Glasgow; *middle:* Phil Burridge, John Ashford, Mike Mills, Derek Rundle;
*front:* Nick Davies, John Hunkin, Brian Caunter, Steve Bower, Arthur Curnow,
Ernie Fradd. RNLI

# 14

# THE *EDWARD BRIDGES*
## *16 APRIL 1975–3 FEBRUARY 1995*

**Type:** *Arun*     **Propulsion:** *2 x 460bhp, Caterpillar D343 Diesel*     **Crew:** *5*

**Length:** *53' 3¾"*     **Beam:** *17' 0"*     **Displacement:** *30T 8Cwt*     **Speed:** *19.1 knots*

**Operational number:** *54-03*     **Official number:** *1037*

**Builder:** *William Osborne Ltd, Littlehampton (No.700)*     **Designers:** *G.L. Watson Ltd*

**Civil Service number:** *37*     **Launches:** *459*     **Lives Saved:** *286*

**Coxswains:** *Kenneth Gibbs (1975–76); George Dyer (1976–78); Arthur L.V. Curnow (1978–91); Dave P. Hurford (1991–95).* **Mechanics:** *Kenneth Gibbs (1975–76); Stephen Bower (1976); Bryan Johnson (1986); Mark Criddle (1995).*

The year 1970 saw the birth of the modern-day lifeboat, with the development of the Arun Class. The first three Arun Class boats were built with a wooden hull. The hull was of a cold-moulded wood construction. A double bottom and inner skin at the sides of the boat extended from the after peak to the forepeak bulkhead. The spaces between the inner and outer skins were filled with expanded polyurethane foam, the volume of which was sufficient to support the boat if the 26 watertight compartments were holed simultaneously. The watertight transverse bulkheads subdivide the hull into: forepeak, cable locker, forward cabin, fuel tank space, engine-room, after cabin and tiller flat. The aluminium superstructure housed all instruments, controls and electronic equipment. Controls were duplicated on the upper bridge. The watertight superstructure provided the self-righting capability of the boat. The forward cabin was fitted with two bunks and a toilet compartment.

Unlike her two Arun predecessors, the *Edward Bridges* was lengthened to a hull length of 54ft. Her transom radiuses were altered to produce an elliptical stern which, it was felt, would give better handling in following seas and also make the corners of the transoms less vulnerable. She had a working range of 260 nautical miles at cruising speed and 250 nautical miles at full speed, giving a radius of action of 115nm. The boat was fitted with fire-fighting and salvage pumps, the fire pump being fitted to the port side engine, and she

was the first Arun to carry a 'Y' class inflatable craft on her cabin roof, in addition to an inflatable life-raft. Her electronic equipment included radar, Decca Navigator, autopilot, VHF, recording and indicator echo sounders, a five-way intercom and MF for the direction finder. First-aid equipment was available for use by the qualified first aiders in the crew. Other equipment carried included stretchers, blankets, a resuscitation appliance, a breeches buoy, parachute flares, emergency rations and storm oil spray. The *Edward Bridges* could accommodate up to 170 survivors before her limit of stability was reached.

The *Edward Bridges* was the first Arun Class to enter service at Brixham and did so on Wednesday 16 April 1975. Her Coxswain was Ken Gibbs. Tuesday 17 June 1975 was a landmark day for the RNLI in Devon. During the morning, His Royal Highness, the Duke of Kent, President of the Institution, accompanied by Her Royal Highness, the Duchess of Kent, attended the dedication and naming ceremony of the new Plymouth lifeboat, *Thomas Forehead and Mary Rowse II*. She was a Waveney Class boat, Operational Number 1028, Official Number *44-010*. Having been withdrawn from operational service, in December 1999 she was moved from a berth in Poole, to Harwich, from where she was to be shipped to New Zealand.

Following the naming of the new Plymouth boat, the Duke and Duchess travelled to Brixham, where they were received by Cmdr

Above: *Mrs Gibbs is presented to the Duchess of Kent at the naming ceremony.* KEN GIBBS

Below: *Children of the crew; Suzanne Gibbs, James Bower and Kelly Dyer.* KEN GIBBS

Above: *Ken's daughter Suzanne presents a bouquet to the Duchess of Kent at the ceremony.* KEN GIBBS

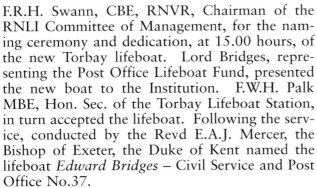

Right: *Second Coxswain George Dyer is presented to the Duke of Kent.* KEN GIBBS

F.R.H. Swann, CBE, RNVR, Chairman of the RNLI Committee of Management, for the naming ceremony and dedication, at 15.00 hours, of the new Torbay lifeboat. Lord Bridges, representing the Post Office Lifeboat Fund, presented the new boat to the Institution. F.W.H. Palk MBE, Hon. Sec. of the Torbay Lifeboat Station, in turn accepted the lifeboat. Following the service, conducted by the Revd E.A.J. Mercer, the Bishop of Exeter, the Duke of Kent named the lifeboat *Edward Bridges* – Civil Service and Post Office No.37.

The boat was named after Baron Bridges (1892–1969), former Head of the Civil Service. She was funded, at a cost of £150,000, from donations made to the Civil Service and Post Office Lifeboat Fund, established in 1866 when a group of PO workers subscribed £220 to purchase a lifeboat to be stationed at Wexford. From this modest beginning, in succeeding years, the Fund has continued to provide and maintain lifeboats. As her number indicates, the *Edward Bridges* was the 37th lifeboat to be purchased in this way. The Fund continues to flourish and has provided 44 lifeboats nationwide to date.

The crew of the *Penny Lass* had a terrifying experience on Tuesday 29 July 1975 when their boat was constantly circled and bumped by a 20ft whale. The party of four had left Salcombe heading for St Peter Port, Guernsey, when their navigation light failed whilst crossing the busy shipping lanes. In total darkness, with their direction-finding equipment out of order and desperately short of fuel, the *Penny Lass* was attempting to motor clear of the shipping lanes when the crew heard a whale blowing. As daylight dawned they could clearly see it swimming around the boat and continually bumping into it. The crew attempted to evade the whale by weaving their course but the whale stuck with them, constantly diving and resurfacing. The skipper of the chartered vessel explained that his companions were terrified that the whale would surface directly beneath their vessel and capsize the boat.

Above: *Ken Gibbs receives his Certificate of Service from the Station Hon. Sec. (Dec. 1976). Left to right, back: Cmdr Porchmouth, Lt Cmdr Miller, J. Churchill, Dick Jackson, George Dyer, John Dew, Arthur Curnow, Steve Bower, Brian Caunter, John Ashford, John Hunkin, Tony Smith; front: Brian Snell, Sam Little, Ken Gibbs, Capt. Anderson, Mike Mills, Mike Kingston.*

*The lifeboat and 'Y' boat (crew John Ashford and Mike Kingston) stand off Babbacombe as a team descends to a car wreckage, 17 May 1977.* COURTESY *WESTERN MORNING NEWS*

*The Duke of Atholl (Vice-Chair., RNLI) visits the Torbay Station, 1976. Left to right: Hon. Sec. Capt. Anderson, Ken Gibbs, Duke of Atholl, Stan Churchill (Branch Chair.).* KEN GIBBS

Right: *Ken Gibbs receives his Bronze Medal from the Duke of Kent, at the London Festival Hall on 8 May 1975, for saving life from the FV* Petite Michele, *16 December 1973.* RNLI

With their fuel supply reduced the *Penny Lass* fired a red flare and put out a distress call, which was picked up by the cruise liner *Camberra* and relayed to the Coastguard at Brixham. Coxswain Ken Gibbs and the crew of the *Edward Bridges* located the *Penny Lass* some 50 miles off Berry Head. The recovery of the vessel was routine; as for the whale, it was reported to have made off as soon as the *Edward Bridges* came into sight!

The Brixham Coastguard received a radio message requesting assistance from the 50ft ketch *Amorel*, when she encountered 25ft waves and wind gusts of 70mph, five miles south-east of Berry Head, in the early hours of Sunday 14 September 1975. The ketch had been en route from Alderney to Brixham when a sudden wind shift, from the south-west to the north-east, produced the gusts, which shredded her headsails. Although the ketch attempted to use her engine, she was unable to make headway in the extremely heavy seas. Ken Gibbs launched the *Edward Bridges* at 01.30 hours and battled through the waves to reach the ketch. In difficult conditions it took some time for the lifeboat crew to get a line on board the *Amorel*. Once this had been established, the lifeboat began the slow, and often tricky, tow to Torquay. The *Edward Bridges* was back on station at 05.30 hours.

An inflatable emergency life-raft, belonging to the 320ft coaster *Hoofinch*, was at the centre of an investigation when it failed to inflate on Wednesday 22 October 1975. The coaster, owned by the Springwell Shipping Company of Hull, which was on passage from Teignmouth to the Channel Islands, lost her engines and steering after being tossed about in heavy seas 15 miles east of Start Point. The initial distress call sent out by the *Hoofinch* reported that her engines were faltering; she then sent a second signal reporting that all was well and that she was heading for shore. Coastguards subsequently received a third signal from the coaster, which indicated

*The crew of the* Edward Bridges *land survivors from the MV Lyrma, 6 December 1976.*
At rail: *Keith Bower (Cox'n), John Dew, Nick Davies.* RNLI

*The crew of the* Edward Bridges *who took part in the 'Gold Medal' rescue of crew from the*
MV Lyrma, 6 December 1976. *Left to right: John Dew, Second Coxswain Keith Bower,*
*Michael Mills, Motor Mechanic Stephen Bower, Asst Mechanic John Hunkin,*
*Richard Brown, Nicholas Davies.*

that her engines were breaking down and that she required immediate assistance. It was when the crew of the *Hoofinch* launched the ship's life-raft that it failed to inflate. The heavy seas and swell made it impossible to launch a second life-raft.

The Torbay lifeboat was launched, under the command of Coxswain Ken Gibbs. British, Russian and French ships in the Channel were alerted and requested to proceed to the location of the *Hoofinch*. A rescue helicopter was scrambled from RNAS Culdrose but was later recalled to base when it had been established that the RFA *Engadine* had launched one of her helicopters to the scene. However, the helicopter winchman was unable to be set down on the coaster due to the motion of the vessel and what were described as 'aerial hazards on the coaster'. After several attempts the helicopter succeeded in establishing a line between the *Hoofinch* and her sister ship the *Hoofort*, which took the crippled coaster in tow until the arrival of the *Edward Bridges*, at about 17.30 hours. The *Hoofort* successfully transferred the tow to the lifeboat and Gibbs and his crew set about the long and difficult tow back to Brixham. The wind strength and direction was so variable during the tow that, as the lifeboat approached Brixham, the Coastguards requested a number of vessels moored at the entrance of the harbour to move in order that Coxswain Gibbs could manoeuvre the *Edward Bridges* and enter the harbour with the *Hoofinch* remaining under tow. This was achieved and the lifeboat arrived back on station a little before 01.00 hours. All in all, the drama had lasted ten hours. The life-raft, which had failed to inflate, was recovered by a Russian trawler and relayed on to the *Hoofort* and taken in to Brixham. The failure of the life-raft to inflate gave cause for great concern and Board of Trade officials subsequently removed the raft for examination.

The relief lifeboat (and former Torbay boat), the *Princess Alexandra of Kent*, was temporarily on station at Brixham in 1976 whilst the *Edward Bridges* underwent a routine overhaul. She was launched on Thursday 26 August 1976, the Coastguard having received a report that survivors from a speedboat, which had been wrecked, were stranded at Forest Cove, Start Bay,

some ten miles south of Brixham. Due to the cove's location, and the fact that it is bordered by overhanging cliffs, access could only be gained from the sea. The lifeboat, helmed by Second Cox'n Keith Bower, reached the cove at 16.00 hours.

The F5 easterly winds in Start Bay were producing rough seas and a heavy swell, with 5ft surf breaking onto Forest Cove. Although the stranded persons were in no immediate danger, concern was foremost for the children in the group. Knowing that the lifeboat would be unable to reach the shore, due to swell, Bower dropped anchor and veered the lifeboat down to within 50 yards of the beach. Amongst the lifeboat crew was John Dew, a professional diver, who volunteered to swim ashore with a line. He removed his sea boots, but kept his life jacket and oil-

*A painting depicting the* Lyrma *rescue.* RNLI

skins on, and entered the sea. He battled through the breaking surf, managed to reach the shore and hauled in the breeches buoy. Where possible John Dew paired an adult with a child. He swam out through the breaking surf assisting the first pair of casualties to reach the lifeboat and then swam back to the shore. John repeated this perilous journey on a further six occasions until he had secured the rescue of all six adults, eight children and an Alsatian dog. Suffering from total exhaustion, John Dew returned to the lifeboat. The *Princess Alexandra of Kent* landed the survivors at Dartmouth before regaining her moorings at Brixham at 20.10 hours. For his outstanding courage and determination John Dew was awarded a Bronze Medal by the RNLI.

On the night of Monday 6 December 1976 a full southerly gale blew, unabated, from the Bay of Biscay directly into the English Channel. Whilst Brixham Harbour was somewhat sheltered by the natural break of Berry Head, conditions were quite different in Lyme Bay. It was at 01.13 hours that the *Edward Bridges* responded to a MAYDAY transmitted by the Greek-owned cargo ship *Lyrma*. The 475-ton vessel sailed under the Panamanian flag. The exact position of the *Lyrma* was not known but Brixham Coastguard estimated her position to be 20 miles south, lying approximately 6 miles off Start Point. The vessel's radar was unserviceable, her steering gear had broken down and she had developed a list.

On this occasion the *Edward Bridges* was

under the command of Acting Coxswain Keith Bower. Keith's crew on this launch were John Dew (Acting Second Coxswain), Stephen Bower (Mechanic), John Hunkin (Assistant Mechanic), together with lifeboat men Richard Brown, Nicholas Davies and Michael Mills.

As they cast off, Keith Bower initially chose to steer from the open bridge position, thus allowing himself clear visibility in negotiating the confines of the harbour. After the lifeboat cleared the breakwater, Keith ordered everyone inside and all doors and hatches closed. He then transferred his control to the wheelhouse. Being sheltered by Berry Head, on an easterly course and in only a slight to moderate sea, the *Edward Bridges* was able to steam at full speed, nearly 19 knots. As the lifeboat rounded Berry Head and set a course southward, conditions altered dramatically as the lifeboat was struck by a mountainous wave that threw the crew members around like rag dolls. The Coxswain immediately reached for the throttles and attempted to reduce the power of the twin 460hp diesel engines, and stabilise the handling of the lifeboat. The sea, which was almost a spring tide, was running at about one knot against the wind. The *Edward Bridges* was now facing directly into the teeth of the F10 storm, with a constant 48–55 knots of wind. Looking out into the Channel, the Coxswain saw huge waves, crested with spray, pounding towards him, the largest being about 40 feet.

On several occasions the *Edward Bridges* was left riding on the crest of a wave, her propellers turning clear of the water, before her bow plunged down into the trough. The weather that night was a true test of the durability and seaworthiness of the Arun lifeboat, together with the bravery and resilience of her crew. In the raging seas, Acting Second Coxswain, John Dew, found navigation impossible, the compass was swinging through 30° and he was experiencing extreme difficulty in keeping his navigational instruments on the chart table. It became abundantly clear to Dew that he would have to rely on the 'Decca' navigator to plot their position.

The Coxswain continued to search for a way to reduce the punishment which was being experienced by both crew and boat; this he did by skilful timing and manipulation of the throttles to ride each wave. As the *Edward Bridges* crested the largest waves, Bower almost completely cut his throttles and then opened them up to about 1,500 rpm (13 knots) to drive the lifeboat down the face of the wave, through the trough, and up to the crest of the next gigantic wave. To a greater degree these actions kept the keel of the boat in the water but on more than one occasion the lifeboat was completely airborne. The Decca fixes showed that in this manner, with the aid of

the tide going with her, the lifeboat made a good ten knots over the ground or nine knots through the water.

Progress towards the *Lyrma* was extremely uncomfortable, but worse was yet to come. Barometric pressure continued to drop and conditions worsened to 'violent storm F11', 56–63 knots of wind. In an attempt to make better progress, and to make conditions more comfortable, Coxswain Bower steered 20° to the east of his intended course, keeping the sea more on the bow. At 01.54 hours, a radar contact was made, five miles on the starboard bow and approximately a mile from the original reported position of the casualty. The *Edward Bridges* altered course and then had the sea and wind across her port bow. John Dew plotted the position of the radar contact by taking its range and applying this information to the Decca fixes. As the contact was making good progress on a northerly course, it became apparent that this could not be the *Lyrma*.

At 02.15 hours the Coastguard updated the lifeboat with the casualty's position, now being 114°T, 7.5 miles from Start Point. The lifeboat altered course to 169°T to intersect the new position. Two radar echoes then appeared five miles ahead and, ten minutes later, Acting Coxswain Bower sighted lights about three miles ahead. Start Point Radio gave the wind strength, at this time, as F10–11. Keith Bower made an assessment of the situation that confronted him and, believing that attempting a rescue would be highly dangerous, if not impossible, requested that the crew be taken off the casualty by Sea King helicopter. The Coastguard subsequently informed Coxswain Bower that a Sea King was not available.

At 02.40 hours, the lifeboat reached the *Lyrma* and found that two other vessels were standing by. Coxswain Bower transferred his control to the flying-bridge position; he was accompanied by lifeboat man John Hunkin who was to act as radio operator. With her steering gear disabled, the *Lyrma*, which was listing heavily to starboard, was slowly steaming round, in a starboard circle, at the mercy of the sea. The Captain, fearing for the safety of his crew, requested that they should be taken off the ship. The wind started to veer a little, although there was no reduction in its intensity, the heavy swell continued from the south and the sea became more confused. Conditions continued to steadily worsen. The lifeboat requested the Captain of the *Lyrma* to instruct his crew to launch and take to the life-raft but there was confusion as only the Captain spoke English. At 02.57 hours the raft was launched but the crew appeared reluctant to get into it. At this time the *Lyrma* appeared to stop her engines and lay bows west port beam to the sea. The Coastguard then informed acting Coxswain Bower that RFA *Engadine* was approaching; she was carrying a Wessex helicopter, which she hoped to get airborne at 03.15 hours.

The helicopter arrived on the scene at 03.30 hours. A winch-man was lowered over the aft superstructure of the vessel but he could not control his descent. A second approach was made but on this occasion the winch-man was injured, when he became entangled in one of the ship's davits, and had to be withdrawn. It later transpired that instruments on board the helicopter had recorded the freighter's deck rising and falling 30 feet during the rescue attempt. The helicopter pilot also requested that the *Lyrma's* crew should take to a life-raft, from which each could be winched to safety.

Despite the pilot's request, there was no response from the crew of the *Lyrma*. Acting Coxswain Bower then made the decision that the rescue would have to be undertaken by the lifeboat and at 03.45 hours he made an initial approach to the casualty's starboard quarter. The 27,000 Eurofreighter was trying to make a lee for the rescue operation, but her presence appeared to make the sea even more confused. As this initial assessment appeared favourable the Captain was requested to muster his crew aft, on the starboard side of the vessel. Fenders were placed along the side of the lifeboat by crewmen John Dew and Michael Mills, in preparation for taking the crew aboard, while Richard Brown and Nicholas Davies prepared to lead them aft and inside the lifeboat. Keith Bower then commenced his first rescue approach and successfully manoeuvred the lifeboat up to the *Lyrma* and took off the only female on board. With both vessels twisting in the corkscrewing sea, the lifeboat pulled away and Bower prepared to make his second approach. This run had to be abandoned, as the two craft rolled violently. During the third the crew took off two men with John Dew standing between the forward guard rails and the inner pulpit rails to catch them. The fourth run resulted in the rescue of another man. In horrendous conditions Coxswain Bower approached the *Lyrma* for a fifth time, but again his approach had to be aborted.

For the sixth time the *Edward Bridges* commenced her approach but as her port bow came alongside the vessel the *Lyrma* rolled violently to starboard, directly on top of the lifeboat, crushing nine of the lifeboat's guard-rail stanchions. Lifeboat men, who were exposed on the open foredeck, had to leap for safety. The lifeboat was in fact trapped under the *Lyrma's* gunwales, and, as the casualty rolled down on top of her, John Hunkin, who was standing

beside Keith Bower at the upper conning position, leaned over to fend off the *Lyrma's* lifeboat which was swinging, still in its davits, about five feet inboard the *Lyrma's* side. The two vessels remained locked together as one more crewman leapt from the *Lyrma* to the safety of the lifeboat; a second hesitated but was dragged onto the lifeboat by John Dew who had again gone forward over the pulpit rails. Engaging both engines full astern, Acting Coxswain Bower pulled the *Edward Bridges* clear of the *Lyrma*.

By this time a further two members of the crew had taken to the life-raft, leaving the Captain and one crewman on the vessel. On the seventh run the crewman was rescued but Coxswain Bower had to make two further runs before the Captain could be rescued. The life-raft, containing the remaining two crewmen, was attached to the port bow of the *Lyrma* by a line. Bower skilfully manoeuvred the lifeboat to windward of the raft and tried to encourage the crewmen to set the raft free. Eventually, language difficulties were overcome, the line securing the raft was cut and a line was thrown, from the lifeboat, to the raft. The last two casualties were rescued at 04.10 hours.

Throughout the rescue operation the Wessex from RFA *Engadine* had stood by. The pilot said later that, in the conditions, he would not have believed it possible that anyone could have been taken off safely by the lifeboat. He described the lifeboat's actions as 'fantastic seamanship'.

The return to Brixham was just as perilous as the outward journey with Coxswain Bower again having to contend with huge waves and poor visibility. To ensure the self-righting properties of the lifeboat worked, it was essential that the watertight doors of the vessel were closed. Coxswain Bower insisted that the survivors from the *Lyrma*, together with his own crew, remained in the wheelhouse with the doors secured. Keith Bower, accompanied by Assistant Mechanic Hunkin, remained on the exposed upper deck the better to observe the huge following seas and thus be readily in a position to take action to prevent broaching. They were fully aware of the possible consequences should the lifeboat have encountered difficulties. The wind had

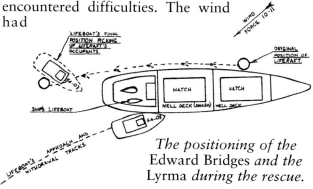

*The positioning of the* Edward Bridges *and the* Lyrma *during the rescue.*

veered to the south-west; the seas reduced somewhat in comparison with the outward journey. Full speed was maintained for the homeward journey and only two broaches occurred. By calling once more on all his skills of seamanship, and placing his total trust in the *Edward Bridges*, an exhausted Coxswain Keith Bower brought the casualties and his crew safely back to Brixham Harbour, arriving at her refuelling berth at 05.10 hours.

It is rare that the RNLI awards a Gold Medal for bravery, but on this occasion it was awarded to Keith Bower for his outstanding courage and seamanship during this demanding service *(above)*. John Dew was awarded a second Bronze service clasp and Bronze Medals were awarded to Motor Mechanic Stephen Bower, Assistant Mechanic John Hunkin, and crew members Michael Mills, Nicholas Davies and Richard Brown.

There is a saying that 'lightning doesn't strike twice', but it did for John Reed, a housemaster at Lupton House School, Churston, and luckily for him Coxswain George Dyer and the Brixham lifeboat were at hand on both occasions. The first occasion was in 1974 when Mr Reed, his cousin and Mr Reed's two-year-old son were rescued after their boat suffered engine failure, when struck by a freak storm whilst sailing from Poole to Bristol. Their craft was towed into Brixham by the lifeboat. On this occasion, Mr Reed had a miraculous escape when he was blown into the sea by an explosion on board his 24ft yacht, *Serenity*. Late in the evening of Monday 18 April 1977, Mr Reed was motor sailing, approximately two miles off Brixham Breakwater, when fire broke out in the engine of his vessel. He attempted to fight the fire but an explosion blew him into the sea. Mr Reed climbed back on to the boat and broadcast a MAYDAY, continuing to fight the fire which had spread to the galley. He repeated his distress call. There was a second explosion, the force of which again blew Mr Reed into the sea. Once more he clambered on board the *Serenity* and managed to lower the mainsail and jib, which were both on fire. The mast then crashed down and just before the lifeboat arrived, a calor gas canister exploded and, for the third time, Mr Reed found himself in the sea.

When Coxswain Dyer reached the casualty she was burning from stem to stern. The lifeboat located and picked up Mr Reed and the crew of the lifeboat fought and extinguished the fire with

a portable pump, which had been donated to the Torbay Station by the Torquay Hotels' Association. It was the first occasion on which the diesel pump, which pumped seawater, had been used. The Honorary Secretary, Captain Barry Anderson, said 'The men said it proved absolutely splendid and is going to be a Godsend in situations like this.'

The Brixham trawler, *Phoenix*, took the *Serenity* in tow and made for Brixham Harbour where two fire appliances were standing by. The *Serenity* burned to the waterline and sank before reaching harbour. Mr Reed was subsequently landed at Torquay and taken to Torbay Hospital, suffering from shock.

Deputy Coxswain Keith Bower was at the helm of the *Edward Bridges* when, on Friday 10 June 1977, she went to the assistance of the 42-ton Dartmouth-registered yacht *Golliwogs*, which was taking part in a race to the Channel Islands. She was one of a fleet of 25 yachts, which set out from Torquay, at 18.00 hours, in favourable conditions with a forecasted wind of F2–3.

The Brixham Coastguard coordinated rescue operations after the vessel *Buffalo* reported sighting a red flare 13 miles east of Start Point. The *Edward Bridges* was immediately launched and the Royal Navy minesweeper, HMS *Cuxton*, was diverted to the scene. Several other vessels, including two fellow competitors, also answered the distress signals.

The *Golliwogs*, with a crew of four, was on course for the Channel Islands when weather conditions deteriorated. At about 21.50 hours, in a F7 south-easterly wind with an accompanying heavy sea and swell, her aluminium mast snapped. The crew cut away the mast and rigging and, being at the mercy of the sea, issued the distress signal. The skipper started the vessel's small engine but in the south-easterly gale the yacht was unable to make headway. The yachts *Skirmish* and *Contessa* immediately responded to the signals and attempted to take *Golliwogs* in tow. The attempts made by these vessels were unsuccessful as in the heavy seas the towline repeatedly parted. A small tanker, the *Tillerman*, which stood by the *Golliwogs* informed Brixham Coastguard that the crew of four was safe. Upon receipt of this information the minesweeper was thanked and released from the operation.

The *Edward Bridges* reached the casualty just before 23.59 hours. In the increasing swell, Coxswain Bower successfully manoeuvred the Arun alongside the casualty and established a towline. The *Golliwogs'* crew of four were landed safely, at Brixham, at 02.30 hours. Mr Courtney, of Torquay, skipper of the *Golliwogs* and an experienced yachtsman, was full of praise

*Coxswain George Dyer receiving the RNLI Bronze Medal from the Mayor of Torbay, for service to the* Leslie H, *19 February 1978. Certificates of Service were awarded to* (left to right) *John Hunkin, Arthur Curnow, Ron Bradford, Brian Caunter, John Ashford and Keith Bower.* A. CURNOW

*HRH the Duke of Kent presents the RNLI Bronze Medal to Cox'n Arthur Curnow for service to the* Fairway, *2 December 1978.* A. CURNOW

for the crew of the lifeboat admitting to a local reporter 'It was pretty frightening in that heavy swell.'

The crew of the *Edward Bridges* were involved in two outstanding rescues during 1978, the first being on the morning of Sunday 19 February. At 11.45 hours the Brixham pilot's boat, the *Leslie H*, left harbour to take a pilot off the container ship *American Archer*. Pilot Captain Bob Curtis was on board the *Leslie H* together with Coxswain Bruce Halford and deck-hand Carl Ansell. Her departure, in winds of F8, gusting to severe F9, which were accompanied by extremely heavy seas and swell, was witnessed by the Lifeboat Station's Deputy Launching Authority, Tony Smith, who immediately telephoned the Hon. Sec., Captain Anderson, who in turn telephoned Coxswain George Dyer, requesting that a crew muster at the boat-house as soon

as possible. At 12.35 hours, when the *Leslie H* was one mile east of Berry Head, she broadcast a MAYDAY, reporting that her steering gear had jammed. Within three minutes of receiving the call, the *Edward Bridges* cast off her moorings and headed out to assist the *Leslie H*. Having negotiated the harbour fairway and rounded the Brixham breakwater, Coxswain Dyer would normally have steadily increased the speed of the lifeboat. On this occasion, however, the seas were of such ferocity that he was required to reduce speed to ten knots, a little over half speed. The lifeboat battled through 30ft waves for 20 minutes before she located the casualty. Mr Halford and Mr Ansell were immediately taken off, leaving only Captain Curtis on board. A tow-line having been secured between the *Leslie H* and the *Edward Bridges*, the lifeboat set a course to clear Berry Head. The pilot boat proved an extremely slow, difficult tow as both of her rudders were locked firmly to starboard; the lifeboat had to compensate for this hindrance by steering a wide, arced course. In the heavy, heaving seas, Coxswain Dyer had to constantly vary his speed of tow and, on occasions, placed the lifeboat's engines in neutral to reduce his speed and compensate for the motion of the sea. 'One of the biggest problems with the tow was that we only had 50 fathoms of tow-line. We could have done with at least 200 fathoms,' recalls Coxswain George Dyer.

With the tow underway, Second Coxswain Keith Bower moved to the upper steering position and took the wheel of the lifeboat; Deputy Coxswain Arthur Curnow, who took over the operation of the engine controls, accompanied him. Coxswain Dyer went to a position, on the port side, from where the progress of the tow could be observed and any necessary advice given. But nothing could have prepared the crew for what followed as the force of the waves caused the pilot boat to veer violently to starboard. Coxswain Dyer ordered the engines to neutral, immediately reducing forward momentum. As both vessels momentarily foundered, the lifeboat, caught by the wind, was swung broadside-on to the breaking seas. Lifeboat man John Ashford was standing by the handrails aft of the flying bridge, when he saw a huge freak wave bearing down on the lifeboat; he immediately crouched down and wrapped his arms under the handrails. The wave was estimated at 35–40 feet in height and was further crested by breaking foam; it crashed down upon the *Edward Bridges* flinging her on her beam-ends. Coxswain Dyer was himself totally immersed in the sea, whilst Second Coxswain Bower managed to stay at the upper steering position. The lifeboat heeled over to such a degree that Captain Curtis, on board the *Leslie H*, reported seeing the entire length of the keel as both of the lifeboat's propellers came clear of the water. The self-righting properties of the Arun came into their own as, slowly, the lifeboat began to right herself; it was at this point that the crew realised that John Ashford had been washed overboard. Second Coxswain Bower attempted to engage the engines into reverse but the cut-out switches had automatically reduced the engines to idling when the lifeboat rolled. Acting Motor Mechanic John Hunkin reset the switches and the engines responded. Coxswain Dyer was able to reach John Ashford with the tow-rope from the pilot boat and he was pulled to safety.

'We towed for about three quarters of an hour and were doing well until we tried to ease her into Torbay,' said Coxswain Dyer, continuing:

*She went over 90 degrees and the motors cut out – as they are meant to when that angle is reached. I was on the port side and went right under the water. She settled there for a couple of seconds and then came up again. With the force of water rushing past I lost my glasses and both of my seaboots were pulled from my feet.*

Coxswain Dyer decided that the risk to life was too great and took Captain Curtis on board the lifeboat. At 13.20 hours the tow-rope parted and Coxswain Dyer abandon the *Leslie H* and returned to station. The *Leslie H* now rests below the cliffs south of Berry Head.

It was some time later that the Station's Hon. Sec., Captain Barry Anderson, attempted to make a ship-to-shore call to George Dyer, who was fishing off Lands End, but eventually a radio-telephone call had to be made by Start Point Coastguards to inform him that he had been awarded the RNLI's Bronze Medal for his courage, fine seamanship and outstanding leadership during this demanding service. The award had been announced only a few hours earlier by the RNLI's Management Committee in London. The Committee also awarded Certificates of Service to Keith Bower (Second Coxswain), Ron Bradford, Arthur Curnow, Brian Caunter, John Hunkin and John Ashford. Captain Anderson described the conditions during the rescue as being 'as bad as during the *Lyrma* rescue in Start Bay in December 1976.' He continued, 'The crew and everybody in Brixham will be delighted that George has received this recognition. He has given 21 years of grand service to the lifeboat.'

The Torbay boat was launched on Tuesday 28 March 1978 to go to the aid of the 70ft sailing vessel *Biche*, which had broken down five miles off Brixham. The 38-year old former fishing vessel, with a crew of six men and a woman, experienced engine trouble whilst making her way up Channel. Whilst she had battled against heavy seas the *Biche* started to take water as seams sprung in her hull. Having informed the Brixham Coastguard of the problems, the skipper turned the *Biche* and in darkness struggled at only two knots, in an attempt to make Brixham.

Main: *Arthur Curnow noses the bow of the* Edward Bridges *into Oddicombe Cliffs, Torquay, to recover a youth injured in a rock-fall, September 1978.*
Insets, left to right: *Coxswains of the* Edward Bridges *George Dyer (1976–78) and Arthur L.V. Curnow (1978–91).* RNLI

The Coastguard contacted the British tanker *Naticina* which located and escorted the *Biche*. The trawler ran into further difficulty when, whilst under escort, her engines failed totally. The skipper of the *Biche* dropped her anchor in an attempt to prevent the vessel from drifting towards the shoreline, as water continued to leak in through her hull. It was acknowledged that the only vessel available to tow the trawler to safety was the *Edward Bridges*, which was launched once it had been established that the *Biche* was in potential danger. The lifeboat recovered the trawler to Brixham Harbour where she underwent extensive repairs and a refit.

Coxswain George Dyer and the crew of the *Edward Bridges* were at the centre of a full-scale land, sea and air search on the evening of Friday 16 September 1978, when it was thought that two skin divers had failed to surface in the waters off Beesands. The divers had entered the sea at 17.15 hours to dive for scallops, with a sufficient supply of air for an estimated 40-minute dive. The dive time having expired and the divers having apparently failed to surface, the occupant of the hired support vessel returned to Beesands and raised the alarm. It subsequently transpired that, while waiting for the divers to surface, the support vessel had crossed and severed the divers' surface marker buoy line. Unaware of this, the boatman followed the marker buoy as it drifted out to sea also unaware of the fact that the two divers had in fact surfaced some distance behind him.

The *Edward Bridges* was called out at the request of the Coastguard, as in their opinion the superior speed of the Arun would achieve a faster response time than that of the nearer, but slower, Salcombe boat. A Sea King helicopter from RNAS Culdrose was also scrambled to assist in the search. Having surfaced, the two skin divers, who were from Gloucester and the West Midlands, located and clung on to a crab pot line, watching helplessly for several hours as the Coastguard teams searched the shoreline, assisted by Prawle Point Coastguard who sent up para-flares to illuminate the scene. The area searched was between Start Point and Torcross, that being the area where the divers' marker buoy was located. The sea that night was a flat calm which undoubtedly assisted the men in their survival.

As the search continued, Coxswain George Dyer 'felt something was wrong' and decided to widen the area of the search. Such intuition can only come with the expertise and knowledge gained by an experienced lifeboat man. The search pattern was widened and, having spent five and half hours in the water, the divers' cries for help were heard by the lifeboat crew. The

crew picked out the orange colour of the divers' buoyancy aids in the searchlight and plucked the two men to safety at just before 22.45 hours. A doctor was lowered from the helicopter to the lifeboat to attend to the men. Following initial treatment the lifeboat conveyed both men, who were suffering from hypothermia and severe shock, to Dartmouth, where, following treatment at the local hospital, they were discharged.

Coxswain Dyer explained that the two men were kept alive by each giving the other the will to live. He said, 'Had they let go of the line they would have been tossed in and out to sea by the flood and ebbing tides and they would probably have drowned.' Captain Barry Anderson, the lifeboat Secretary, met the *Edward Bridges* on her return to Brixham. Captain Anderson explained how close he had been to considering withdrawing the major rescue operation. He had intended to leave a small rescue boat in the area to continue an all-night search, whilst planning to recall the lifeboat to Brixham in order that she could refuel and start her search afresh in the morning.

Arthur L.V. Curnow was appointed Coxswain of the Torbay lifeboat on Saturday 11 November 1978 and that evening celebrated his appointment by dining with his wife, Barbara, and friends at a local restaurant. As if fated, the waiter had no sooner served the main course than Arthur was summoned to his first launch as Coxswain. The vessel seeking assistance was the motor yacht *Petrellen*, which had suffered engine failure, one and a half miles off Start Point. The yacht was located and taken in tow to Dartmouth.

The lifeboat was again launched to assist a vessel, which had suffered engine failure, on Thursday 30 November 1978, the vessel in trouble being the Brixham fishing boat *Mi Amore*. Off Lyme Regis, she was not in imminent danger but deteriorating weather conditions prompted the launch, at approximately 01.00 hours, of the *Edward Bridges*. The Coastguard particularly requested the launch of the Torbay boat, as she was faster than the Weymouth boat, albeit further from the location of the casualty. The predicted winds were such that, in making her way to rendezvous with the casualty, the lifeboat passed the oil rig *Off Shore Mercury*, which was entering Lyme Bay to seek shelter. The lifeboat encountered no difficulty in recovering the fishing vessel and returned to her mooring, at Brixham, at 05.00 hours.

The 123ft trawler *Fairway*, of Brixham, suffered mechanical failure during the night of Saturday 2 December 1978, eight miles south of Lyme Regis and, her anchor warp having parted, started to drift towards the shore. The trawler crew did not feel in imminent danger, but having established that neither a tug nor a helicopter was available to render assistance, the launch of the Exmouth lifeboat was requested. As low tide and heavy seas prevented the launch of the Exmouth boat, the *Edward Bridges* was launched at 02.00 hours. The lifeboat battled through heavy seas and a gale, of F9–10, reaching the distressed trawler at 03.45 hours. Rolling and pitching in seas measuring 30 feet from trough to crest, the trawler's skipper was informed that it would be daybreak before either a tug or helicopter could be expected to reach the scene. He continued in his attempts to effect repairs but was unsuccessful and made the decision to 'abandon ship'. The skipper and crew, however, remained on board until the arrival of the lifeboat.

Coxswain Curnow stationed his crew along the starboard rail of the lifeboat and after the trawl board had been dropped by the *Fairway*, he manoeuvred the lifeboat alongside. One member of crew was taken off the trawler but the lifeboat had to 'hold off' as the two vessels rolled together. In atrocious sea and weather conditions, the *Edward Bridges* came alongside for a second time and three men were successfully taken aboard; another man leapt for the lifeboat's guardrail, grabbed it, and hung suspended over the raging sea. Coxswain Curnow saw a large wave approaching and, on realising the man's vulnerability to being crushed between the two vessels, he immediately put the lifeboat's engines into full reverse. The trawler rolled heavily, scraping the man's back, but he was pulled to safety. The *Edward Bridges* approached the *Fairway* yet again and the last crew member jumped from the trawler and gained the safety of the lifeboat. An official RNLI report said:

*Mr Curnow's leadership was outstanding as he conducted the rescue in a most responsible and seamanlike manner throughout, displaying cool judgement and skill and an alertness of reaction which probably saved the life of the man on the guardrail.*

For his action that night, Coxswain Arthur Curnow was awarded the RNLI's Bronze Medal.

Three Brixham fishermen and a 15-year-old boy were rescued from the 74ft trawler, *Trevarth*, on Monday 14 May 1979 when fire broke out on board. The trawler was one mile north-east of Start Point when the crew noticed smoke coming from the engine-room. The skipper, Mr Edward Cudd, later explained that he initially took little notice of the smoke as he had experienced diesel overflows from the engine on previous occasions. On this occasion, however, the diesel oil overflow ignited on the engine and quickly engulfed the engine-room. The crew immediately sent distress signals to the Coastguards and abandoned ship

into a life-raft. The lifeboat was launched and successfully located the life-raft and rescued the four casualties.

The Royal Navy Fisheries Protection vessel HMS *Jersey* was dispatched to assist the trawler, with fire-fighting gear on board. As the lifeboat stood by, a fire-fighting team from HMS *Jersey* fought the fire with foam. The intensity of flames was such that additional foam had to be flown to the scene by helicopter from HMS *Ardent*, which was anchored in Torbay. It took four attempts before the fire was finally brought under control. With the fire extinguished, the 15-year-old boy remained on the lifeboat as the three men returned to the *Trevarth*. She was towed back to Brixham, arriving at 04.00 hours. The lifeboat crew were congratulated on the speed of the launch, the lifeboat having left her mooring three minutes after the firing of the maroons.

An exhausted lifeboat crew returned to Brixham on the evening of Thursday 9 August 1979, having spent some nine hours at sea battling with 30ft waves, only to be immediately sent out on a second call for assistance. As gale-force winds swept the South-Devon coastline, the lifeboat was launched at 08.00 hours following a report being made to the Coastguard, from a British freighter, to the effect that the sailing sloop *Contessa Gabriel* was in difficulties 28 miles east of Berry Head. The sloop, with a crew of four on board, was listing badly having had her sails blown out and having been swamped by the sea on at least two occasions. The lifeboat located the casualty and took the 26ft yacht in tow to Brixham Harbour. During the tow, which took six hours, both the lifeboat and the sloop continued to be battered by the huge waves. The owner of the *Contessa Gabriel*, Mr Farmer of Exeter, said:

*The seas were really high and I was wondering whether the boat would actually get over them, but it ended all right thanks to the wonderful men from the lifeboat.*

Having returned to harbour, the lifeboat had just completed refuelling when she put to sea once more following reports of a swimmer being in difficulty off Hopes Nose, Torquay. Upon arrival at Hopes Nose, the Coxswain was informed that the swimmer had safely reached the shore. An hour later, the exhausted crew returned to their station.

Many distress calls answered by the RNLI are in respect of persons who have become stranded on, or fallen from, cliffs; one such call was that to which the *Edward Bridges* responded on Tuesday 14 August 1979. Initial information indicated that three men were stranded on the rocks below

Southdown Cliff, which is two miles south of Berry Head. With south-westerly F8 winds, gusting to F9, which were accompanied by extremely rough seas, the lifeboat was launched at 11.00 hours for the 12-minute journey to Southdown. The three stranded men were located but the approach of the lifeboat was severely hampered by a 6ft swell that was breaking over the rocks and along the base of the cliffs. Coxswain Curnow assessed that conditions were such that the safest way to approach the men would be by using the inflatable 'Y' boat, which the Arun carried stored on the roof of the cabin. Acting Assistant Mechanic Brian Caunter and lifeboat man Michael Kingston were respectively designated helmsman and crew of the 'Y' boat. The *Edward Bridges* was halted some 100 yards from the cliffs and, by using a combination of line and the outboard engine, the 'Y' boat was veered down towards the shore.

In order to keep the 'Y' boat flat in the water and prevent it from flipping over, Michael Kingston had to transfer all his weight to the bow. As Brian Caunter eased the boat forward into a narrow gully, Michael Kingston grabbed hold of a rock, his grip being firm enough to allow two of the stranded men to get into the 'Y' boat. With the additional weight, and being in the backwash from the cliffs, the 'Y' boat started to ship water. As the boat headed back out of the gully, the propeller struck a rock, shearing the drive-pin. Using the veering-line the lifeboat crew pulled the 'Y' boat clear and back to the *Edward Bridges*. Coxswain Curnow then manoeuvred the lifeboat, taking her in towards the rock where the third man remained stranded. Using paddles Kingston and Caunter again took the 'Y' boat in to the heavy swell. They were dangerously close to the rocks when the last man jumped aboard.

The recovery of the 'Y' boat to the Arun was not plain sailing; as the crew started to pull her back she grounded on a rock and was at the mercy of the waves that broke over her. Coxswain Curnow ordered the veering-line to be made fast as, very slowly and cautiously, he went astern and began to pull the 'Y' boat clear. The boat inched clear when, without warning, the hand-grip to which the veering-line had been attached on the 'Y' boat gave way allowing the force of the sea and swell to wash the boat back in towards the rocks. The two lifeboat men used their paddles in an attempt to slow their rate of drift and prevent the boat from once more grounding on the rocks. Without hesitation Coxswain Curnow took the *Edward Bridges* in even closer until he reached a point where he had less than two feet of water beneath his keel. A second line was passed to the 'Y' boat crew, which they held, and the boat was pulled to safety.

In recognition of an outstanding service, the Chairman of the RNLI, his Grace the Duke of Atholl, subsequently presented framed Letters of Thanks to Coxswain Arthur Curnow, Acting Assistant Mechanic Brian Caunter and lifeboat man Michael Kingston.

Controversy surrounded the launch of the Torbay relief boat, the *Lilla Marras, Douglas and Will*, a 47ft Watson Class boat, on Tuesday 20 November 1979, following the loss of the local fishing vessel *Our Venture* and her skipper, Michael Perry. The crabber capsized and sank 500 yards north-east of Berry Head. At 11.18 hours the 30ft crabber was seen to be very close to the shore, at the foot of Berry Head; weather conditions were good and the skipper was thought to be trawling. Coastguards at Berry Head saw the vessel suddenly capsize, they saw Mr Perry get himself clear of the vessel, and float on his back, before disappearing from view. It was surmised that the trawl net had snagged an underwater obstruction, which caused the crabber to capsize.

The Royal Navy training ship *Loyal Chancellor*, which was in Torbay, was requested by the Coastguard to attend the scene. The Brixham pilots intercepted the radio message and reached the casualty within minutes. The skipper of the pilot boat said:

*We saw the crabber going down as we rounded the breakwater. We made straight for her but when we were about 200 metres away she sank in about 50 feet of water.*

Debris and traces of oil from the crabber covered the water; the pilot boat recovered two lifebelts that bore the name *Our Venture*. The *Loyal Chancellor*, the pilot boat, a helicopter that had been scrambled from RAF Chivenor and the lifeboat subsequently made a comprehensive search of the area. In a hope that Mr Perry may have been trapped in an air pocket aboard his vessel, two divers attempted to locate the crabber. Due to extremely strong currents and the darkness of the water, their efforts were unsuccessful.

The controversy surrounding the lifeboat's involvement in this tragedy stemmed from the timetable of events leading up to the launch, which were reported as follows:

*11.18 hours* Coastguard observed and recorded incident
*11.22 hours* Torbay lifeboat Honorary Secretary requested to place the lifeboat on stand by
*11.35 hours* Lifeboat requested to launch
*11.44 hours* Lifeboat at scene

A full 17 minutes had therefore elapsed between the reporting of the incident and the request for the lifeboat to be launched; a further nine minutes elapsed between the launch and the lifeboat's arrival at the scene, the latter being unavoidable in any event. The Hon. Secretary, Captain Barry Anderson, said:

*We pride ourselves on trying to launch as quickly as possible because we believe that speed is of the essence. If there is an unnecessary gap in the time it took to call us out I would be very interested to know why.*

In a statement the Coastguard responded:

*There were two other vessels under way and the duty officer wanted to see whether anything else was necessary, bearing in mind that the replacement lifeboat is slower than the regular vessel. If the lifeboat is the best boat to go then we will call it, but if there is another vessel on the spot we shall use it.*

What started out as a 'routine' launch of the lifeboat, on Friday 28 December 1979, could have ended up as a full-scale emergency for the town of Brixham. The *Butaseis*, a 1300-ton tanker of Spanish origin, was on passage from Le Harve to Spain, when she caught fire whilst in Torbay, sheltering from hurricane-force winds. The fire was reported to be in the crew's cabin. The crew activated the ship's sprinkler system and abandoned ship, in lifeboats, as soon as the fire was discovered. The relief lifeboat *Lilla Marras, Douglas and Will*, was launched under the command of Coxswain Arthur Curnow. Arthur recalls:

*As we cleared the breakwater I called the Coastguard and asked what cargo the* Butaseis *was carrying; imagine my reaction when I was told 740 tons of butane gas. We didn't have fire-fighting gear to tackle that kind of fire, so we returned to the Western Lady steps to pick up the Fire Brigade. We told them the problem but life jackets were not readily available for the firemen and we had to wait for them to be brought from Torquay before we could set off again.*

The fear that the tanker could explode was such that the Civil Aviation Authority was immediately made aware of the situation. The blazing tanker lay immediately beneath Flight Path 'Amber Two-Five', the air lane used by aircraft flying between Britain, the Channel Islands and Southern Europe. The CAA immediately closed the lane and aircraft which were already committed to the flight path were instructed to increase altitude from 9,000 to 10,000 feet.

At the same time that the lifeboat set out for the *Butaseis*, Captain Bob Curtis of the Brixham Shipping Agents also set out in the pilot boat. Captain Curtis and Mr Bart Thomas boarded the tanker with the intention of releasing the anchor chains in order that the vessel could be taken in tow, only to find that the gear was snagged. They eventually succeeded in burning the anchor free using borrowed cutting equipment. The vessel was lying approximately one mile north of the breakwater and it was intended to tow her out to a distance of about eight miles. As it became obvious that the *Lilla Marras, Douglas and Will* would be incapable of towing the *Butaseis*, Coxswain Curnow returned to Brixham in order to take out the *Devon Ray*, a stores ship, which had the required towing capability. Coxswain Curnow had just returned to the casualty, when the Cypriot coaster *Deneb*, out of Teignmouth, offered to take the tow. 'I handed the tow over to her as I was allowed to hand over to a commercial vessel,' recounts Coxswain Curnow.

HMS *Anglesey*, a Royal Navy minesweeper from Britannia Royal Naval College, Dartmouth, arrived, intending to put a fire-fighting crew aboard the stricken vessel. Coxswain Curnow said:

*The minesweeper launched her inflatable; they got over the first wave and the second one completely swamped their boat. We then had to go alongside, take off the crew and put them on the Spanish boat. We gave our galvanised bucket to the one remaining crewman to bail out the inflatable. By this time things were heating up and we could see steam coming off the side plates of the* Butaseis.

Whilst the tow was under way, the small group of vessels was joined by the Royal Navy's ocean-going tug *Typhoon*, of Plymouth, and later, the fire-fighting tug, *Robust*, which carried 3,000 gallons of foam. Coxswain Curnow recounts:

*The tug was accompanied by a man who demanded that the* Deneb *surrender her tow. It was obvious that she was reluctant to do so because she wanted to claim salvage. The man told the* Deneb *that if she did not surrender the tow he would cut the towline. He obviously had clout and guaranteed the* Deneb *her salvage money. She dropped the tow and the* Typhoon *took it on. The* Typhoon *was then joined by the tug* Robust, *of Plymouth, which had fire-fighting equipment on board. I was later told that had the* Butaseis *gone up, the blast would have spread out over a four-mile radius – some bang!*

The man referred to by Coxswain Curnow was the Admiralty's Chief Salvage Officer, Mr J. Evans.

The *Deneb* succeeded in towing the *Butaseis* into Lyme Bay and the fire, which had been burning since Friday morning, was finally extinguished on Sunday morning by more than 25 firemen from Torbay and Dartmouth, under the leadership of Devon's Chief Fire Officer John Killoran. The *Butaseis* was eventually towed to Devonport by the *Robust*. The boat-house Service Boards record that on this occasion the lifeboat crew 'Gave help'.

A few weeks after this incident, attending a formal dinner at the Britannia Royal Naval College, Dartmouth, with his wife, Arthur Curnow was formally presented with a galvanised bucket!

On Monday 16 June 1980, a distress call was received from the yacht *Nymonic*, which was returning from St Malo, France, where she had been competing in a race. She requested 'immediate assistance' at a position given as ten miles south-east of Start Point. Coxswain Curnow launched the *Edward Bridges* into heavy seas and gale-force winds and set a course for Start Point. Whilst the lifeboat was on passage, it was established that the yacht had no engine and was under bare poles. It was further established that the *Nymonic* was in fact 11 miles south of the Eddystone Light. Although the vessel's corrected position lay within the Plymouth lifeboat's service area, it was mutually agreed that the Brixham boat would continue with the operation. The oil tanker *Esso Cardiff* had located the *Nymonic* and, in acting as a windbreak, provided some shelter to the stricken yacht until the lifeboat arrived. Upon locating the casualty, Coxswain Curnow assessed the sea state to be too bad to transfer the crew from the yacht to the lifeboat. A tow-line was established and, under very difficult conditions, the *Nymonic* was towed by the *Edward Bridges* to Salcombe. The lifeboat saved the yacht and her crew of four.

The *Edward Bridges* was launched twice, on two separate services, on Friday 14 November 1980, the lifeboat crew that day saving a total of nine lives. The first service provided was to the crew of the 64ft Plymouth crabber *Marie des Isles* which, in gale-force winds and heavy seas, began to take in water whilst returning from a fishing trip 60 miles off Start Point. The crabber's skipper, Phil Bradbury of Paignton, radioed Brixham Coastguard at about 10.30 hours, requesting assistance as water was pouring into the engine-room and the crew were unable to start the pumps. The distress call was also acknowledged by the 120ft Brixham trawler *Big Cat 1*, which established a line and took the *Marie des Isles* in tow.

When the lifeboat located the casualty, they were at a position approximately 17 miles off Berry Head. As sea conditions were too heavy to allow pumps to be passed from the lifeboat to the crabber, the skipper of the crabber requested that the lifeboat take off his crew. In the extremely bad weather and heavy seas, Coxswain Curnow manoeuvred the lifeboat and made his approach to the crabber. He skilfully held his position, allowing all five members of the crew to be taken aboard the lifeboat at the first attempt. The *Big Cat 1* continued with the tow but with wind gusts reaching F10, the crabber continued to take in water. The engine-room of the *Marie des Isles* became flooded and, at 16.30 hours, she sank by the stern. The wreck lies, north-east to south-west, at 50°28'.04N 03°16'.38W, and is 'festooned with nets'.

The second service that day was to the trawler *Pietja Antje*, when tragically three lives were lost. Red flares were fired from the trawler at 19.15 hours whilst she was fishing in the Channel, 23 miles south-east of Start Point. The crew had hauled in the starboard beam and were in the process of retracting the port beam, when the vessel was struck by two freak waves. One of the survivors, Mr David Bubeer, of Brixham, recalled at the time:

*The trawler was lying slightly lower on her port side because one beam had not been retracted yet, when we were hit by two freak waves. As she took the second wave, she started slowly to go over. There was nothing we could do about it.*

The crew attempted to attract the attention of one of their number, who was below deck, and then launched their life-rafts; that was the start of their terrifying ordeal.

The alarm having been raised, the *Edward Bridges* was launched to assist in combing a search area, which was established as 20 miles south-west of Berry Head and 20 miles east of Start Point. Five ships joined in the search for the

The *Pietja Antje, which tragically sank with the loss of three lives, 23 miles off Start Point, 14 November 1980.* RNLI

trawler. Two helicopters assisted them in turn. Coxswain Curnow made excellent passage in poor visibility, in a north-westerly gale, rough seas and a long swell. On arriving at the scene, the lifeboat found the *Esso Frawley* and the SS *Clymene* to be in attendance. The SS *Clymene* had been successful in rescuing the trawler's mate, Will Gillespie, and deckhands Dusty Spicer and Joe Young, from a life-raft. It was established that the *Pietja Antje* had sunk some nine hours earlier, and that five of their colleagues were still missing. The vessel had in fact sunk 21 miles south-south-east of Start Point.

The Royal Fleet Auxiliary Fort Grange was sent to the scene and took over 'on scene command' to coordinate the seven boats now engaged in the rescue operation. Throughout the night a bitterly cold wind of F5–6 blew, accompanied by a big swell. The life-raft occupied by Mr Bubeer and Mr Gary Coley was tossed about in the 30ft swell and capsized on two occasions. The men lost all their emergency provisions, including their distress flares. After nine and half hours in the life-raft, a Sea King helicopter located the two men, but that was not the end of their ordeal. Hovering over the long 30ft swell, the helicopter pilot tried, for half an hour, to pick up the two casualties without success. However, at about 21.00 hours, they were successfully rescued by the Torbay boat.

Together with the other vessels, the lifeboat continued to search for the remaining members of the *Pietja Antje's* crew; the skipper Don Williams, engineer Peter Morgan, and deckhand Phil Kingham. A helicopter sighted a life-raft which, upon investigation, proved to be that from which the SS *Clymene* had previously rescued the three men. At 23.00 hours the RFA Fort Grange advised the lifeboat 'Sufficient in area – return to Brixham with your casualties.' The *Edward Bridges* stood down and landed the casualties at Brixham at 01.15 hours. The search was subsequently abandoned without the missing fishermen being located.

For the 'skill and the very high standard of seamanship displayed on this occasion', Coxswain Curnow received a Letter of Appreciative Thanks from Rear-Admiral W.J. Graham, CB, MNI, Director, RNLI.

On Sunday 24 May 1981 the *Edward Bridges*, whilst at sea for the annual service of the 'Blessing of the Sea', received a report of a person having fallen over the cliffs at Berry Head. The casualty, an 11-year-old boy, was stranded on a ledge having sustained head and arm injuries. Due to the extent of his injuries the youth could not be recovered by cliff rescue. Upon arrival, Coxswain Curnow held the lifeboat away from the rocks and launched the 'Y' boat to recover the

injured person. The action of the sea against the base of the cliff was such that the motion of the 'Y' boat was deemed too lively to embark the casualty. The 'Y' boat withdrew and the Coxswain skilfully nosed the lifeboat forward until the bow was almost against the face of the ledge, a crewman fending her off. The lifeboat was held in this precarious position as the casualty was safely transferred to her deck before being conveyed to Torquay and a waiting ambulance.

During the last week of May 1981, the *Edward Bridges* was temporarily withdrawn from service in order to undergo a major refit; she was replaced by the relief lifeboat, the *52-17 Sir Max Aitken*, ON 1071. This was the first occasion on which the Torbay boat had been relieved by another boat of the Arun Class. The *Sir Max Aitken* was built at a cost of £350,000 and purchased with a gift from the Beaverbrook Foundation. She was heavier than the *Edward Bridges*, being constructed of glass fibre as opposed to wood. Although she was fitted with twin V8 diesel engines, which produced an additional 15hp, she was two knots slower that the resident lifeboat. Previous relief boats had been capable of only eight knots.

On Thursday 4 June 1981, Coxswain Curnow was again in charge for another dramatic rescue, this time in a 'borrowed' boat. The latest addition to the RNLI's Arun Class fleet, the *52-18 Robert Edgar*, ON 1073, called at Brixham to refuel, whilst undergoing sea-trials. Whilst refuelling, the lifeboat monitored a radio transmission stating that two men, one of whom was blind, were being swept towards rocks near Hollicombe Beach, Paignton. With the permission of the boat's own Coxswain, Coxswain Curnow 'borrowed' the *Robert Edgar* and responded to the distress call.

Upon arriving at Hollicombe, the lifeboat found the 14ft open boat, *Midge*, only 10 feet from the lee shore, at the foot of rocks. The vessel had suffered engine failure and had been disabled for more than an hour before a local resident raised the alarm. As the casualty was found in an insufficient depth of water to allow the *Robert Edgar* to approach, the 'Y' boat was launched. A tow-line being established between the 'Y' boat and the cruiser, the *Midge* was towed to safety. Both men were taken aboard the lifeboat unhurt, and landed, with their boat, at Torquay Harbour. 'If it had been left any longer the cruiser would have been wrecked on the rocks and the men could have drowned,' commented Coxswain Curnow.

The Torbay lifeboat answered two emergency calls on Sunday 13 December 1981, on what proved to be an extremely dangerous and exhausting day for the crew. The first call was to go to the aid of the 30ft Dartmouth-based sloop *Talvez*, with a crew of five. The yacht had set out from Cherbourg earlier that morning, with a good weather forecast, but as they approached the Devon coast the weather deteriorated drastically and the seas became mountainous. 'We ended up drifting out of control, without the power to steer ourselves in the heavy seas,' explained the skipper, Mike Pickering. The lifeboat slipped her mooring at 13.47 hours; the exact location of the *Talvez* was unknown but using their skill and knowledge, the lifeboat located the stricken yacht at 15.45 hours, six miles east of Berry Head. In a gale-force wind and huge waves, the lifeboat passed and secured a tow-line to the yacht. With extreme difficulty, the *Edward Bridges* towed the *Talvez* and her crew to Brixham, arriving at 17.45 hours.

The *Edward Bridges* refuelled, took on three extra crew members and dry clothing, and, within 15 minutes, put to sea in support of one of her sister lifeboats. She was to head towards the scene of what was to be one of the South West's largest rescue operations to date, centred on Brixham. One man lost his life and three were seriously injured when huge seas swamped the 10,000-ton cargo vessel *Bonita*, 30 miles southeast of Berry Head. In all 36 members of the crew were rescued.

It was just after midday that Start Point radio picked up a MAYDAY from the coaster. The St Peter Port lifeboat, the *52-02 Sir William Arnold*, ON 1025, was immediately launched. In the English Channel weather conditions were atrocious, the lifeboats having to contend with mountainous waves, which one lifeboat man likened to 'going uphill'. The wind was of hurricane F11–12, making the task even more dangerous for the lifeboat crew. It was getting dark when the *Sir William Arnold* reached the casualty, at 16.30 hours, and found that the *Bonita's* cargo of banana fertiliser, which she was carrying from Hamburg to Panama, had shifted, resulting in the vessel having a 50° list. Battling against the hurricane-force winds, showing great skill and bravery, helicopter crews from RNAS Culdrose and Lee-on-Solent had already airlifted five of the crew to safety. Coxswain Michael Scales of the *Sir William Arnold*, who at the age of 30 was then the youngest RNLI Coxswain in the country, found it impossible to approach close enough to the *Bonita* to take off the remaining crew, which included three women and two children. With the hurricane continuing to blow and the huge seas continuing to run, he took the unprecedented course of action of ordering the crew to jump into the sea. There were obvious language barriers, the crew being Norwegians, Spaniards and Ecuadorians, but one by one they

jumped; lifelines were thrown, and one by one they were pulled through the raging sea to the safety of the *Sir William Arnold*.

The crew member who lost his life was Chief Steward Luis Alvardo. Norwegian Chief Electrician Nils Fossveilt, in describing the terrible accident, said:

*He lost his handhold and fell over the wrong side of the ship. He didn't have a chance. The waves smashed him up against the side of the ship. He must have died immediately.*

The *Sir William Arnold* landed the casualties at Brixham at 23.15 hours. Following medical checks the casualties were housed at the Northcliffe Hotel, Brixham, which had been utilised as a casualty centre. The *Edward Bridges* had been at hand in support of the Guernsey lifeboat. The lifeboat had battled her way through turbulent seas into the very teeth of the storm and was within less than a mile of the casualty when a radio message from the Coastguard informed Coxswain Curnow that he could return to station as his services were no longer needed in the rescue operation. Having landed the casualties, the Guernsey lifeboat men, being totally exhausted, were looked after by their colleagues at Brixham. The *Sir William Arnold* moored in Brixham overnight, returning to Guernsey the following morning. The Coastguard believes that the *Bonita* sank early on Monday 14 December.

Coxswain Michael Scales of the St Peter Port lifeboat was awarded the RNLI Gold Medal for this service. Captain Barry Anderson, Honorary Secretary of the Torbay Lifeboat Station, received a letter from the Director of the RNLI, Rear-Admiral W. Graham, expressing the Institution's thanks for the assistance given to the crew of the St Peter Port lifeboat by members of the Torbay Lifeboat Station. Letters of appreciation, signed by Rear-Admiral W. Graham, were also received by Coxswain Curnow and his crew for their service to the sloop *Talvez*.

The crew of a 35ft yacht had a miraculous escape on Saturday 24 April 1982, when, on her maiden voyage from the Hamble Marina to Falmouth, she was in collision with an oil tanker off Brixham. The £40,000 *Jay Bee* had her mast severed as the Bombay-registered tanker, *Abul Kalam Aziz*, sliced through her guardrails. The tanker, on passage from New Orleans to Hamburg, was making for a point off Brixham where she was to pick up a North Sea pilot. The accident, which was witnessed by a member of the tanker's crew, took place 14 miles south of Berry Head. The crew member raised the alarm and the Brixham Coastguard monitored a MAYDAY call. All shipping in the area was

*Launching the 'Y' boat from the Arun.* Left to right: ?, *John Ashford*, ?, *Peter Hoskings*. RNLI

*The 'Y' boat launched from the* Edward Bridges. *Steve Bower and Phil Burridge crew. Derek Rundle helms.*

alerted and the *Abul Kalam Aziz* turned back to the scene of the accident. The tanker *BP Scorcher*, which was lying five miles away, also steamed to the scene. The *Edward Bridges* was launched and within an hour had located the yacht. Coxswain Curnow placed three of his crew, Dave Hurford, Derek Rundle and Ernie Fradd, aboard the stricken vessel, who cut away the mast and rigging and remained on the vessel as she was taken under her own power into Brixham, escorted by the lifeboat. It is believed that the ship's ladder caused the damage to the yacht. The yacht's owner, his wife and son were uninjured. Second Coxswain Fradd commented, 'It was lucky that the tanker did not sink the yacht. The yacht crew did not see the tanker at all. It took them completely by surprise.'

Coxswain Arthur Curnow, who was called away from his daughter's 18th birthday

celebrations to attend the service, paid tribute to the quick reactions of the Captain of the *Abul Kalam Aziz* as, in making an immediate turn-about, engine problems were caused which necessitated repairs before the pilot could be picked up. He also commented upon the skill of the yacht's skipper in keeping his damaged rigging clear of the propeller.

The *Edward Bridges* and a helicopter from RAF Brawdy, South Wales, were launched at about 04.00 hours on Saturday 18 September 1982 to go to the aid of the 500-ton, Irish-registered coaster, *Majorca*. She carried a crew of five; three Dutchmen and two Portuguese. The vessel, which was on passage from Holland to Teignmouth with a cargo of fertiliser, had developed a list in the early hours and broadcast a distress call that was acknowledged by Brixham Coastguard.

The lifeboat, which was launched under the command of Second Coxswain Ernie Fradd, reported nil visibility within Brixham Harbour, the visibility improving to about 50 yards once the lifeboat was clear of the breakwater; the sea was calm. Coxswain Fradd set his course for the reported position of the coaster, some 20–25 miles south-east of Straight Point, Exmouth. Being subsequently given an amended position he altered his course towards Portland. Coxswain Fradd later explained:

*We were going for about one and a quarter hours when we saw a red flare rise over a fog bank on the bow, this was from the life-raft. When we got there the helicopter had just arrived and it took up two and we went alongside and picked up three. Two of these were from a small rubber boat and one from the raft.*

Because of the fog ashore, the helicopter pilot lowered the crewmen he had rescued onto the deck of the lifeboat, which then recovered the rubber boat and life-raft.

The skipper of the *Majorca*, Captain Klviter, spoke little English but explained that the coaster had experienced trouble with her rudder and started to take in water from the stern. Coxswain Fradd noted: 'The *Majorca* was listing to port and we saw her go down slowly, and finally stern first. It was sad to watch the crew as they saw their ship go down.' The crew were landed safely at Brixham and cared for by the Brixham Shipping Agents.

The Torbay lifeboat had to undertake a rather protracted tow on Tuesday 23 November 1982 when she went to the assistance of the 70ft Salcombe crabber, FV *Burutu*, of Guernsey. The vessel was drifting 37 miles south-east of Start

Point, having suffered engine failure following the flooding of her engine-room. The crew fought to stop the flooding but were unable to do so and requested assistance from the Berry Head Coastguard. The *Edward Bridges* was launched and made her way to the scene. In appalling weather she was launched in preference to the closer, but slower, Salcombe boat. A Wessex helicopter from RNAS Culdrose was scrambled and was first to reach the scene. Chief Petty Officer Arthur Matthias and Leading Airman Paul Dennett were lowered onto the *Burutu* with a portable pump, in an attempt to stem the flooding.

In the strong winds and heavy seas, it took the lifeboat three and a half hours to reach the casualty. She arrived to find that the efforts of the Royal Naval personnel had paid dividends, and the engine-room of the crabber had been pumped clear of water. By this time the Wessex, piloted by United States exchange flyer Al Gaston, was running low on fuel and left the scene to refuel at Guernsey, her personnel remaining on board the crabber. The lifeboat secured a tow-line and in 30-knot winds and heavy seas the tow, which was to become a six-hour struggle, commenced. Towing another vessel in such conditions requires great skill and seamanship, the vessel under tow being completely at the mercy of the sea. On this occasion slow but steady progress was made until, when off Brixham, the tow rope slackened in the surging sea and fouled the lifeboat's propeller; both vessels managed to limp into harbour. A local diver and salvage man, Mr Tony Ridd, immediately dived to inspect the lifeboat and upon freeing the propeller found that no other damage had occurred.

Coxswain Arthur Curnow recalls the 36-foot long trawler *Llamedos* as 'the boat that had nothing'. It was at 05.00 hours on Friday 4 February 1983 that the Brixham Coastguards received a radio message from the *Llamedos*, requesting assistance as her compass had failed. The trawler had only been purchased by her owner on the previous day and was ill equipped, to say the least. The lifeboat was launched but had difficulty in locating the trawler that was estimated to be 31 miles from Berry Head. Coxswain Curnow explains:

*I contacted the* Llamedos *by VHF, only to be told that she had started to make water. I asked if they had a life-raft, they said 'No.' I asked if they had a working compass, they said 'No.' I asked if they had flares or life jackets, again the answer was 'No.' The boat had nothing. I asked if they could see my lights, they answered 'No.' I asked if he could see the lights of French trawlers, which were nearby, again the answer was 'No.' I said, 'Can you see the moon?' the skipper replied, 'Yes.' This was a start! I said, 'Which way are the waves moving along the moonbeams, towards the moon or away?' The trawler replied, 'Along the moonbeams, straight at us.' Don't ask me why, call it intuition but I steamed for 30 minutes on 090° and located the* Llamedos.

Having located the trawler the crew of three were taken off and the vessel was taken in tow. At a tow speed of three knots the journey to Brixham was expected to take ten to eleven hours. The lifeboat, towing the crippled trawler, had reached

*The Salcombe boat, the* **Baltic Exchange,** *with self-righting bag inflated, makes for Brixham following her capsize on 10 April 1983.* RNLI

a point approximately eleven miles from Brixham when the tow broke and the *Llamedos* sank. She now lies at 50°11'.30N  03°34'.30W and stands 15 feet proud of the seabed. The trawler's crew were landed safely.

Every rescue has the potential to become a tragedy and when answering a distress call every lifeboat crew must be fearful of what they might find. No call can be more heart-rending than that received from one's own family, friend or colleague. Such was the call to which the *Edward Bridges* responded on Sunday 10 April 1983, when the 47ft Watson Class Salcombe lifeboat, *Baltic Exchange*, ON 964, capsized off Start Point. The Salcombe boat had been launched as mountainous seas and hurricane-force winds in excess of 63 knots wrought havoc on the South-Devon coastline. In these horrendous conditions, a group of skin divers from the Exeter Sub-Aqua Club found themselves in difficulties off Start Point. Circumstances took a turn for the worse when an inflatable with two of the six divers aboard capsized. The remaining members of the team fired a flare and then made their own way back to Hallsands to raise the alarm. In addition to the lifeboat being launched, a helicopter was scrambled from RAF Chivenor. Whilst searching for a missing diver, the *Baltic Exchange* was struck by a 20ft wave that capsized the lifeboat. The capsize occurred within a few miles of the spot where Rob James, the husband of the yachtswoman Dame Naomi James, had drowned only three weeks earlier. Lifeboat man Mike Hicks was thrown into the sea and it was a full 20 minutes before his crewmates on the *Baltic Exchange* could rescue him. It could have been disastrous as two other members of the crew were on the open deck of the lifeboat when the wave hit. Mike Hicks told a reporter:

*It was frightening. Worst of all was seeing the boat completely flipped over. A picture flashed through my mind of all my crewmates joining me in the water.*

The lifeboat's self-righting system immediately took effect and the boat righted herself within seconds, although Coxswain Graham Griffiths said, 'It seemed like a lifetime. I have never been so frightened in all my life. I thought we'd had it.'

As soon as it was known that the *Baltic Exchange* was in trouble, the *Edward Bridges* was launched, skippered by Coxswain Curnow. The lifeboat punched her way through the heavy seas and hurricane-force winds, which were reported as reaching 75mph. Referring to the *Baltic Exchange*, Coxswain Curnow recalls:

*She had lost her radar and radio equipment when she went over and by the time we got there the helicopter from Chivenor had picked up the two divers and a German tanker had recovered the inflatable. I thought to myself, 'If I was in their position, I'd go into Beesands for a bit of shelter.' We went in and sure enough there was the Salcombe boat. As we approached her, she signalled 'All Well'. We started to escort the* Baltic Exchange *back to Brixham but were diverted to another casualty, believed to have been a drifting dinghy or dory. After a fruitless search, when all we recovered was a dustbin, we were ordered to return to port. The Salcombe boat got in under her own power.*

Former Honorary Secretary, and now Station Administrator, Tony Smith reflects:

*When I knew that the* Baltic Exchange *was coming in to Brixham, I contacted the Harbour Master to request a mooring buoy. I was unable to speak to the Salcombe boat as she had lost her radio, but of all the buoys in Brixham Harbour her Coxswain brought her straight in on to the allocated buoy. It was quite uncanny. The men came ashore and, as we had just installed a new shower in the boathouse, we proudly offered them our facilities – it didn't work. Someone started to laugh and they all joined in and just kept on laughing. It was marvellous to hear it. I think it was the build-up of tension and emotion being released.*

It was the first time that the 21-year-old *Baltic Exchange's* enormous 'black bag' self-righting unit had been deployed. The bag only inflates when the boat reaches 115 degrees from the vertical. Mr Leslie Vipond, South West Divisional Inspector of Lifeboats for the RNLI, later examined her at Upham's Boatyard, Brixham, and commented:

*The* Observer/Europe *single-handed Trans-At. Race entry,* Biotherm II, *required help after losing her mast and rig, 26 May 1984.* RNLI

Above: *HRH the Duchess of Kent during a visit to the Torbay Station, 24 September 1983. Left to right: Derek Rundle, Arthur Curnow, Phil ?, Ray Foster, Mayor of Torbay, Steve Simons, Brian Caunter, Mayoress, Ernie Fradd, Nigel Coulton, Capt. Anderson.*

Right: *HRH Princess Anne visits the Torbay Station, 11 June 1984, accompanied by Lt. Commander R.H. Bew (Station Hon. Sec.) and Coxswain Curnow.* A. CURNOW

*It is absolutely incredible, there is so little wrong with her. If there was an incident now, she would be able to go to sea. There is no question about it, without the lifeboat's self-righting equipment, yesterday, lives would have been lost.*

In responding to distress calls where fellow lifeboat crews are in peril, surely every crew member must reflect upon the phrase 'There but for the Grace of God.'

Even the most luxurious motor cruisers can find themselves in difficulty, particularly if the vessel is ill equipped and the crew inexperienced. Such was the fate of the £70,000, 42ft motor cruiser *Bubble Trouble* on Saturday 4 June 1983, when she set out at 20.00 hours from Yarmouth, Isle of Wight, her crew of two intending to deliver the craft to Poole, Dorset, a distance of about 15 miles. The Solent Coastguard were alerted when the vessel was reported overdue at Poole.

The *Edward Bridges* was launched at just after 03.00 hours on Sunday 5 June, after a survey vessel off Hopes Nose, Torquay, sighted an SOS signal being flashed from a motor cruiser. It was a routine recovery for the lifeboat as it was quickly established that the craft had purely run out of fuel. The craft was furnished with a microwave oven and a heart-shaped bed, but did not carry charts or a radio. Having recovered the *Bubble Trouble* to Brixham, Coxswain Curnow commented:

*The situation was absolutely ridiculous. I advised them to get charts and a radio before*

*they went anywhere else. They were about 60 miles off course; you can almost see Poole from the Isle of Wight.*

Some 95 racing yachts from all over the United Kingdom and Europe gathered in Plymouth in May 1984, to compete in the Observer/Europe Single-handed Transatlantic Race. One competitor, making her way towards Plymouth on Saturday 26 May 1984, was the 26-year-old French yachtswoman Florence Arthaud, sailing her trimaran *Biotherm II*. The relief Arun Class lifeboat, the *Sir Max Aitkin*, ON 1071, was launched to assist the multihull, which had broadcast a MAYDAY after being dismasted in atrocious weather conditions 24 miles south-south-east of Start Point. One other person accompanied Mlle Arthaud. The cargo vessel *Autobahn* had also responded to the distress call and was standing by the *Biotherm II*, awaiting the arrival of the lifeboat. Even when being assisted in such conditions, some individuals cannot show gratitude. Coxswain Curnow said:

*Having located the multihull, we took her in tow and headed for Dartmouth, the woman insisting that she be taken to Plymouth. Obviously with the weather as it was, and the extra distance involved, I could not afford to be away, off station, for that amount of time. We had gone about 18 miles when the woman threatened to cut the towline if I didn't turn for Plymouth. A commercial vessel came along and accepted her request to tow her boat to*

*Plymouth. I handed over the tow and I assume she got to her race.*

Mlle Arthaud sought an alternative tow as she wished to reach Plymouth in order to register her race entry before the race inspection deadline. The vessel that offered the tow was the Dartmouth crabber *Sancris*; the tow being accepted for a fee of £1,000. Coxswain Curnow summed the situation up:

*It takes some swallowing when you have seven fellows doing this sort of thing for nothing when all of a sudden a £1,000 fee is agreed and they are off. We are a lifeboat and all we are concerned with is life.*

The Torbay lifeboat saved the crew of four from a Royal Navy yacht that got into trouble in Start Bay on Sunday 23 February 1985. The incident occurred near to the point at which the Salcombe lifeboat had capsized the previous year. The 34ft training yacht *Blue Eyes*, from HMS *Raleigh*, Plymouth, which left Dartmouth in gale-force winds and heavy, icy seas, immediately found herself being driven towards Start Point. The yacht's crew realised that they were not making headway, even when under power, and immediately radioed for assistance. The *Edward Bridges* was launched with Coxswain Curnow in command. The lifeboat was initially directed to a location three miles off Dartmouth, but upon her arrival they found that the wind had already driven the yacht two miles east of Start Point. The lifeboat used a VHF direction finder to locate the *Blue Eyes*, and was also assisted by the yacht putting up a red flare. In extremely difficult conditions, the lifeboat was taken alongside the yacht and a tow-line established. Coxswain Curnow, fearing that the waves would flip the yacht, moderated the speed of the recovery. The seven-mile tow back to Dartmouth took three hours.

Tragedy struck the fishing community of Brixham once again on Friday 12 April 1985. The Brixham crabber, *My Emma*, was reported overdue, between Dartmouth and Brixham, having failed to return to port by nightfall. The Brixham crabber *Newbrook* was already searching for the overdue vessel when the alarm was raised. *My Emma* was known to have a crew of three on board; Mark Lane, Mark Tyler and Stuart Dutton – all local men.

In darkness, the *Edward Bridges* searched downwind from Datum, but did not locate the crabber. The search was subsequently called off until first light. At 06.20 hours, Coxswain Curnow and his crew resumed their search; they were joined in this by a helicopter from RAF Chivenor. The lifeboat returned to the original

Datum Point and again backtracked downwind. Whilst proceeding downwind, the lifeboat sighted a life-raft, dead ahead; this was found to contain one survivor, Stewart Dutton. Stuart was found to be physically fit, but in shock. He was able to reveal that the 23ft crabber had foundered at 13.10 hours the previous day, two miles from Dartmouth. He had been alone in the life-raft for 20 hours. Stuart also revealed that the crabber had overturned and sunk 'bow first', and that Mark Lane and Mark Tyler had 'floated away from him' after the raft had been inflated.

It was at 12.45 hours, on Saturday 27 July 1985, that the 32ft ketch, *Sea Sable*, with her crew of three, the skipper, his wife and their 16-year-old son, departed St Peter Port, Guernsey, to cross the Channel. The ketch was sailing in the company of the 34ft Moody *Barnacle*. The two vessels cleared the Little Russell and, with a fair forecast and a south-westerly wind, looked forward to a pleasant crossing. It was a little after 16.30 hours when the crew of the *Sea Sable* noticed that a large piece of nylon fishing net had become entwined around their propeller. Their efforts to clear the net with a boat hook were unsuccessful. Although her speed was reduced to about five knots, the ketch continued to sail well, although her crew experienced difficulty in manoeuvring between container vessels in the shipping lanes. The accompanying Moody reefed her sail in order to reduce her speed to that of the ketch, and continued to escort the vessel to Dartmouth.

During the course of the evening the weather deteriorated, with a corresponding increase in wind, causing the *Sea Sable* to reef down. A check of the Decca navigator gave the skipper an ETA for Dartmouth of 01.40 hours. In steadily worsening seas and weather conditions, Start Point light became visible on their port bow, but just after midnight the wheel steering jammed, rendering the craft incapable of turning to starboard. The crew fitted an emergency tiller but this was to no avail as the rudder still refused to move. With the sea increasing and the wind now at F6–7, the skipper made the decision that there would be too much risk involved in requesting the *Barnacle* to come to his assistance and broadcast a MAYDAY. This was acknowledged by the oil tanker *Esso Avon*, which was only two miles away from the casualty; the broadcast was also acknowledged by the Brixham Coastguard who coordinated the rescue. The Torbay lifeboat was immediately launched and proceeded to the scene. Other shipping, including HMS *Ark Royal*, gave an offer of assistance.

At 01.00 hours, the *Esso Avon* arrived at the position of the casualty, 50°10'.27N 03°23'.80W; the wind was now south-south-westerly, accompanied by a rough sea and swell. The lifeboat reached the scene at 02.20 hours, and launched a parachute flare to illuminate the scene. The *Esso Avon* manoeuvred closer to provide a lee for the *Sea Sable*. The lifeboat made two approaches, the second being successful, and two lifeboat men were transferred to the ketch. They found that both the skipper and his son were suffering from severe seasickness and that the wife was effectively in command.

At 02.40 hours, a tow-line having been established between the *Sea Sable* and the lifeboat, the *Esso Avon* continued her passage. Visibility had now reduced to approximately one and a half miles and the position of the casualty was about three miles off Salcombe. A drogue anchor was set from her stern and the lifeboat commenced to tow the casualty to Dartmouth, arriving at about 05.00 hours. The wife of the *Sea Sable's* skipper, Mrs Angel Keates, wrote:

*The circumstances which put us in our predicament were not of our making, but our rescue was wholly due to the courage and skill of the Torbay lifeboat men.*

The Master of the *Esso Avon* recorded: 'The lady in question earned the admiration of all of us, keeping calm and collected, acting under stress in the correct manner.' He also noted:

*The last communication we heard from the yacht to the lifeboat was by one of the lifeboat crew who boarded the yacht asking for the lifeboat to slow down as they were spilling the scotch – I wonder if all the West Country pirates are extinct!*

The £35,000 French yacht, the *Lady Maya*, put out a MAYDAY on Sunday 9 August 1987, after striking an underwater object in Start Bay. Due to the fact that the French family of Pierre Couzigh could not speak English, Brixham Coastguard had extreme difficulty in pinpointing the yacht's exact position. The Coastguard established that the yacht was making water and that the family intended to make towards the shore at Slapton. Two mobile Coastguard units were set up to scan Start Bay from the shore and when a distress flare was sighted, the position of the yacht was relayed. The *Edward Bridges* had been launched and, whilst proceeding to Start Bay, was given the updated position indicating that the yacht was half a mile east of the Slapton War Memorial. Upon the arrival of the lifeboat, the *Lady Maya* was just 100 yards from the shore and about to founder. It was established that, in striking the submerged object, the propeller and shaft had been ripped from the vessel. The

casualty had taken in four feet of water. The lifeboat crew utilised the boat's fire pump, to pump the water from the *Lady Maya*, and plugged the stern tube with wooden bungs. The yacht was then taken in tow to Brixham where she was moored with other French yachts, the crews of which assisted with the language problems.

Lifeboats are required to undertake rather unpalatable tasks from time to time, which involve neither the saving of property nor lives. So it was on Friday 15 April 1988, when the crew of the *Edward Bridges* launched to the 2,000-ton German Coaster MV *Waseberg*, at a position 17.8 miles, on 137° from Berry Head (50°13'N 03°08'W). The vessel was carrying a cargo of waste metal from London to Plymouth. Brixham MRSC had received a signal from the *Waseberg* stating that two of her crewmen were in the hold and running out of air. One crewman had been recovered from the hold and attempts were being made to resuscitate him. The lifeboat was requested to launch and convey a doctor to the coaster and, although visibility was poor, less than two miles, helicopter assistance was also requested.

On the arrival of Doctor David Langley, the Station's Honorary Medical Advisor, the lifeboat was launched at 10.57 hours. The Devon Ambulance Control at Exeter confirmed that visibility in the vicinity of Torbay Hospital, Torquay, was half a mile and at 10.32 hours rescue helicopter No.172 was scrambled from Portland. The coaster continued to steam at approximately ten knots and the lifeboat used her VHF direction finder in order to rendezvous at 11.28 hours with the *Waseberg* at a point approximately five and a half miles off Berry Head. Having made fast, Second Mechanic Brian Caunter and crewman Steve Birchenall accompanied Dr Langley aboard the coaster. They were taken forward to the location of a well, forward of the main hatch and adjacent to the hold access, where they found two male persons lying athwartships. The coaster crew appeared to be attempting to resuscitate one of the men. The HMA pronounced both men dead. It was believed that the two men, who were from the Pacific island of Tarawa Kiribati, asphyxiated from a lack of oxygen combined with a build-up of poisonous gases in the ship's hold. Coxswain Curnow requested, and took possession of, the casualties' passports, from which their identities were established. The bodies were landed at Brixham at 12.20 hours and handed over to the Police.

The Torbay Borough Council bestowed Civil Honour upon the RNLI, Torbay Lifeboat Station, on Friday 29 April 1988, when it was granted the Honorary Freedom of the Borough of Torbay. At a ceremony held at Oldway Mansion, Paignton,

Above: *Simon Littlewood receives his personal copy of the Freedom of the Borough certificate from the Mayor of Torbay Cllr Eloise Armes.* COURTESY *HERALD EXPRESS*

Left: *Copy of the Freedom of the Borough scroll presented to the Torbay Lifeboat Station.* RNLI

the Mayor of Torbay, Councillor Eloise Armes, presented the illuminated scroll to Mr G. Anthony (Tony) Smith, the Hon. Secretary of the Torbay lifeboat. Coxswain Curnow and 18 members of the crew of the *Edward Bridges*, received personal copies of the scroll.

The Mayor said she thought that all of Torbay was proud to have a lifeboat station in the bay, and all were proud of the crews past, present and future. 'I believe the station is one of the institutions that helps bind the three towns of Torbay together,' she said.

Past Mayor, Mr Len Blogg, said:

*They go out in all weather conditions, to risk their lives not only rescuing people but doing unpleasant tasks like searching for and recovering bodies of those who have perished.*

He paid tribute not only to the crews but also their families and supporters, 'On behalf of all of us I wish them safe passage on whatever call they go out to.'

Brixham Councillor and past Mayor, Mrs Mary Thairlwall, said that it was especially an honour for Brixham. 'It is very encouraging that there is always a waiting list of young men wanting to join the lifeboat.' In accepting the scroll, Tony Smith commented that Torbay was the first

lifeboat in the South West and only the fourth in the country to be awarded such an honour. The citation reads:

*At a Special Meeting of the Council of the Borough of Torbay, held on the twenty-ninth day of April, one thousand nine hundred and eighty eight:*

*It was RESOLVED that, the Council of the Borough of Torbay being desirous of recognising the great record and tradition of the Royal National Lifeboat Institution Torbay Lifeboat Station over many years of service since 1866 in the humane cause of preventing loss of life at sea, especially in Tor Bay and around the coast of Devon, and the Council wishing to give public expression to such recognition DO CONFER upon the ROYAL NATIONAL LIFEBOAT INSTITUTION TORBAY LIFEBOAT STATION the privilege, honour and distinction of the HONORARY FREEDOM of the BOROUGH OF TORBAY.*

*The Common Seal of the Borough of Torbay was hereunto affixed in the presence of*
***Mayor** Eloise Armes*
***Town Clerk & Chief Executive Officer***
*David Hudson*

In addition to bearing the flag of the RNLI, the scroll depicts lifeboat *54-03 Edward Bridges* Civil Service No.37.

After the ceremony Coxswain Curnow admitted to having a lump in his throat but added that throughout the ceremony his crew would have been ready to answer the call of the maroons. 'We have had to leave occasions like this before, and we would have been ready to go now,' he said.

At 16.28 hours on Sunday 29 May 1988, Start Point Radio monitored a Pan Pan message from the 25ft sloop, *Siouxsie*, indicating that she had run into trouble and was held fast to the ground by a large bundle of net and cordage. The netting had become entangled with her propeller and rudder. Two persons were reported to be on board, giving their position as being west of the Casquets separation zone. The wind was recorded as south-westerly, F8, accompanied by a 5ft sea and 3ft swell. Visibility was three miles.

If the crew's estimated position was correct, the vessel was 32 miles on 155° from Prawle Point and 20 miles west of the Channel Light Vessel. Neither Brixham MRSC, Portland MRSC nor St Peter Port Radio monitored the call. A good DF bearing of 157°T, was obtained, on the East Prawle equipment, locating the vessel at 50°02'N 03°34'W. At one stage Lands End Radio thought that the vessel had broken free and requested the casualty to maintain contact via Start Point Radio. Contact was established and Start Point Radio confirmed that the casualty was still held fast. The crew of the *Siouxsie* were in a poor state and the *Edward Bridges* was launched at 17.44 hours, and at 17.59 hours Search and Rescue helicopter, No.169, was scrambled. The helicopter flew down a bearing of 155°T from Prawle requesting the sloop to make several radio transmissions, for DF purposes. Eventually the helicopter pilot obtained visual contact with the casualty and remained overhead until the arrival of the lifeboat. The crew of the sloop declined evacuation by helicopter. The lifeboat also determined the position of the casualty by DF and arrived on scene at 19.19 hours. The lifeboat crew freed the *Siouxsie*, attached a tow-line and towed the vessel into Dartmouth. The lifeboat was back on station at 23.07 hours.

The relief lifeboat, the *Ralph & Bonella Farrant*, came off second best to a Royal Navy ship when engaged in transferring casualties on Friday 15 July 1988. The lifeboat was engaged in a three-hour rescue operation following a report that a vessel was sinking in Start Bay. Two Plymouth-based Royal Marines, Chris Johnson and Paul Harry, on board the racing catamaran *Alien II*, which was owned by the Round Britain yachtsman, Rob Wyngate of Poole, put out a distress call when their craft started to take on water off Dartmouth. The Torbay boat was launched under the command of Second Coxswain Ernie Fradd and local shipping was alerted. The two

men, having taken to their life-raft, were in fact rescued by HMS *Ambuscade*. In heavy seas Coxswain Fradd approached HMS *Ambuscade* to take off the two men and it was during this hazardous operation, in heavy seas, that the Royal Navy vessel was lifted onto the lifeboat causing superficial damage to her starboard side. Having completed the transfer Ernie Fradd manoeuvred the *Ralph & Bonella Farrant* up to the catamaran and placed lifeboat man Steve Simons on board with a view to securing a tow-line; unfortunately he had to be taken off immediately as the stricken craft started to sink. A tow-line was eventually secured to the *Alien II* and the lifeboat commenced a long, difficult tow to Brixham. It was later established that the catamaran had been sailing at a speed of approximately 25 knots when a plate had lifted leaving a 3ft wide gap in her starboard hull.

At the end of February 1989, the *Edward Bridges*, which had by this time been in service for 14 years, was to be laid up for six months to facilitate a major refit. Deputy Coxswain Dave Hurford and a five-man crew, including Nigel Crang, Simon Littlewood, John Ashford and Brian Caunter, made their way to Donaghadee, Ireland, to collect the relief Arun Class lifeboat, *52-25 A.J.R. & L.G. Uridge*. The crew found themselves in action long before reaching their home port of Brixham for, as Dave Hurford and his crew crossed the Irish Sea, they came across the trawler *Antigua*, floundering in exceedingly

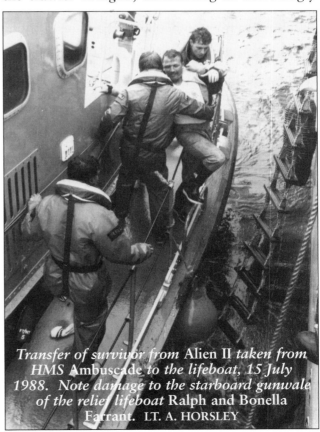

*Transfer of survivor from* Alien II *taken from* HMS Ambuscade *to the lifeboat, 15 July 1988. Note damage to the starboard gunwale of the relief lifeboat* Ralph and Bonella Farrant. LT. A. HORSLEY

*The trawler* Antigua *located by the Torbay relief boat in the Irish Sea and escorted in to Milford Haven, February 1989.* JOHN ASHFORD

heavy seas. The *Antigua* had been taken in tow by a sister ship having sustained mechanical failure. The Torbay lifeboat rendered assistance and undertook to escort the vessels into port. At a point during the long, arduous tow the line parted; it was re-established and the *A.J.R. & L.G. Uridge* escorted the vessels safely into Milford Haven before continuing to Brixham.

On 22 April 1989, Ron Littlewood, Honorary Secretary, Torbay Lifeboat Station, received a letter from RNLI Headquarters, Poole, confirming the appointment of Dave Hurford as Second Coxswain of the Torbay lifeboat. Dave's appointment was to take effect upon the retirement of Ernie Fradd on 9 May 1989.

The annual Skerries Race, hosted by the Brixham Yacht Club, got off to a good start on Sunday 10 September 1989 in north-easterly winds gusting to F6 and a heavy swell, with the fleet setting their course to round Berry Head. One of the leading yachts was the 35ft Beneteau, *Double First*, skippered by Chris Garraway. At 10.29 hours, the yacht *Diamond Chaser* reported by MAYDAY Relay that the yacht *Double First* had been dismasted close to Berry Head. The Beneteau had been about to round the headland when, suddenly and without warning, she lost her mast. The manner in which the mast fell prevented her skipper from using the yacht's engines and, out of control, she found herself being blown nearer and nearer to the rocks at the foot of Berry Head. Other race competitors, including *Friendship Rose* and *Sigmagnifique*, immediately sought to render assistance to *Double First* but were unable to secure a line in the 12ft swell. Mr Les Playle, on his yacht *Papillion*, was successful in establishing a tow-line and pulled her away from the rocks, for a distance of about 50 yards, before the line parted at 50°24'N 03°29'W.

The lifeboat had been alerted and reached the scene within a matter of minutes. The yacht was so close to the shoreline that there was only time to make one rescue attempt. Coxswain Curnow took the *Edward Bridges* in and held her steady in the swell as his crew successfully attached two

tow-lines to the Beneteau. The £54,000 four-month-old *Double First* and her crew were towed to safety. Mr Garraway later commented:

*We were just 20 feet away from sheer rocks, I don't see how we could have got off onto them. It was great to see the lifeboat but she only had time to do one pass to put on the tow ropes. If she had missed that time we would have been on the rocks I'm sure.*

This was in fact the first service to be provided by the *Edward Bridges* on her return to station, following a six-month absence for a major refit. During the refit, which cost several thousand pounds, she was fitted with new steering, had a major engine rebuild and new paintwork, in addition to the replacement of equipment.

The Torbay boat was called upon on Thursday 2 November 1989 to rescue six men from their cargo ship off the South-Devon coast in mountainous seas and storm-force winds. The dramatic operation was launched following a MAYDAY broadcast being received by the Brixham Coastguard from the 1,500-ton cargo freighter *Ibis*, on passage between Poland and Northern Ireland. The vessel, which was taking in water following a shift in her cargo of timber and chipboard, was running for the shelter of Torbay. It was shortly after 02.00 hours that Coxswain Arthur Curnow, Second Coxswain Dave Hurford and the crew slipped the *Edward Bridges* from her mooring and headed to a rendezvous point 14 miles east of Berry Head, the exact position of the freighter having been pin-pointed by the Brixham control room. The lifeboat battled through 15ft waves and on reaching the *Ibis* at 03.20 hours found her to be listing, at times, to 45°.

At the same time that the lifeboat was tasked, a frigate of the Dutch Navy, the *Bloys van Treslong*, also made her way to the scene. As conditions on board the freighter deteriorated, the ship's German Master, Captain Helmut Demski, requested that his crew be evacuated by helicopter. A Royal Navy helicopter was subsequently scrambled from RNAS Culdrose. A car carrier and a petrol tanker also stood by as the *Bloys van Treslong* launched an inflatable dinghy in an attempt to save the Polish crew of the *Ibis*. The First Mate of the *Ibis*, Andrzej Babicki, later described how the Dutch inflatable craft had developed an engine fault and how he and his colleagues had to row 100 metres to the frigate before they could be landed. Captain Demski was reported 'missing' at the scene, having jumped into the sea. He was later rescued suffering from exposure and severe shock and was airlifted directly to Torbay Hospital.

In seas which were described by the lifeboat Coxswain as being 'horrendous', the crew of five were transferred from the Dutch frigate to the *Edward Bridges*. No problems were encountered during the transfer; indeed the lifeboat crew reported that 'all had gone smoothly'. The Arun returned to Brixham at 04.45 hours; the casualties were landed and cared for by the Royal National Mission for Deep Sea Fishermen.

The 74ft trawler, *Carhelmar*, radioed for medical assistance at 21.00 hours on Monday 22 January 1990, after a crew member was hit in the stomach by a heavy steel block, as she recovered her trawl. Her location was 14.5nm on a bearing of 095°M from Berry Head. The lifeboat was launched into a severe, south-westerly gale F9 and heavy seas; she reached the casualty at 22.20 hours. To provide the necessary medical assistance, Doctor Ray Foster accompanied the crew. When the lifeboat reached the *Carhelmar*, the trawler was stationary with both beam trawls extended, one of which had apparently fouled either the seabed or an underwater obstruction. Coxswain Curnow realised that in darkness, with beam trawls extended, he would have great difficulty in manoeuvring alongside the trawler. He approached the *Carhelmar*, placing starboard quarter to starboard quarter. 'We had to go in stern first, which was unusual, but it was the only way we could get alongside. It's a manoeuvre I use quite frequently with my own tugboat,' explained Coxswain Curnow.

With expert manipulation of the throttles, he held the lifeboat steady as Dr Foster and lifeboat man Mark Criddle, who was the nephew of the injured man, transferred a stretcher and medical kit to the trawler. In a 15ft swell the two men then leapt from the lifeboat to the deck of the trawler, Dr Foster administered medical treatment to the injured man and then, with the casualty firmly strapped to the stretcher, he had to be transferred back to the lifeboat.

Coxswain Curnow again approached the *Carhelmar* and once more, with great skill, manoeuvred the two vessels quarter to quarter; he maintained this position by the use of the engines and securing ropes. The injured man was successfully transferred to the lifeboat. Mark Criddle jumped and regained the safety of the deck of the *Edward Bridges*, but in jumping Dr Foster slipped. Coxswain Curnow explained:

*Unfortunately he jumped on the wrong side of the rail. It could have been very nasty for him if the boats had touched at that point, but he managed to jump over by himself.*

He added, 'The doctor did a magnificent job in very difficult circumstances.'

Once all were safely aboard, the securing lines were cut and the lifeboat pulled clear. The lifeboat again fought its way through the F9 winds, landing the casualty at Torquay, and returning to her mooring at 01.30 hours.

For his skill and expert seamanship, Coxswain Curnow received the RNLI's Thanks on Vellum, which was presented at Oldway Mansion by the President of the Torbay Station, the Mayor of Torbay, Mrs Frances Johnson. Certificates were also presented to Second Coxswain David Hurford, Deputy Coxswain Ricjard Morphett, Station Mechanic Bryan Johnson, Assistant Station Mechanic Brian Caunter, and crewmen Steve Bower, Cyril Yeoman, Mark Criddle and Dr Raymond Foster.

A full-scale search involving the *Edward Bridges*, the ILB and SAR helicopter R172, was initiated at 19.23 hours on Monday 21 May 1990, following a report from the *Solent Searcher*, that she had recovered a person from the sea. The man was located in the water at 50°18'N 03°29'W, approximately eight miles south-east of Berry Head; he was suffering from shock and was unable to explain which vessel he had come from or how he came to be in the water. Although sea and wind conditions were calm and visibility was approximately four miles, the *Solent Searcher* reported that no other vessel was in the vicinity. Brixham MRSC made attempts, via the skipper of the fishing vessel, to establish how many other persons were likely to have been involved in the incident, but no useful information was forthcoming. The Torbay lifeboats were launched and a helicopter scrambled from RNAS Portland; a PAN broadcast was also initiated. The lifeboats rendezvoused with the *Solent Searcher* at 20.02 hours, at a position approximately four miles south-east of Berry Head. They were joined shortly afterwards by the helicopter, the F/V Jacoba and the motor yacht *Solar Eclipse*, which also joined the search.

The casualty was transferred to the lifeboat where he was examined by an ambulance man, who was a member of the lifeboat crew; he considered that it would be detrimental to the health of the casualty to airlift him to hospital. The lifeboat conveyed the man to Torquay Harbour from where he was taken to hospital by ambulance.

Further questioning of the skipper of the *Solent Searcher* revealed that he had been following a yacht and saw it collide with another vessel. He had been asked by the F/V Maggie Marie to check the yacht. The skipper explained that whilst en route to the yacht, he had located the man in the water but did not connect the two incidents. The yacht in question, the 26ft Dartmouth-registered vessel *Red Advantage*, was located by the helicopter and boarded by the crew of the *Jacoba*. The yacht was unmanned, and the sails were not set; the autohelm was engaged and the engine set in 'ahead' gear. The cabin was found to be under water, the sea entering through a seacock from which the hose had been disconnected. The water was baled out and the *Solar Eclipse* took the *Red Advantage* under tow to Brixham Marina. A quantity of money and a large number of pain-killing tablets, which were on board the yacht, were handed to the Police. The ILB returned to the boat-house at 20.30 hours and the ALB at 21.33 hours.

The Torbay Lifeboat Station underwent renovation during the early part of 1990, the costs being defrayed by a bequest of Miss Marjorie Olive Heath and Institute funds. Raymond Baxter, RNLI Vice-President and television personality, officially opened the newly refurbished boat-house on 7 June 1990.

The Torbay lifeboats again responded to a report of 'missing divers' that was received at 21.06 hours on Thursday 28 June 1990. On this occasion the dive boat *Torbay Diver* reported that two divers were missing off Orestone. The divers had dived at 19.00 hours and, being equipped with sufficient air for 60–75 minutes, were expected to return at 20.00 hours well within their time tolerance. RCC, Plymouth were requested to supply air support and a diver. The helicopter, R172, was scrambled from RNAS Portland and arrived on scene at 21.35 hours. The ILB was launched at 21.16 hours and the *Edward Bridges* at 21.23 hours, arriving on scene at 21.32 hours and 21.35 hours respectively. The vessels *Dart Princess* and *Deep Mystery* were also at the scene having been tasked to search the area by Brixham MRSC. Helicopter R172 commenced an expanding square search whilst the lifeboats proceeded to the datum selected as the dive point, at 50°27'N 03°28'W, and commenced to check the numerous dan buoys which are to be found in the area.

At 21.46 the Torbay boat located the two divers who were safe and well and did not require medical attention. They had surfaced away from their dive boat, *Torbay Diver*, and drifted on the surface. The lifeboat landed the divers, who were both local men, at Torquay. Both lifeboats were back on station by 22.39 hours.

The MRSC, Brixham, monitored a PAN PAN broadcast, from the yacht *Daydream*, at 07.13 hours on Saturday 14 July 1990. The 25ft Dragon Class sloop with four people on board reported that she had a broken compass and had been dismasted. The yacht gave a position of '15 mile off Lyme Bay', stating that she was in no immediate danger and did not request any assistance. A good DF bearing was obtained of 084°T, from Berry Head, but before the position

could be clarified, VHF working had to be suspended whilst St Peter Port Radio received a MAYDAY call from a vessel close to Guernsey. Attempts by the MRSC to re-establish contact with the *Daydream* were unsuccessful. It was established that the initial PAN call had not been received by Portland MRSC and no further DF bearings were available.

Brixham MRSC estimated that the casualty was probably within 15 miles of Berry Head and requested the launch of the Torbay boat. The *Edward Bridges* was launched at 08.16 hours and commenced a search on the bearing of 084°T, out to a 15-mile limit. MRSC also commenced an hourly PAN broadcast for the information of other shipping. Enquiries revealed that a vessel named *Daydream* had left Exmouth the previous evening on passage to Portsmouth. A description of that yacht was passed, by MRSC, to the Torbay lifeboat.

It was not until 10.22 hours that a further radio broadcast was monitored by MRSC from the *Daydream*. On this occasion a DF bearing of 054°T from Berry Head was obtained. Further DF bearings were obtained by Teignmouth and Exmouth, and the lifeboat was instructed to search an area north of her current track. The Exmouth Station Deputy Launching Authority used the Exmouth lifeboat's direction-finding equipment, whilst the boat remained on her mooring, to obtain his DF bearing. The *Daydream* was requested to fire a smoke flare which was spotted by the FV *Ringtail*, who closed on the casualty at 50°27'N 03°03'W, and stood by until the arrival of the lifeboat at 11.30 hours. The *Daydream* was taken in tow by the lifeboat to Exmouth, arriving at 12.36 hours. The lifeboat reported back on station at 14.15 hours.

The *Edward Bridges* was launched at 15.03 hours on Saturday 13 October 1990, on receipt of a report from the Coastguard that the 20ft cabin cruiser, *Nearly But Not Quite*, was disabled seven miles off Berry Head (50°30'N 03°23'W). The two anglers on board were fishing off the Coal Boat wreck, two miles off Teignmouth, when their propeller had fouled with the mooring line that tethered the marker buoy, placed to indicate the position of the wreck. One of the anglers sustained an injury to his ribs when, whilst attempting to free the mooring line from the propeller, he was crushed against the side of the boat by the heavy swell. At 15.15 hours the new Teignmouth ILB, B538 the *Lord Brotherton*, which was in the vicinity, went to and stood by the casualty. The occupants of a local dive boat, *Deep Mystery*, Mr Alan Smith and Mr C. Yarwood, offered their assistance and accompanied the lifeboat crew to the scene, arriving at 15.39 hours. The divers were able to cut the vessel free but were unable to totally free the rope from the boat's propeller. The divers were transferred to the *Lord Brotherton*, tow-lines were attached by the *Edward Bridges* and the *Nearly But Not Quite* was towed in to Torquay Harbour. The lifeboat returned to her mooring at 16.05 hours. For their assistance, the RNLI's Chief of Operations, Commodore Cooper, sent letters of appreciation to Mr Smith and Mr Yarwood.

The *Edward Bridges* was launched at 15.25 hours on Saturday 23 February 1991, following a report from the Coastguard that a Nab 21 speedboat had capsized off Compass Point, at the mouth of the River Dart. The position of the incident was given as 50°20'N 03°33'W. Initial reports indicated that five persons were clinging to the upturned hull of the powerboat, which had been on a demonstration run at the time of the incident. As the lifeboat made her way towards Dartmouth, helicopter No.193 was scrambled from RNAS Culdrose. Coastguard units were dispatched to Kingswear and Compass Cove. Weather at the scene was a southerly wind, F9, with a heavy sea and swell. At 15.39 hours, the HM Customs Cutter, *Venturous*, reported monitoring a PAN PAN broadcast and that her *Searider*, with three officers aboard, was making its way down the river to assist. At 15.46 hours the survivors were taken from the water, on board the *Searider*. By now the continuing strong winds and sea were driving both the powerboat and the RIB towards Newfoundland Cove and onto the very rocks where the *Broadmayne* had foundered on 2 January 1921. Shortly afterwards the *Searider* was swamped by the heavy swell and failed to respond to her radio. Land-based Coastguard units continuously monitored the situation. At 15.50 hours the helicopter arrived on the scene, followed two minutes later by the lifeboat. The helicopter lowered a SAR diver who searched the hull and accounted for all casualties. The skipper of the speedboat, who was suffering from the cold, had slipped into unconsciousness and needed urgent medical attention; the helicopter recovered her diver and airlifted the man to Torbay Hospital. As the two vessels continued to drift towards the lee shore, Coxswain Curnow manoeuvred the lifeboat alongside the *Searider* and the remaining seven persons were taken aboard, some showing symptoms of hypothermia. The casualties were immediately taken to Dartmouth, where they were transferred to a waiting ambulance.

Conditions in the area remained too hazardous for salvage of either the speedboat or the Customs *Searider*. Both craft were subsequently driven ashore and broke up at Newfoundland Cove. The *Edward Bridges* booked back on station at 17.50 hours.

The 34ft sloop, *Dorothy Hackforth*, left her moorings at Brixham late on the evening of Tuesday 23 July 1991. Owned by the Poole Sailing Trust, Dorset, she carried a crew of seven on a training voyage from Poole to Alderney, via Brixham. At about 01.30 hours on 24 July the *Dorothy Hackforth*, with the skipper Sean Barlow and two trainees on watch, collided with the Danish liquid-gas carrier *Lisbet Kosan*, 14 miles on a bearing of 158°T from the Torbay station. The cargo vessel was on passage from Southampton to Swansea. On arriving at the scene, Coxswain Curnow manoeuvred the lifeboat alongside the sloop and took off the crew of seven. Coxswain Curnow reported to the Brixham MRSC that the *Dorothy Hackforth* had sustained 'an enormous hole in her port side, a metre across.' The hull of the sloop was constructed of a fibreglass/foam sandwich, which kept her afloat, albeit she was quickly taking water. Coxswain Curnow advised against recovery, the yacht was abandoned and an alert on its location was broadcast to shipping. The seven men were landed at Brixham. The exact reason for the collision remained unclear.

Sunday, 25 August 1991 started out as another glorious summer day; Brixham was in full festive spirit with the streets and the harbour being decorated for the Regatta. The Regatta sailing events, hosted by the Brixham Yacht Club, were reaching a climax with a good fleet of yachts and dinghies assembling for the day's events. However, during the morning large areas of the bay became enveloped in dense fog. By mid morning, the Brixham Yacht Club Race Committee Boat was on station waiting to start the first race, when Brixham became shrouded in fog. The fog was very localised and close to sea level to such an extent that a race competitor, taking advantage of a delay in proceedings, climbed his mast to make a masthead adjustment and reported that he was above the fog and could see Torquay bathed in sunshine.

On this day, the Royal Torbay Yacht Club was hosting the Cowes to Torquay Powerboat Race. The craft were scheduled to enter the bay, round a mark off Paignton Pier and finish at an approved line off Torquay Harbour. During the time that areas of Torbay were fogbound, these high-powered craft entered the bay in virtually nil visibility and ran amuck with little or no consideration for the safety of other boat owners.

The *Edward Bridges* was launched in response to reports of a powerboat running aground at Saltern Cove, Paignton. Coxswain Curnow proceeded with extreme caution in poor visibility, being constantly aware of the engine sounds of other competitors entering the fogbank. He designated a member of the crew to give running commentary on the movement of other vessels, as seen on the radar. The powerboat in question, the *Bagutta*, ended up on the shore, 110 metres from the tide-line. Being assured that other emergency services were already at the incident, the lifeboat proceeded to Fairy Cove where another powerboat, the *Fiat Uno*, was reported ashore. The Master of a 'super tanker', which was anchored in Torbay, repeatedly attempted to make radio contact with the race competitors, in order to prevent further incident. These attempts failed and a competitor's powerboat actually collided with the tanker; luckily the Master was able to signal 'All Okay'. Other high-speed boats continued to enter the fog unaware of their position or the dangers that lay before them. The lifeboat was successful in directing some back to sea. The Brixham Yacht Club Race Committee Boat had by this time withdrawn to a position approximately 100 yards north of the entrance to Brixham Harbour, and had, by signal and radio ordered the Regatta fleet to return to harbour. At least one powerboat, at speed, passed between the Committee Boat and the entrance to Brixham Harbour. The Race Officer, Chris Brimecombe, contacted MRSC and the Royal Torbay Yacht Club Race Control by radio, requesting curtailment of the race; he was informed that Race Control had little or no radio contact with the competitors. On returning to station, Coxswain Curnow expressed his concern regarding the unacceptable level of danger in which his boat and crew had been placed. The Station's Honorary Secretary lodged an official protest with both the Coastguard and the RNLI's Operations Room at Poole.

The Teignmouth boat was launched in support of the *Edward Bridges*, late on the evening of Friday 20 September 1991, following a number of reports of red flares being sighted east of Hopes Nose. Brixham MRSC received the first call at 00.23 hours both by way of the '999' emergency system and a radio call from the fishing vessel *Starlight*. The MRSC requested that the *Starlight* investigate. From information gained, it was estimated that the flares were fired from a position approximately four and a half miles on compass bearing of 085° from Hopes Nose. The lifeboats were launched and instructed to proceed to the position 50°29'N 03°21'W.

At 01.09 hours on Saturday 21 September, the *Starlight* reported that she was alongside a life-raft with two people on board; the *Starlight* stood by the raft until the arrival of the Teignmouth lifeboat which rescued the two men and shortly afterwards transferred them to the *Edward Bridges*. It transpired that the men were the crew of the 50ft fishing vessel, the *Quest*, which while sailing at about eight knots had struck a submerged object, which had stopped the vessel dead in the water. The *Quest* had remained afloat for approximately 20 minutes during which time the crew had radioed for assistance but had not received a reply to their call. They had abandoned their sinking vessel and remained in the life-raft for about one hour before being rescued. The men were subsequently landed at Brixham.

Having just returned from a Combined Emergency Demonstration at Torquay, at 16.05 hours on Sunday 6 October 1991, the *Edward Bridges* was ready for an immediate launch when Brixham MRSC monitored a VHF broadcast from a motor vessel in Torbay. The broadcast requested assistance as the vessel had experienced electrical failure. The broadcast had not been repeated, but the MRSC had a DF bearing of 317°T from Berry Head.

The lifeboat proceeded on the course without locating the casualty. The ILB was also launched to assist. The vessel seeking assistance was the 28ft motor-cruiser *Toyakwai*. The name was recognised as belonging to a vessel which had been moored on Brixham Marina and was due to be taken to Torquay to be hauled out. Subsequent enquiries located the *Toyakwai* at Torquay Marina. Following the distress broadcast, the crew had restarted the vessel's engines but continued to experience radio failure. The crew failed to notify their safe arrival at Torquay.

On Sunday 6 October 1991 Brixham MRSC requested the launch of the lifeboat following receipt of a MAYDAY broadcast by the *Lucy Jane* reporting that she was disabled off Eastern Blackstone Rock, Dartmouth. The casualty had attempted to anchor to prevent grounding on the rock. The Dartmouth-based crabber *Excel* stood by pending the arrival of the lifeboat, which towed the casualty into Dartmouth.

After 27 years of service with the RNLI, Arthur Curnow retired as Coxswain of the *Edward Bridges* on Monday 11 November 1991. In the New Year Honours List of 1992, Her Majesty Queen Elizabeth II awarded Arthur the British Empire Medal. The award of the RNLI's official Certificate of Thanks further marked his retirement. Oldway Mansion provided an impressive setting for the latter presentation, which was made on behalf of the RNLI by the Mayor of Torbay, Wallace Dolman. Coxswain Dave Hurford and all the crew of the Torbay lifeboat, together with officials and members of the Torbay Branch of the Lifeboat Guild, attended the ceremony. During the 13 years that Arthur Curnow was Coxswain of the *Edward Bridges*, the boat and her crew were credited with the magnificent tally of 340 launches and the saving of 229 lives.

*Arthur Curnow and Brian Caunter with lifeboat men from Ouistreham, Normandy, on the bridge of the* Edward Bridges, *following the twinning of their Lifeboat Station with the Torbay Station.* COURTESY TORBAY NEWS AGENCY

On Monday 11 November 1991, David Hurford became the third Coxswain of the *Edward Bridges*.

Brixham Coastguard coordinated a major search operation, which involved the Torbay and Teignmouth boats and a SAR helicopter from RNAS Portland, late on the afternoon of Monday 27 April 1992. The search was in response to a report that a canoe, containing two canoeists, had overturned off Mansands, Brixham. Further reports of 'an abandoned boat' and of 'bodies floating in the sea' were received. 'There were several independent sightings of the tragedy,' said Torbay RNLI spokesman Tony Smith, 'including one man who drove hotfoot from Berry Head to the life-boat house to warn us about the upturned boat he'd apparently seen.' In rough seas and with winds gusting to 38 knots, the lifeboat was launched with paramedic John Ashford as Coxswain. Together with the SAR helicopter they searched the area between Mansands and Hopes Nose, Tony Smith explaining: 'If there were people in the water in that weather they would have needed medical attention immediately.' It was later learned that two men, in a white canoe, had in fact paddled from Teignmouth to Dartmouth, and back, quite safely. The men were totally unaware of the search that they had inadvertently sparked off. 'There were reports from the public with good intent. Better safe than sorry,' commented Tony Smith after standing down the operation.

A Brixham fisherman, Richard Mead, owes his life to the actions of two brave members of the Torbay lifeboat crew who dragged him from the sea on Sunday 15 March 1992. The dramatic incident unfolded at 12.15 hours when the crew

of the trawler *Boy Jamie* radioed Brixham Coastguard reporting that they had monitored a report, on a non-emergency channel, that the 30ft stern trawler *Julie Ann* was sinking. A further report, monitored by the *Sido*, indicated that the skipper of the trawler was attempting to return to his home port of Brixham. The message was immediately relayed to other vessels in the area and a helicopter was scrambled from RAF Chivenor.

It would appear that as the launch of the lifeboat was requested, six members of the lifeboat crew were about to leave the boat-house having been assisting a group of children undertaking the Duke of Edinburgh Award Scheme. There was a former Coxswain present who volunteered to make up the seventh member of the crew. The exact location of the *Julie Ann* was unknown, but local knowledge suggested the she would be fishing in the vicinity of the Mewstone. It transpired that the *Julie Ann* had in fact last been seen about seven miles off the coast between Berry Head and Dartmouth. Assessing time and tide, Coxswain Dave Hurford altered course and headed the *Edward Bridges* to a location that he estimated the trawler would have reached. Unknown to the lifeboat crew, the trawler had already sunk. Luck was with the lifeboat as, from the elevated steering position, Mr Mead's red jumper was spotted in the water from 200 yards away. He was not wearing a lifejacket.

As Mr Mead's motionless body was being washed by the waves, lifeboat men Nigel Crang and Dr Ray Foster dived into the freezing sea to rescue him. Nigel Crang held Mr Mead's head above water while Dr Foster gave him mouth-to-mouth. With the aid of a harness, Mr Mead was

*Crew of the* Edward Bridges. Left to right, back: *Phil Burridge, Derek Winning, Derek Rundle, Steve Lunn, George Glasgow;* front: *Brian Caunter, Ernie Fradd, 'an American visitor', Arthur Curnow, Steve Bower, Richard Brown (crouching).* RNLI

*A 'relief lifeboat' plays host to Standard Telephones & Cables' local Beauty Queen contestants seeking to find 'Miss S.T.C.' Arthur Curnow and Brian Caunter did not enter!*

lifted onto the lifeboat where he was wrapped in foil and blankets in an attempt to prevent further loss of body heat. Dr Foster successfully stabilised Mr Mead's condition and together they were winched onboard the helicopter and airlifted to Torbay Hospital. 'It would be nearly impossible to find someone in similar conditions,' said Dave Hurford, who continued:

*We weren't going to the actual position given. The swell was over his face and he was submerged in the water. If you imagine the vast amount of sea there is, he could have been anywhere. He was so lucky it's unbelievable. I really cannot praise Dr Foster enough.*

Subsequently, Coxswain Dave Hurford and his six-strong crew received an RNLI Letter of Commendation. The Station's Hon. Secretary, Tony Smith, commented:

*Dr Foster and Nigel Crang both showed great presence of mind, but the certificate goes to all the crew because it was a team job and they had to search for the casualty, locate him and then treat him before getting him to hospital.*

A journey from Guernsey to Starcross, Devon, nearly ended in tragedy for two sailors on Sunday 24 April 1992. Robert Wilkie and Delia Siedle, joint owners of the 27ft sloop, *Aquila*, feared for their lives when their craft almost capsized off the South-Devon coast. In gale-force winds, mounting seas and driving rain, their sails blew out, equipment jammed and they lost all steerage. The F10 winds and 12ft swell threatened to snap their mast. The terrified couple put out a MAYDAY call to Brixham Coastguards who immediately alerted the lifeboat.

Coxswain Dave Hurford and his crew took the *Edward Bridges* to the *Aquila's* reported position, 18 miles east of Berry Head, but they were unable to locate the stricken vessel. Coastguard direction-finding equipment located the yacht closer inshore. The lifeboat immediately set a new course and located the yacht, just five miles from the shore. As the sea and weather conditions were too hazardous to allow Coxswain Hurford to place his crew on board the yacht, a tow-line was thrown to the sailors, in order that the vessel could be towed to Brixham. Dave Hurford explained to a reporter from the *Herald Express*:

*The yacht wasn't making any headway because it only had a little engine and the foresail was flapping about like a helicopter. We could see it keep disappearing from view under the swell and the owners were worried that the mast was*

*going. The whole lot was shaking in the wind. We got them to take the mainsail down and started the tow – but we could only travel at two knots and it took well over an hour to get back to Brixham.*

Mr Wilkie and Miss Siedle were provided with hot drinks at the lifeboat house, Mr Wilkie commenting, 'It was touch and go whether we would make it and I can't thank the lifeboat enough.'

On Wednesday 1 July 1992 the *Herald Express* carried the headlines, 'Councillor steps up Bring back maroon's campaign', 'Bleep failed to alert lifeboat coxswain'. The headlines alluded to the fact that during the previous year the RNLI had abandoned the 168-year-old tradition of using maroons to call out the lifeboat crews and now depended solely on electronic pagers. This procedure had once again been highlighted as the previous weekend the pager issued to Coxswain Dave Hurford had failed to operate at the time of a call-out. It was revealed that Dave Hurford was less than 200 yards from the boathouse when his pager failed, leaving him totally unaware of the emergency. Torbay Councillor Vic Ellery, who led the campaign seeking the return of the maroons, said that in a potentially dangerous situation a back-up sound signal was a necessity.

The Deputy Launching Authority, Ron Littlewood, who was responsible for authorising the launch of the lifeboat on this occasion, explained that sometimes a crewman could be in a blind spot for a signal and that sometimes the pager batteries ran down. Whilst the matter had caused some embarrassment, he reassured the public that there was no danger and that he had every confidence in the crew that put to sea that day. Mr Littlewood also confirmed that the RNLI was looking into the reintroduction of a sound signal. The sound signal was subsequently reinstated.

Storm-force winds swept South Devon during the weekend of Saturday 24–Sunday 25 October 1992, resulting in the Torbay, Teignmouth and Exmouth lifeboats being launched following emergency calls. The most serious incident was that to which the Torbay boat, under the command of Acting Coxswain Richard Morphett, responded. The alarm was raised following the receipt of a radio message from the dive boat *Solent Searcher*, stating that she was in trouble three miles off Berry Head. The vessel, a converted trawler, had lost her propeller and was drifting in gale-force winds, gusting to F9, leaving a team of six skin divers stranded in the water. Coxswain Morphett located five of the divers clinging to their marker buoy, and took three of their number on board the lifeboat. Two divers remained in the sea waiting for the sixth member of the team to surface; he was ascending more slowly to avoid the bends. The lone diver was located and the remaining three persons were taken on board the lifeboat. By this time the *Solent Searcher* had drifted approximately half a mile, she was taken in tow by the lifeboat and, together with the skin divers, was taken to Brixham.

That day the lifeboat crew also rescued a Gloucester couple who remained sound asleep as their yacht broke its mooring chain in Brixham Harbour, drifted through the crowded anchorage and smashed against the breakwater. Luckily no one was injured and no other vessel was damaged.

A 23ft cabin cruiser, the *Rose Wind III*, with a crew of two on board started to take in water when on passage from Falmouth to Weymouth on the afternoon of Wednesday 16 June 1993. The Brixham Coastguard, who scrambled a helicopter from RNAS Portland and the Torbay boat, had monitored a distress call from the vessel. Coxswain Dave Hurford launched the *Edward Bridges* and, in a heavy swell, located the casualty at a point 20 miles east of Dartmouth.

A SAR helicopter was first on the scene and intended to lower a pump to the *Rose Wind*, but the diver who was lowered from the helicopter to inspect the vessel realised that the pump was far too big and its weight might well have sunk the small craft. The helicopter stood by and awaited the arrival of the lifeboat, as their pump could then be utilised. Water was pumped from the cabin cruiser and she was then towed very slowly to Brixham. The Hon. Secretary, Ron Littlewood later commented that the *Rose Wind* was far too small a craft to have been attempting such a passage in the prevailing sea conditions.

The crew of the *Edward Bridges*, under the command of Coxswain Dave Hurford, were engaged on a five-hour rescue mission following a launch at 21.00 hours on Sunday 25 July 1993. The lifeboat initially went to Torquay to pick up Dr Ray Foster, before heading out to the 80,000-ton Turkish tanker, *Urgup*, which was lying 16 miles east of Berry Head. The Captain of the tanker, which was bound for the USA from Rotterdam, had requested assistance as a crewman had sustained injury in a fall.

When the lifeboat reached the *Urgup*, lifeboat men Roger Good and Toni Knights boarded the tanker to prepare the casualty for transfer. In F6 winds and 15ft waves, Coxswain Hurford made repeated attempts to approach the tanker but was unable to come alongside the boarding ladder. Coxswain Hurford manoeuvred the *Edward Bridges* to the stern of the tanker, while his two crewmen strapped the casualty to a stretcher. In a hazardous operation, which lasted more than

an hour, Toni Knights and Roger Good lowered the injured man 60 feet from the stern of the tanker onto the pitching deck of the lifeboat. The lifeboat took the casualty to Torquay Harbour from where he was transferred to Torbay Hospital by ambulance. The lifeboat had returned to her station by 02.00 hours.

The lifeboat crew of the Torbay boat reached an historic milestone on Sunday 22 August 1993. Lifeboat man Nigel Crang raised the alarm just after 13.00 hours, when he saw the upturned hull of a dinghy floating about 1,000 yards off Brixham breakwater. Two persons were clinging to the upturned hull and a third person was seen to be in the water. The *Edward Bridges* was launched and located the three sailors floundering off Shoalstone Beach, their 14ft dinghy, having turned turtle, had been dismasted. The three persons were rescued and the dinghy righted and taken in to Brixham Harbour.

The historic milestone achieved that day was that the rescue marked the 1,000th person to be rescued by a Torbay boat since the service began with the inauguration of the *City of Exeter* in October 1866.

Coxswain Dave Hurford and his crew took the Torbay boat on a 22-mile dash to reach two Brixham trawlers that had collided in Lyme Bay on Saturday 26 March 1994. The two trawlers involved in the collision were the 50ft *Canari*, with a crew of two, and the 80ft *Jacomina*, with six persons on board. No one was injured in the collision but the *Canari* sustained extensive bow damage and started to take in water. The *Edward Bridges* reached the scene of the collision, which occurred at approximately 21.00 hours, at a position approximately 20 miles south-west of Portland in an hour and three-quarters.

Two Royal Navy ships, the mine-hunter HMS *Quorn* and the RFA *Fort Victoria*, also responded to the vessel's distress call. HMS *Quorn* took the *Canari* in tow but she was relieved from the task upon the arrival of the lifeboat. Coxswain Hurford, having put two of his crewmen and two pumps on board the *Canari* to assist the trawler crew, commenced to tow the stricken vessel to Brixham in conditions described as being 'reasonable with a slight sea and good visibility', at speeds up to eight knots. As the lifeboat and her tow closed on Berry Head, the weather conditions deteriorated but both vessels gained the safety of Brixham Harbour. The *Jacomina* was able to continue to fish.

The Hon. Secretary of the Torbay Station, Captain Alistair Paterson, said: 'If the weather had worsened very much I think it could have been a loss. I think we were lucky that the weather held up as it did.'

The Mayor of Torbay, Councillor John Nicholls, and his wife Elizabeth had a first-hand experience of a lifeboat rescue on Thursday 18 June 1994 when they witnessed a drama unfolding before their eyes, during the annual Brixham Trawler Race. The Mayor and Mayoress were on the bridge of the race rescue vessel, the relief lifeboat the *A.J.R. & L.G. Uridge* with Coxswain Dave Hurford, having earlier been transferred from the race guard ship, the minesweeper HMS *Bicester*.

The race was under way with the competing vessels approximately one mile offshore, when the trawler *Girl Debra* found herself in trouble and began to sink. The Brixham trawler, the *Guyona*, and two other competitors immediately went to the assistance of the stricken trawler and stood by until the lifeboat arrived at the scene. Coxswain Dave Hurford commented:

*There was no panic. As we got alongside we took the women and children off and put a pump on board. She was going down by the bow so we knew something was obviously wrong... to be on the safe side we towed her in.*

On entering the engine-room of the *Girl Debra* her owner/skipper, Mr Dave Driver of Exmouth, found it to be awash with oil and water and further investigation revealed that a pipe, running off the engine-cooling system, had become disconnected causing the engine-room to flood.

The *A.J.R. & L.G. Uridge* saved the vessel and 12 persons, including seven children, one of whom was the trawler skipper's 16-week-old daughter, Zöe. Mrs Debra Driver praised the manner in which the rescue was carried out:

*The lifeboat men were wonderful. They were very good taking the children off, particularly little Zöe. They took a lot of time and trouble to make sure the kids weren't frightened.*

Following 20 years of distinguished service, the *Edward Bridges* was withdrawn from active service, as the Torbay lifeboat, on Friday 3 February 1995. During a routine inspection, weaknesses had been found in the vessel's hull, deck and some beams. Coxswain Dave Hurford said at the time:

*We'll be really sorry to lose her we know every inch of her. She was so familiar to the whole crew we had a lot of confidence in the* Edward Bridges, *especially in really bad weather. She'd roll badly but we always knew she would right herself eventually.*

The *Bridges*, as she was affectionately known, is now on display as part of the National Lifeboat Collection at Chatham. Her name board is preserved at the Torbay Lifeboat Station, Brixham, proudly declaring 'RNLI *Edward Bridges* Civil Service No.37.'

**Edward Bridges** *off Berry Head.* DEREK RUNDLE

*The 52-19* Marie Winstone, *at her mooring in Brixham Harbour.*

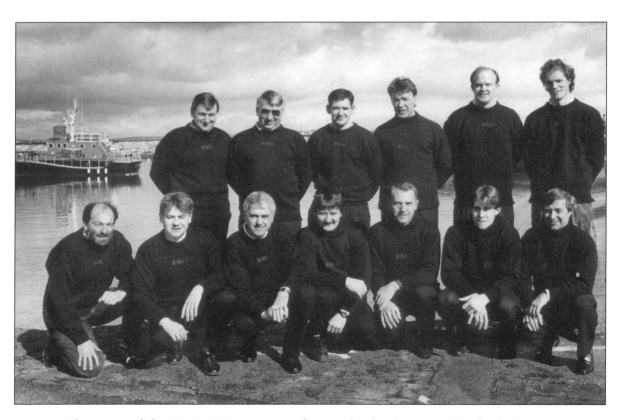

*The crew of the* Marie Winstone. *Left to right, back: Dave Hurford (Cox'n), Richard Morphett, Mark Criddle, Toni Knights, Simon James, Mark Pope; front: John Ashford, John Horner, Andy Constable, Nigel Crang, Chris Ram, John Heale, Cyril Yeoman.* RNLI

# 15

# THE *Marie Winstone*

## 3 FEBRUARY 1995–31 OCTOBER 2001

**Type:** *Arun*    **Propulsion:** *2 x 500hp, Caterpillar 3408 TA Diesel*    **Crew:** *7*

**Length:** *52' 9"*    **Beam:** *17' 9"*    **Displacement:** *31T 10Cwt*    **Speed:** *15 knots*

**Operational number:** *52-19*    **Official number:** *1076*

**Launches:** *277*    **Lives Saved:** *63*

**Coxswain:** *Dave Hurford (1995–2001)*    **Mechanic:** *Mark Criddle (1995)*

The *Marie Winstone* took up service in Torbay on Friday 3 February 1995, having served at Fishguard for 13 years between 1981 and 1994. Like her predecessor, the *Edward Bridges*, she was an Arun Class but differed primarily in that her hull was constructed from the now standard glass reinforced plastic (GRP) and was 52 feet in length.

The replacement lifeboat was immediately put to the test on the night of 9 February 1995 when she went to the assistance of a small sailing vessel, the *Perelandra*, which, with a crew of two, was being blown on to 60ft rocks adjacent to Streete Gate. The Torbay lifeboat Honorary Secretary, Barry Foster, commented:

*The lifeboat had only one chance to save the two sailors. To get a line aboard, the lifeboat had to come in so close she was in the surf. Another five minutes and the sailing boat would have been on the rocks.*

Having secured a tow-line, Coxswain Dave Hurford, assisted by Mechanic Mark Criddle and the crew, towed the *Perelandra* in to Dartmouth.

The *Marie Winstone* was initially allocated to Torbay in the capacity of a relief lifeboat and remained on station as such until 27 February 1995. She was out of service between 28 February and 2 March, during which time she underwent a propeller change and heat exchanger replacement. The *Marie Winstone* returned to station on 3 March 1995 after being confirmed as the Torbay boat, the official replacement for the

*Edward Bridges*. A service of rededication for the new boat was held at the Lifeboat Station, Brixham, at 15.00 hours on Sunday 26 March 1995. The service proved to be what has been described as 'the most emotional service of dedication ever to have taken place at Brixham.' Mr Peter Hoskings, Chairman of the Torbay Station Branch, opened the proceedings and Captain Hugh Fogerty, Divisional Inspector of Lifeboats, delivered the boat into the care of the Station. Mr Barry Foster, the Honorary Secretary, accepted the *Marie Winstone* on behalf of the Branch. With music being provided by the Royal British Legion Band, Brixham Branch, under the musical direction of Mr Peter Robinson, Paul Jarrett, MBE, JP, Senior Superintendent of the Royal National Mission to Deep Sea Fishermen, conducted the service. It was as the Coxswain David Hurford read the Lesson that Brixham Harbour reverberated to the all-too familiar sound of the two maroons. Coxswain Dave Hurford

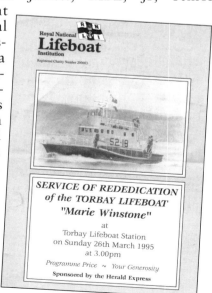

SERVICE OF REDEDICATION
of the TORBAY LIFEBOAT
*"Marie Winstone"*
at
Torbay Lifeboat Station
on Sunday 26th March 1995
at 3.00pm
*Programme Price ~ Your Generosity*
**Sponsored by the Herald Express**

and his crew immediately readied the lifeboat and, as the assembled congregation raised their voices and sang 'Eternal Father, Strong to Save', the *Marie Winstone* pulled astern, turned, and headed seawards on yet another errand of mercy. Superintendent Paul Jarrett made comment that this was the first occasion on which a congregation had walked out on him!

The *Marie Winstone* had put to sea as the result of receiving an 'immediate launch' request from the Brixham Coastguard. The lifeboat headed for the site of the wreck of the *Orangeman*, four and a half miles off Berry Head, where a diver had been reported missing. Tragically the diver, a 36-year old Teignmouth schoolteacher, Dominic Rowbottom, became separated from his 'buddy', Peter Milner, who had surfaced without problems. Together with a Royal Navy helicopter, the Customs cutter *Valiant* and the three dive-support vessels, *Glencoe*, *Fastrack Diver* and *Solent Searcher*, Coxswain Dave Hurford and his crew systematically searched the area for three hours and 20 minutes, in the knowledge that Mr Rowbottom's air supply would have already run out before the time the official search was commenced. The lifeboat found the diver's fins floating on the surface but, unfortunately, the diver himself was not found. The launch received the classification 'No Service Rendered'.

The Brixham harbour-master, Mike Wier, reported a vessel and the owner to the Marine Safety Agency, Plymouth, on 4 August 1995, following a rescue by the relief lifeboat the *Duke of Atholl*. He disclosed: 'I reported it on the grounds the vessel was not seaworthy and insufficiently manned.'

The circumstances that lead to the rescue began when one of the crew of three slipped down steps and reactivated an old back injury. The vessel had left Weymouth the previous evening bound for the USA. It had been heading for Cape Finistere before changing course and heading for Plymouth, then Dartmouth and latterly Weymouth. At approximately 05.30 hours Brixham Coastguard received a radio signal to the effect that Francis Machorn, the skipper of the 90ft *Mul 16*, a former Swedish minelayer, had been injured. The vessel gave her position as being off Start Point. The lifeboat was launched and, as Second Coxswain Richard Morphett explained at the time: 'We had to catch up with the boat. We asked them to steer west but she kept going east.' The *Duke of Atholl* eventually located the *Mul 16* and put five lifeboat men on board the vessel. Having transferred the injured man and his daughter to the lifeboat, Richard Morphett together with crewmen Roger Good and John Horner set about manning the vessel

that now had only one crewman on board. The lifeboat crew had difficulty coping with the vessel's faulty steering controls, a spokesman explaining:

*We couldn't get anything working on the bridge and we ended up steering inside and running outside to operate the engine controls from the wing of the bridge.*

The lifeboat crew were successful in their efforts, the *Mul 16* being berthed at Brixham at 09.00 hours.

The *Marie Winstone* and her crew had to battle against F10 winds (48–55 knots) to save a 1,000-ton cargo vessel, which was in danger of running ashore at Broadsands Beach, Paignton, on Wednesday 7 February 1996. The drama unfolded when the Dutch-registered coaster, the *Deina Jacoba* with a crew of five, which had sought the shelter of Torbay from the storm-force winds and 10ft waves, found herself in difficulty. The vessel, which was bound for Istanbul with a cargo of metal, had been anchored in Torbay when, just after 11.00 hours, she started to drag her anchor, at the same time being unable to fire up her engines due to a faulty starting motor.

The Brixham Shipping Agents' craft *Bay Protector* answered the coaster's request for assistance and managed to get a tow-line on board but with the weight of the line dragging in the raging sea, her crew found that they were unable to haul the line in. The *Marie Winstone*, which was skippered by Dave Hurford, attached a second tow-line to the *Deina Jacoba* and held her fast while a tow-rope was secured between the coaster and the *Bay Protector*. When finally secured, the coaster was less than half a mile from the beach. Later that day, the *Marie Winstone* escorted the *Deina Jacoba* and the *Bay Protector* into Brixham Harbour, having saved the coaster and five lives.

A member of the public raised an alarm at 13.00 hours on Friday 23 August 1996, three red distress flares having drawn his attention to a boat which appeared to be drifting perilously towards the rocks between Thatcher Rock and Hopes Nose, Torquay. Brixham Coastguard requested the immediate launch of the *Marie Winstone* to assist the casualty, a 16ft Orkney 'Fastliner'. The lifeboat successfully saved the crew of two, who had been bottom netting and crab potting when the fishing boat suffered engine failure. The lifeboat towed the vessel to Torquay Harbour.

Headlines in the *Herald Express* of Saturday 24 August 1996 read, 'Is this a lifeboat I see before me?' The Brixham Coastguard coordinated the *Marie Winstone*, the Brixham pilot boat and a land-based Coastguard team, together with several other fishing boats which were in the area, following cries for help being reported at Berry Head. A thorough search was made of the area but nothing untoward was found. A spokesman for the Coastguard later explained that it was suspected that the cries could have come from the Illyria Theatre Company's open-air performance of Shakespeare's *Macbeth*, which was taking place at the Berry Head Country Park. The launch received the service classification 'false alarm, good intent'.

The 50-year-old trawler *Mourn Lass*, which at the time was the second oldest trawler in the Port of Brixham, narrowly escaped sinking after holing her bow on rocks off Dartmouth on Saturday 7 December 1996. The alarm was raised just after 19.00 hours when the vessel, which was returning to port after a two-day fishing trip with £2,000 worth of fish on board, struck a small rock off the Eastern Blackstone Rock at the mouth of the River Dart and started taking in water. The owner of the vessel, Lindsey Kittle, later confirmed that the trawler had struck a shallow rock, which was barely picked up on the boat's radar. The *Marie Winstone* was launched and made her way to the scene. The skipper of the *Mourn Lass*, Jim Thompson, and his crew-mate were rescued by the Dartmouth-based fishing boat the *Michelle Louise* after her crew had spotted two red flares fired from the stricken trawler. The fishing boat's crew managed to get a tow-line on board the trawler and, despite fears that the boat would sink, commenced to tow the 40ft vessel. The vessels had made progress for some two miles before the *Marie Winstone* took over the tow into Dartmouth. Lifeboat men Tony Knights, Roger Good and Steve Simons were placed on board the *Mourn Lass* to work salvage pumps in a bid to clear the floodwater. Although their efforts were unsuccessful, the vessels made port. Alistair Paterson, the Honorary Secretary of the Torbay lifeboat, later commented:

*The bow was badly damaged and wide open to the sea, but the watertight bulkheads held. I would say they were quite lucky the boat stayed afloat with the bulkhead doing its job.*

Following a distress call for 'immediate assistance' at midnight on Saturday 28 December 1996, the *Marie Winstone* saved a craft and a crew of two. The vessel in distress was the 25ft yacht *Bacarolle* which had lost its rudder ten miles south-east of Berry Head. The lifeboat towed the casualty into Brixham Harbour.

The lifeboat was launched to the scene of a tragic incident on Thursday 10 July 1997, which

the local press dubbed 'The Marie Celeste Fish Tragedy.' The lone crewman of the 44ft Brixham trawler, *BM 145 Spartacus*, was seen shooting his nets at about 06.30 hours. The *Spartacus* would normally not have fished beyond a 12–16-mile limit but the alarm was raised around 13.00 hours when skipper David Murphy of the *Carhelmar*, heading out to sea, spotted the trawler some 32 miles south-east of Brixham. The vessel was dangerously close to the separation zone, which is largely restricted to merchant vessels using the English Channel. Mr Powder failed to respond to the *Carhelmar's* attempts to contact him both by radio and mobile telephone. In answer to the alarm the *Marie Winstone* and a rescue helicopter were scrambled. It was David Murphy and the *Carhelmar* who first reached the trawler, which had been sailing on autopilot, Skipper Murphy placing two of his crewmen on board the *Spartacus*. Their worst nightmare was realised when the nets were raised and they retrieved the body of their friend Tony Powder. Mr Powder's body was transferred to the *Marie Winstone* and taken back to Brixham. In May 1998, the family and friends of Tony Powder took a last trip on the *Spartacus*, for a special memorial service off Berry Head. Following the service the *Spartacus*, which in 1962 had been one of the last working trawlers to be built on the River Dart, at Galmpton, was decommissioned and sailed to Hull, where it was placed in a fishing museum.

The Torbay Station answered three calls within a period of one hour and ten minutes, on 30 July 1997, two calls being answered by the ALB and one by the ILB. The first call came at 15.10 hours when the yacht *Oyster* was reported to be in difficulty 11 miles east of Berry Head. The single-handed crewman was reported to be suffering from exhaustion. The Torbay boat was launched and immediately made her way to the scene, together with a Coastguard helicopter and numerous other vessels, which had monitored the distress call. The first craft to reach the casualty was the fishing vessel *Our Joel*, which put a crewman aboard the yacht in order to stabilise the situation. The *Oyster* was recovered to Brixham.

Emergency services along the South-Devon coast prepared for potential devastation following a mid-Channel collision approximately 35 miles off Berry Head at 06.40 hours on Wednesday 2 October 1997. The collision was between the 20,000-ton Liberian-registered tanker, *Allegra*, on passage from Liverpool, and the 2,000-ton St-Vincent-registered grain carrier *Ciboney*, which was on passage with a cargo to Spain. The force of the collision ruptured the port cargo tank of the *Allegra* releasing

*David P. Hurford, Coxswain of the* Edward Bridges *(1991–95) and of the* Marie Winstone *(1995–2001).* RNLI

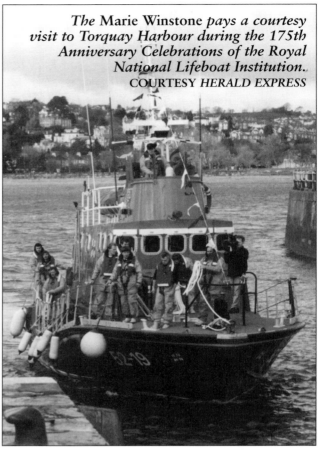

*The* Marie Winstone *pays a courtesy visit to Torquay Harbour during the 175th Anniversary Celebrations of the Royal National Lifeboat Institution.* **COURTESY** *HERALD EXPRESS*

approximately 900 tonnes of oil into the sea. The spillage resulted in a slick, which covered around 1,000 square metres. The *Ciboney* sustained a 20ft-wide gash from her deck to below the waterline.

The *Marie Winstone* and a Sea King helicopter from RAF Chivenor were launched, as it was unclear whether or not crew members from the stricken vessels required evacuation. The tanker carried a crew of 32, the coaster 11. The Marine Pollution Control Unit sent a Cessna surveillance aircraft to the scene. A Coastguard spokesman said that computer modelling was also being used to predict the movement of the slick. Thankfully the spillage was identified as palm oil, a natural, harmless substance that dispersed naturally. Lifeboat Coxswain Dave Hurford commented: 'When we got there most of the oil had already leaked out of the number-one tank. Luckily there weren't any casualties.' The *Marie Winstone* stood by until clearance was given for the *Allegra* to limp into Rotterdam and for the *Ciboney* to be escorted to Portland for repair.

A Paignton man, filming giant waves, was swept to his death off Goodrington North Sands sea wall on the evening of Monday 21 October 1997. In darkness, the *Marie Winstone* was launched into the teeth of the gale; a helicopter from RAF Chivenor was also scrambled. The sea and weather conditions were such that waves were swelling up to 20 feet and although Coxswain Hurford made every effort to take the *Marie Winstone* in close to the sea wall, the lifeboat could not get within 400 yards of the shoreline. For the safety of his own crew,

Coxswain Hurford was forced to abandon his rescue efforts. The helicopter crew were also advised to curtail the search, as conditions were perceived as being too dangerous for any rescue attempt. The final decision to withdraw was in the hands of winch-man Jamie Hamilton, who elected to continue the search. As mountainous waves, driven by winds gusting to F10 pounded the shore, sightseers ignored the warnings and advice of the Coastguard and diced with death in their efforts to watch the spectacular seas. The body of the drowned man was recovered from the water by the helicopter at 21.20 hours.

The combined courage, skill and outstanding seamanship of the crew of the Torbay boat, Coastguard, Torbay Harbour pilot boat, Torbay Shipping Agency support vessel, trawler-men and the assistance of the emergency services, averted what was potentially the biggest shipping disaster to hit Torbay in more than 30 years on Thursday 1 January 1998, when the 22,600-ton oil tanker *Santa Anna* drifted helplessly towards the shore. In F9 winds, gusting to F10, the Panamanian-registered vessel, laden with 250 tonnes of fuel oil and 50 tonnes of lubricating oil, dragged her anchor and was driven against Thatcher Rock. The vessel, which had come from Hamburg, spent several days sheltering in Torbay awaiting orders to proceed to its next destination. She had the capacity to carry in the region of 170,000 tonnes of oil and was manned by a crew of 29 from Greece, Romania and the Philippines (from whence her Captain came).

It was at 16.06 hours that the *Santa Anna* started to drag her anchor and started her drift towards Thatcher Rock. The first rescue vessel on the scene was the *Marie Winstone*, under the command of Coxswain Dave Hurford. On the arrival of the lifeboat crew rockets were immediately fired in an attempt to establish tow-lines aboard the tanker. Coxswain Hurford recalls:

*When we reached her the weather was atrocious and spray was breaking over her stern. We tried to get lines on board but the wind suddenly veered to the west and within two minutes the tanker completely shifted position and this caused us a lot of problems. I knew that we didn't have the engine power to pull her off so the arrival of the* Marbella *was good news.*

The combined efforts of the lifeboat, pilot boat and the *Marbella* were eventually rewarded when they succeeded in attaching lines to the stricken vessel. They used every rope in their possession, the *Marbella* using her own mooring lines and steel hawsers. Coxswain Hurford said:

*At the time his power was the only option of saving the ship. The tug* Far Minara *eventually arrived and took over the tow while we stood by in case the tow parted and the crew had to be rescued.*

The lifeboat and the pilot boat checked the *Santa Anna's* list and she was deemed stable enough to be towed out to the safety of Torbay.

In the local press Coxswain Hurford refuted claims that the actions of the lifeboat crew had been totally overlooked by the national media, who failed to mention their role in averting the disaster. He said: 'It was all down to team effort, our own lads, the pilot boat and the skipper of the *Marbella*. They're all a good bunch of lads.' The reported timetable of the event was as follows:

**16.06** Santa Anna *drags its anchor and begins to drift towards Thatcher Rock.*
**16.30** *Tanker hits Thatcher Rock.*
**16.45** *Tanker is buffeted towards Hopes Nose where it runs aground.*
**17.00** *Coastguard teams, ambulance and police on full alert. Torbay Hospital Casualty Unit was also put on alert.*
**17.15** *Brixham pilot Rob Cumbes is taken by helicopter out to the ship to help with communications.*

**17.30** *Landing site for Coastguard helicopter cleared at Daddyhole Plain in case of evacuation from the ship. Helicopter flies back to Exeter to refuel.*
**18.00** *Lines put out to the vessel by Torbay lifeboat, trawler* Marbella *and Torbay Shipping Agents'* Bay Protector.
**18.30** *Coastguard Teams set up searchlights from shore.*
**20.00** *High tide.*
**21.15** *Coastguard tug* Far Minara *arrives on scene from Falmouth.*
**22.30** Santa Anna *pulled off the rocks and taken to middle of Torbay for assessment of damage.*

The operation became the subject of a Motion placed before the House of Commons. A copy of that motion is proudly displayed in the Torbay boat-house; it reads:

*HOUSE OF COMMONS*
*No.99*
*Notices of Motion: 22nd January 1998*
*2695*

*626    SANTA ANNA INCIDENT 1.1.98*
*Mr Adrian Sanders*
*Lynne Jones*
*Mr Norman A. Godman*
*Mr John Cummings*
*Mr Jeremy Corbyn*
*Mr Mike Hancock*
*Mr David Chigney*
*Mr Donald Gorrie*

*That this House commends the courage, skill and outstanding Seamanship of the Torbay Harbour Pilot, Captain Rob Cumbes, Torbay lifeboat Coxswain, David Hurford and his crew, Graham Vass and Tim Morgan from the Brixham pilot boat, Billy Tribble, Sam Thompson, Paul Duncombe and Lionel Uden from the Brixham shipping agents' support vessel* Bay Protector. *Skipper Charlie Waddy from the fishing vessel* MARBELLA, *the Brixham Coastguard Duty Officer, Ralph George, Watch Manager Mrs Jan Neal, Section Officer, Paul Aggett and Coastguard helicopter pilot, Captain Kevin Balls, together with all those individuals involved in averting a major disaster off Torbay on 1/1/98 when the* Santa Anna, *a 27,000 tonne tanker, dragged its anchor in stormy weather and smashed into Thatcher Rock before going aground off Hopes Nose, Torquay, and further notes the widely held view that the above named individuals should receive the appropriate commendations from their superiors.*

Five Brixham fishermen were exceedingly lucky to escape with their lives when they were forced to jump to safety from their blazing trawler on the night of Saturday 5 September 1988. The five were three days into a fishing trip when the 161-ton, Fleetwood-registered *Christina*, was hit by a freak wave 15 miles south-east of Berry Head, Brixham. The wave smashed the windows of the wheel-house, shorting-out and igniting electrical circuits. The resultant fire quickly took hold of the wheel-house. Realising that they were in imminent danger, the skipper broadcast a MAYDAY, which was monitored by Brixham Coastguard, who relayed the emergency to other shipping in the area. The Coastguard helicopter from Portland was scrambled to the scene.

The *Marie Winstone* was launched at 19.16 hours, under the command of Coxswain Dave Hurford, into a slight sea and westerly F3 winds. As the lifeboat made her way to the scene of the incident the vessels *Maraverma* and the *Lady T Emile*, which were in the vicinity of the *Christina*, went to her assistance. The *Maraverma* was successful in passing fire-fighting equipment to the crew of the *Christina* but the fire continued to spread throughout the vessel, until smoke filled the entire boat. The skipper of the *Christina*, Peter Boyce, said that with the intense heat and flames the crew had no choice but to abandon the 28-metre beam trawler and leap to the safety of an inflatable life-raft. Mr Boyce and his crew, Dean Atkinson, Chris Hilton, George Tiller and Mark Watts, were picked-up by the crew of the *Lady T Emile* and conveyed back to port.

By the time that the *Marie Winstone* reached the *Christina* at 20.25 hours, the winds were south-westerly F5–6, the seas were rough and the swell height was 15 feet. The lifeboat crew of eight immediately set about fighting the fire that had now engulfed the interior of the trawler. The crew fought the blaze for a full three hours. Lifeboatman Simon James told the *Herald Express*:

*We carry specialist fire-fighting equipment and a hydrant and used these along with our salvage pump to fight the fire. The wheel-house was already gone when we arrived and it was looking in a sorry state. The damage was pretty severe as the fire spread below the deck.*

The warship HMS *Guernsey*, which was in Torbay, also went to the scene to assist in dousing the fire. When the fire was extinguished, lifeboat men Richard Fowler and Gareth Dallow were put on board the *Christina* to secure tow-lines. The *Marie Winstone* towed the hulk to Brixham, arriving back on station at about 03.36 hours.

Reflecting on the operation Coxswain Dave Hurford explained:

*When we started fighting the fire we were almost touching the fishing boat, and because its fishing gear was made of polythene and polyester nylon, the smoke and smell coming away was horrendous. At one stage I did not think we would beat the fire. We were pouring in water but we had a real job getting close to the wheel-house because the big derricks were out at 45 degrees and we had to watch them for the crew's sake. The fishermen were really lucky, the whole deck could have caught fire and they were fortunate that there were other vessels in the area and they were picked up quickly.*

For his seamanship and skills in keeping the lifeboat close to the fishing vessel, so that the fire could be fought and extinguished, Coxswain Hurford received a Letter of Congratulation from Michael Vlasto, Chief of Operations, RNLI.

Many of the calls to which the RNLI respond are 'false alarms', usually made 'with good intent'. Indeed, at times crews are called out on what turns out to be a totally wild goose chase, but on very few occasions do they turn out to follow a ghost hunt! One such call, however, answered by the Torbay lifeboat, was explained away as just that.

At 17.49 hours on New Year's Day 1999, Brixham Coastguard requested the launch of the Torbay boat after two anglers reported seeing an elderly lady staring out to sea near Goodrington Beach, Paignton. The anglers spotted her as they were preparing their tackle, and when they next looked in her direction she had literally vanished into thin air. The anglers thought that they could see something floating in the water and alerted the Coastguard by using their mobile phone and a major search commenced. The Torbay ALB, the *Marie Winstone* and the ILB, 'D 504', *Spirit of the RPC*, were launched and were subsequently joined by the Portland-based helicopter, Whisky Bravo, together with shore-based Coastguard teams and the Police. An extensive search was carried out but was abandoned when no trace of the lady could be found.

The mystery came to the attention of a local resident and businessman, John Wallis, who was convinced that the anglers had seen the apparition of a French nun who had worked at a hospital, tending soldiers, during the Napoleonic wars. The apparition is known locally as 'Sister Mary' and the hospital buildings, in which she tended the sick and wounded, now form part of the popular tourist pub, the Inn on the Quay, on Goodrington promenade. Two French nuns worked at the hospital until it closed in 1817 and when they died, they were buried in a cemetery within the hospital grounds. Eventually the land was developed and the graves were relocated to another part of the town; ever since then sightings of 'Sister Mary' have been reported. Mr Wallis told the *Herald Express* that Sister Mary comes to this part of the sea wall to gaze across the sea towards her native land. As for the Torbay lifeboat crew, they say that they are ready to answer any call for assistance – whether from this side of the hereafter or the other!

On Christmas Eve, 1999 the ILB 'D 504' *Spirit of the RPC* and the *Marie Winstone* were launched at 08.46 hours and 08.49 hours respectively, as part of a massive air-and-sea search for two stowaways who jumped from the Libyan-registered cargo vessel, the *Ebn Batuta*, into the cold waters of Torbay. The *Ebn Batuta* was on a return passage from Hamburg to its home port of Tripoli. The stowaways, both of whom were from Sierra Leone and about 35 years of age, had boarded the vessel at Benghazi, Libya, on her outward passage.

The ship had sought the shelter of Torbay and was at anchor approximately one and a half miles off Paignton. The men had last been seen on board the cargo vessel at about 04.00 hours and when they could not be found the Master of the vessel raised the alarm at about 07.00 hours. The crew of a helicopter saw one of the men in the water but, as the winch-man was lowered, the man disappeared. Thermal imaging equipment was used in an attempt to detect body heat, but no trace was found. Coastguard Auxiliaries patrolled the coastline from Roundham Head to Hopes Nose in the hope that the men had been washed ashore. The men were not located and feared drowned in the cold sea and F4 south-westerly winds. At 10.00 hours on 26 January 2000, the ILB was launched to assist the Police with the recovery of a body from the sea just off Brixham breakwater. The body was subsequently identified as being that of one of the two missing stowaways from the *Ebn Batuta*.

The *Marie Winstone* was launched at 07.08 hours on Saturday 26 February 2000 to go to the assistance of the 65ft Brixham-based trawler, *Sara Maria*. The vessel, with her crew of two, skipper John Porter and crewman Lee Wicks, was returning to port following a week-long fishing trip when, nine miles off Start Point, she started to take in water. The engine-room of the trawler flooded and she became dead in the water, having lost all power. The *Sara Maria's* sister ship, the *Mareverma*, which was in the vicinity, answered her call for assistance and began towing the trawler to Brixham. When the lifeboat located the casualty at 07.45 hours she had some five feet

of water in the engine-room, and had a 20° list with her port side decks awash. Coxswain Dave Hurford placed Motor Mechanic Mark Criddle and crew members Roger Good, Gareth Dallow and Colin Bower aboard the trawler with a portable salvage pump. The lifeboat men stabilised the vessel by pumping out the flooded engine room and re-connecting a broken inlet hose, which had caused the problems. Coxswain Dave Hurford summed up the situation:

*She was in real danger of sinking – no doubt about it. She was listing about 20 degrees, her decks on the port side were awash, and she was dead in the water because her engines had cut out and she had lost power. They had to resort to a hand pump, which could not keep up with the flow of water. When we got there the pair had their lifejackets on and their life-raft ready to throw over – they had already released the straps from the cradle. The trawler was very unstable because of the list, and the* Mareverma *had a real job trying to tow it. If the weather had worsened there could have been a real problem. Fortunately, the weather was on our side and our pump brought down the water level in the engine-room, where Mark was able to reconnect the hose.*

Fortunately the weather remained favourable and the *Mareverma* was able to continue to tow the *Sara Maria* safely to Brixham, where she transferred the tow to the *Marie Winstone* for the task of bringing the trawler into the fish quay. The vessel was berthed at Brixham at 10.17 hours.

It was lucky for a lone Trans-Atlantic sailor that a resident of Stoke Fleming spotted his plight on Monday 24 April 2000. The sailor, Jim Lee, was attempting to sail his 20ft yacht, *Waxwing*, to his home in Brazil. Mr Lee had left Poole, Dorset, 18 days earlier, heading for the Bay of Biscay. He had encountered problems with his mast and altered his course in an attempt to reach Lands End. During the voyage his auxiliary motor had failed and he now found himself in rough seas and a south-easterly wind of F6–7, perilously close to The Dancing Beggars rocks, Dartmouth.

The alarm was raised with the Coastguard and the Torbay boat was launched. The first persons to reach the *Waxwing* were Auxiliary Coastguard Ray Hill and charter boat skipper Dave Harrison. Despite attempts they were unable to board the *Waxwing* for fear of driving the vessel on to the rocks, but they stayed with her awaiting the arrival of the lifeboat. The lifeboat was launched at 15.20 hours, and on reaching the casualty at 15.48 hours, with seas breaking right over the craft, Coxswain Mark Criddle manoeuvred the

*The* Waxwing, *under escort by the* Marie Winstone *at the mouth of the Dart, 24 April 2000; the sailor had been headed for Brazil.*

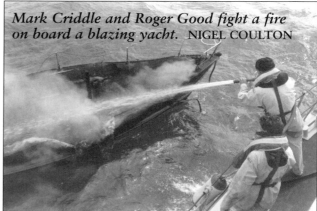

*Mark Criddle and Roger Good fight a fire on board a blazing yacht.* NIGEL COULTON

Right: *Angela Morris, who became the first, and, at the time of writing, only, female crew member of the Torbay lifeboat in April 2000.*

lifeboat into a position where he was able to place crewman Steve Lunn on board the yacht. A tow-line was secured and the *Waxwing* was taken safely in to Dartmouth. It subsequently transpired that Mr Lee was completely disorientated, having run out of fresh water some days earlier. He was taken to Dartmouth Hospital suffering from hypothermia and dehydration.

An historic chapter was written in the 134-year history of the Brixham Station in April 2000, when 28-year old Angela Morris became the first female crew member to join the Torbay lifeboat. Angela was no newcomer to the Royal National Lifeboat Institution; she had been the first female member of an offshore crew in Wales and had served as a member of the Fishguard lifeboat crew for nine years. Angela had not only proved herself as an extremely capable crew member of the all-weather lifeboat, but was also an award-winning helmsman of the inshore lifeboat. Angela had learned her RNLI life-saving skills as a crew member on the *Marie Winstone* when it was stationed in Pembrokeshire; ironically she once again found herself as a crew member of the same lifeboat, this time at Brixham.

The old cliché 'stranger things happen at sea' was certainly proved true when the Torbay lifeboat was launched, at 17.25 hours on Saturday 6 May 2000, following reports that a vessel appeared to be going round in circles 11 miles off the South-Devon coast. One can only imagine the astonishment of the lifeboat crew when they located the 22ft motor yacht, 25 minutes later, and found it to be crewed by two Romanians and a dog, intent on finding Southern Ireland. The Romanians explained that their only navigation aid was a map and that they were following the dotted line of the route of the Roscoff to Plymouth ferry. The men had sufficient food and water for a long journey. Coxswain Dave Hurford recalled:

*They didn't seem entirely keen to see us. We have no idea if there was anything untoward about them but the Police were waiting on the quayside and they were detained.*

A Police spokesman told the *Herald Express* that the dog, which was 'large and foreign looking', had been put into quarantine.

The FV *Providing Star*, with a crew of two on board, found herself in difficulty 14 nautical miles north-east of Berry Head on the morning of Sunday 9 July 2000. The vessel, which had fouled her propeller, also suffered generator power loss and hydraulic failure. The *Marie Winstone*, under the command of Deputy Coxswain Roger Good, was launched at 05.01 hours and reached the casualty at 06.07 hours. A tow was established and the fishing vessel was towed to the safety of Brixham Harbour.

The country awoke on the morning of Monday 18 September 2000 to find itself in the grip of a national fuel blockage. The crisis, which lasted for four days, brought certain parts of the country to a near standstill and affected not only road transport but also, surprisingly, the RNLI. For several weeks the *Marie Winstone* had been 'off station', being fitted with replacement Caterpillar V8 engines. Due to the diesel shortage, her impending sea trials were classed as 'non-essential' and her return to the Torbay Station was delayed. During her absence, the Arun Class relief boat, *52-12 Walter and Margaret Couper*, ON 1059, was placed 'on station'.

The *Marie Winstone* was launched into the teeth of a severe gale, at 21.29 hours on Tuesday 21 November 2000, following a report that the fishing vessel *Girl Debra*, with three persons on board, had suffered steering gear failure 12 miles east of Berry Head. In heavy seas and a south-westerly wind of F6–8, the lifeboat reached the casualty at 22.20 hours. A tow-line was successfully secured to the trawler and at 22.45 hours Coxswain Dave Hurford commenced the long, slow and hazardous tow to Brixham.

The tow had reached a point off Berry Head, when, at 01.11 hours, Coxswain Hurford was requested to respond to a MAYDAY call, transmitted by the 46,000-ton *Ming North*, reporting a 'man overboard'. The cargo vessel, on passage from Antwerp to Singapore, was 4½ miles off Hopes Nose, Torquay, preparing for her pilot to leave ship, when a 33-year-old Burmese crewman was lost overboard. On reaching the scene, the *Marie Winstone* and the pilot boat commenced a search pattern at 01.30 hours. The Exmouth lifeboat, the Trent Class *14-12 Forward Birmingham* and the warship HMS *Gloucester* also joined in the search. Searchlights from two American Navy vessels, which were anchored nearby, further illuminated the scene. The Coastguard Search and Rescue helicopter, 169, was scrambled and also joined the search. At 02.28 hours the missing crewman was located and picked up by the Search and Rescue helicopter and flown direct to Torbay Hospital. Unfortunately the seaman was pronounced dead on arrival.

After a search lasting over one hour, Coxswain Hurford returned to the trawler, *Girl Debra*, and completed the tow to Brixham. The *Marie Winstone* regained her station at 04.15 hours.

The lifeboat was launched at 03.06 hours on Sunday 4 March 2001, to go to the assistance of the 44ft French yacht, *Etachon*, which was at a position 3–4 miles south-east of Dartmouth. The yacht had reported losing all power and that several of the seven crew on board were suffering from seasickness. The *Marie Winstone* located the yacht and towed her to Dartmouth. The lifeboat was back on station 06.05 hours.

After 26 years with an Arun Class lifeboat at Torbay, the station took delivery, on Wednesday 24 October 2001, of a new replacement lifeboat; she was the 17m, Severn Class *17-28 Alec and Christina Dykes*. The proud history of the Arun Class was crowned by the *Marie Winstone* which, during her service time at Torbay, was launched on 277 occasions and is credited with 63 'lives saved', 122 persons 'landed' and a further 206 persons 'brought in'.

After having served for just over six and a half years as the Torbay boat, at 17.30 hours on Wednesday 31 October 2001, the *Marie Winstone*'s status was amended by the RNLI to that of relief lifeboat. At 18.30 hours *17-28 Alec and Christina Dykes* (ON 1255) was officially placed 'on station' at Torbay.

*Severn Class lifeboat,* 17-28 Alec and Christina Dykes, *arriving in Brixham, 24 October 2001.*
ALAN SALSBURY

*Torbay's first dedicated D Class inshore lifeboat D-354 Alfred George Martin with Mark Criddle at the helm and Steve Simons and John Nicholls crewing.* RNLI

*The A-512. Arthur Curnow at the helm and Phil Burridge and Brian Caunter crewing.*
RNLI

# 16

# THE *INSHORE LIFEBOATS*

## *1963–2002*

***Senior Helmsmen:*** *John Ashford (1988–93);*
*Cyril Yeoman (1993–96);*
*Nigel Crang (1996–).*

In May 1963 the RNLI introduced the first of the fleet of high-speed, inflatable, Inshore Rescue Boats, later to become known as the D Class lifeboats, or ILBs (inshore lifeboats). The purpose of these small, agile, neoprene-nylon-hulled boats is to operate in shallow water or confined spaces where the larger lifeboats cannot manoeuvre, or when the full service of the all weather lifeboat (ALB) is not necessarily required. ILBs are manned by a crew of two or three, depending upon the service requirement, and have proved a success in assisting with cliff rescues and medical evacuations, in addition to dealing with small craft, swimmers and sailboards.

The first Inshore Rescue Boat was stationed at Torbay in April 1964 – she was unnamed and did not bear a registered number. The craft was designed and built by the RFD Company Limited of Godalming and had an overall length of 15'6" and a beam of 6'3". Her weight (less the engine) was 295lbs. She was driven by a 40hp outboard engine, which was fitted to an integral transom and gave her a top speed of more than 20 knots, the engine being fed from two flexible fuel tanks, providing a serviceable operating time of at least two hours. The boat had a hull constructed of neoprene nylon, which was divided into five separate buoyancy compartments and was capable of operating in wind conditions up to a F5. She carried equipment, which included a compass, lifeline and fire extinguisher. The craft was designed to operate with a crew of two but was capable of carrying up to ten persons. One of the first to try out the new Torbay boat was Lt P. Gladwyn, the RNLI Inspector for the South West region. As he wiped spray from his face, he told a reporter from the *Herald Express*:

*She handled very well. The craft has been developed for the yachting and small boat casualties which require a faster type of boat than the lifeboat.*

The IRBs were on station for the summer months only, the period usually extending from one week before Easter until 31 October.

The Brixham craft was first launched during the early evening of 11 June 1964, when she was summoned to assist a small boat that was reported in difficulty off Walls Hill, Torquay. Whilst en route the IRB was notified that a passing fishing vessel had rendered assistance to the stricken vessel and taken it in tow into Torquay. The crew therefore returned to station without rendering service.

The first recorded service rendered by the IRB was on 1 July 1964, when she was launched at 14.40 hours following information from HM Coastguard that a boy had fallen some 50 feet down the cliffs at Berry Head. A passenger launch had picked up the injured boy and was returning to Brixham Harbour. The IRB rendezvoused with the launch, transferred the casualty, and landed the injured boy.

Royal National Lifeboat Institution

**HANDING OVER CEREMONY**
and
**SERVICE OF DEDICATION**
of
TORBAY'S 'D' CLASS LIFEBOAT
at
The Lifeboathouse, Breakwater Hard, Brixham
on Saturday, 8th October 1988 at 2.30 p.m.

This lifeboat was generously provided from the bequest of
Dorothy Joan Martin, in memory of her husband,
Alfred George Martin

Price of Programme          Your generosity

The ILB recorded her first 'saved' service on 13 July 1964, when she attended the area off Thatcher Rock, Torquay, where the crew of a capsized yacht were seen clutching to the upturned hull. The crew of the ILB quickly located the capsized yacht, rescued the crew and returned both the two sailors and their yacht to Torquay Harbour.

In 1967 the RNLI introduced a new type of craft that was capable of being used as either an inshore lifeboat or a 'boarding boat', a boat used to take crews out to deep-water moored lifeboats. These boats were known as 'Hatch boats' and, like the ILBs before them, normally had a crew of two. The boats were driven by a 68hp Volvo 'Penta' inboard engine with an outboard drive, that produced a top speed of 20 knots. On 1 July 1969, the Torbay Station received its first 'Hatch', she was the 20'0" wooden-hulled boat, ILB *18-03* and remained on service until 31 October 1971. She was first called into service on 6 July 1969, when the sailing dinghy *Muriel* capsized off Fishcombe. Upon her arrival, it was found that the dinghy had been righted and that the crew was safe. The dinghy and crew were towed into Brixham by another vessel and no useful service was undertaken by the ILB. The *18-03* was called out for a second time that day following a Police report that a small motorboat was in difficulty near Paignton Harbour. Again, the casualty made port and no useful service was undertaken.

It was on the afternoon of 5 October 1973 that the Police received a report that a woman was seen in the sea at Meadfoot Beach, Torquay. The weather conditions at the time in Torbay were a south-south-westerly F7 wind accompanied by rough seas.

Crewed by Coxswain Kenneth Gibbs and Motor Mechanic Barry Pike, *18-03* left her moorings at 15.50 hours. At Meadfoot Beach conditions were causing the seas to break amongst the rocks and masses of seaweed which littered the sea, producing 8–10ft waves. Coxswain Gibbs commenced a search of the beach, being all too aware that the crashing waves could at any time drive the wooden hull of his boat onto any one of the number of submerged rocks. With great skill and seamanship, he held the Hatch boat just inside the line of the breaking waves.

It was Barry Pike who first spotted the woman amongst the breakers and without thought for his own safety, dived into the surging sea in an attempt to rescue the casualty. At that moment Coxswain Gibbs saw a large wave bearing down and, fearing for the safety of his colleague and the casualty, used all his expertise to keep the ILB from being swept onto them. Barry recalls:

*I saw the girl and made a grab for her but I was thrown over and over, in a cartwheel, by the force of the waves. I think I had hold of her at one time but as I tried to stand up I lost my footing because of the undertow and the shingled beach being swept away from under me.*

Becoming more and more exhausted by his efforts, Barry Pike was washed up onto the beach. Regaining his breath Barry once again entered the water but, due to his exhausted condition, was beaten back by the breakers and pulled from the surf by a Police Constable. Again and again Barry tried to reach the woman; he eventually grabbed hold of her and the Policeman pulled him to safety:

*I was thrown up on the beach at one stage and after catching my breath I tried to find her again. I didn't realise the problem that I was in but the Policeman saw it and threw me a line. He saved my life.*

The Police Officer who came to Barry's aid was Constable Doug Trethowan, a dog handler stationed at Torquay. Doug recollects:

*I was on patrol and driving along Meadfoot Sea Road when I saw a group of people looking out to sea. It was a lousy day and blowing a gale; waves were crashing against the sea wall and breaking over onto the road. I parked the dog van and crossed to the wall to see what was going on. I was told that there was a woman in the water. I saw the inshore lifeboat, I think it was a Zodiac or similar, at the edge of the waves and I saw a lifeboat man dive into the water in an attempt to rescue her. The lifeboat man was washed into the beach and then out again. I could see he was in difficulty in the surf so I went back to the van and got the tracking harness with a 32ft lead. I waded out as far as I could but the waves were breaking over me and pebbles were hitting my head. Luckily Barry reached out and got hold of the harness and I was able to pull him in. He went out again to rescue the woman and luckily I got him back with the harness. I was soaked through, cold and covered in seaweed, so I went home and had a bath.*

Regrettably the life of the woman could not be saved.

In recognition for his outstanding courage and bravery during this operation, the RNLI awarded Barry Pike a Silver Medal; the RNLI's Thanks on Vellum were awarded to Coxswain Ken Gibbs. Barry Pike subsequently received the 'Ralph Glister Award' for 'the most meritorious service

*Cox'n Ken Gibbs (left) receives the RNLI's Thanks on Vellum, and Barry Pike (centre) the RNLI Silver Medal for a service by the ILB, at Torquay, on 5 October 1973 from the Station Hon. Secretary Alderman Fred Parkes. The silver salvers were donated by Joyce Upton of the Falcon Hotel, Denham Village, Buckinghamshire.* COURTESY *HERALD EXPRESS*

of the year by a member of the crew of an inshore lifeboat.' Barry Pike personally acknowledged Constable Trethowan's actions by presenting the Officer with a suitably inscribed tankard.

In March 1975 *18-03* was replaced by *A-512*, an 18'0" McLachlin Class, GRP-hulled, twin-engine ILB. Like her predecessor she was moored in the corner of the harbour adjacent to the boathouse.

*A-512* was first launched for service at a little after 20.00 hours on 26 April 1975. A report was received that red flares had been sighted approximately half a mile east of Hopes Nose, Torquay. Upon their arrival at Hopes Nose, the crew found the casualty to be the cabin cruiser *Santa Lucia*, her crew of two suffering from slight exposure. The ILB landed the crew at Torquay Harbour whilst a pilot boat towed the cabin cruiser into port.

The very next day, 27 April 1975, at 22.50 hours, *A-512* went to the assistance of the motorboat *Pegasus* which was experiencing difficulties in St Mary's Bay, Brixham. The boat was taken in tow and the crew of two, along with the boat, were landed safely at Brixham.

On Sunday 19 April 1987 the *A-512* was on exercise in Torbay when she responded to a report of a small vessel having broken down off Princess Pier, Torquay. Her crew on that day were Cyril Yeoman (helm), Roger Good and a trainee. Whilst making their way across the bay to Torquay, the crew were notified that the casualty had entered Torquay Harbour unaided; the ILB was immediately diverted to a position off Goodrington Beach, Paignton. This second service was to a speedboat that was reported to be erratically circling at a high speed, the sole occupant having been thrown from the craft into the sea. Cyril Yeoman recalls:

*The McLachlin was no match for the speed of the speedboat. We were unable to gain on her or break into her circle. We looked across to Brixham and saw the big boat coming out and initially thought that she was going on another shout but she turned towards us and we realised that she was coming to our assistance.*

The Arun Class lifeboat, the *Ralph & Bonella Farrant*, which was on relief duty at Torbay, had

147

*John Ashford and John Hunkin in the McLachlin Class* A-512. NIGEL COULTON

been launched at 11.23 hours, under the command of Coxswain Arthur Curnow. Upon joining the *A-512* a decision was made to attempt to halt the speedboat by fouling her propeller. To stop a runaway craft using this method, a rope is securely fastened to the ALB with the loose end being carried by the ILB. The two lifeboats then proceed on a parallel course, ahead of the casualty, with the snag rope skimming the surface or lying just under the surface of the water. As the runaway crosses the rope, it is released by the ILB, the loose end fouling the propeller of the craft. Cyril Yeoman recalled:

*We strung a mooring line between the Arun and the McLachlin to act as a snag and Coxswain Curnow and myself manoeuvred our lifeboats into a position ahead of the speedboat. We held a course so that the speedboat had to pass between us and we succeeded in fouling her prop and bringing her to a stop. The boat was taken in tow by another craft to Paignton.*

This proved to be the final service provided by the *A-512*, as she was replaced by a D Class 'relief' lifeboat and subsequently the *D-354*.

A handing-over ceremony and service of dedication was held on the Breakwater Hard, in front of the lifeboat house, at 14.30 hours on Saturday 8 October 1988 to mark the acceptance of the *D-354*. This new D Class boat was delivered to the care of the Torbay Station Branch by Captain A.G. McCrum, RN, a member of the Committee of Management of the RNLI. The boat was accepted on behalf of the Branch by the Branch Hon. Secretary, Mr Tony Smith. The service of dedication was conducted by the Reverend Edwin Clements, former Vicar of All Saints, Brixham, assisted by Mr Paul Jarrett, JP, and Superintendent of the Royal National Mission to Deep Sea Fishermen, Brixham. The new craft was generously provided from the bequest of Mrs Dorothy Joan Martin in memory of her late husband. The boat was named *D-354, Alfred George Martin.*

This craft had an overall length of 15'6", a beam of 6'4" and weighed 550lbs. Like her predecessor she was fitted with a 40hp outboard motor, her hull was flexible and the inflatable sponsons were divided into compartments. The fabric construction was nylon, coated with neoprene/hypalon. The craft was completely stable and could be launched in surf up to 7 feet in height and could not be sunk, due to its buoyancy tubes. She carried a crew of two or three and was fitted with VHF radio, first-aid kit, flares and a spare propeller.

At the time that she was introduced into service, D Class craft accounted for more than one third of all lifeboat services and lives saved.

The summer of 1994 saw an extraordinary event take place by a team of men and women of 12th Supply Regiment, The Royal Logistic Corps. Led by WO1 Keith Black and Sergeant Mike Smith, they undertook a megatriathlon. The phases of the Megatriathlon comprised: a 275-mile road run, from their base in Wulfen, Germany, to Cap Gris Nez on the French Coast, a relay swim across the English Channel and a long-distance cycle ride, taking in the Isle of Wight and the coasts of Devon and Cornwall.

Combining monies raised from a sponsored cycle ride the previous year, with contributions from the Regimental Association, the Royal Engineers and Trustees of the Royal Logistic Corps, sufficient funds were raised to provide the RNLI with five D Class lifeboats. The gruelling trial of the 1994 megatriathlon ended in Looe, Cornwall, on the very day that Looe's new D Class lifeboat the *Spirit of the RAOC* was named. One of the five D Class craft provided by the megatriathlon funding was placed at the Torbay Lifeboat Station in April 1996; she was the *D-504*.

On Saturday 31 May 1997, WO1 Keith Black, of the Royal Logistic Corps, was present at the naming ceremony and service of dedication of the Torbay Lifeboat Station's lifeboat *D-504*. The lifeboat was handed over to the RNLI by Colonel R.F. McDonald, Chairman of the Royal Pioneer Corps Association, and was accepted, on behalf of the Torbay Station Branch, by Captain Howard East, Secretary of the Station. Following the service of dedication, which was conducted by the Reverend Graham Dench, Superintendent of the Royal National Mission to Deep Sea Fishermen, WO1 Black poured Devonshire vintage cider over the bow of the lifeboat and named her the *D-504, Spirit of the RPC*.

Within minutes of the naming of the new lifeboat, with Nigel Crang at the helm, the boat sped out towards the harbour mouth. VIP guests were impressed by the craft's turn of speed, believing that Nigel was just putting her through her paces but for some time the *Spirit of the RPC* just simply did not return. Unknown to those present at the ceremony, the helmsman had responded to a service call to rescue a man, who had been cut off by the tide at Roundham Head, Paignton. Only 30 minutes after responding to this incident, the ILB was diverted to Blackpool

*Simon James* (left) *and Nigel Crang* (centre) *receive the RNLI's special Thanks on Vellum and Nick O'Brien a framed Letter of Appreciation from the RNLI following their ILB rescue of three youths at Roundham Head, Paignton, 19 April 1999.* RNLI

*D Class ILB D-354 Alfred George Martin with crew Cyril Yeoman, Nigel Crang and Simon Littlewood.* LENT BY SIMON LITTLEWOOD

*The ILB D-504 Spirit of the RPC with John Ashford at the helm and Andy Constable as crew.* RNLI

Sands, near Stoke Fleming, to assist in a search for a missing swimmer.

The new craft was the largest D Class to be stationed in Torbay having an overall length of 16'3", a beam of 6'7" and a weight of 745lbs. D Class craft continued to be powered by a 40hp outboard engine but improved fuel facilities allowed service time to be increased to three hours, at 20 knots. The neoprene/hypalon hull construction continued to be compartmentalised, maintaining stability should one section of the sponson become damaged. The *Spirit of the RPC* operates with a crew of two or three and, in addition to the equipment carried by her predecessor, carries an anchor.

The lifeboat was launched at 19.21 hours on Friday 19 April 1999 when three Paignton youths became trapped by the incoming tide at Roundham Head, Paignton. The alarm was raised when one of the youths dialed 999 on his mobile phone. The *D-504*, manned by Nigel Crang (helmsman), Simon James and Nick O'Brien, was launched into a moderate to rough sea with a 3-metre swell. The lifeboat took only five minutes to cover the three miles distance and reach the stranded youths. After searching the cliffs below the headland, the lifeboat crew spotted the three casualties in a cave, huddled against a rising tide. Having located the youths, during a lull in the swell, Simon James, at great personal risk of being dashed against the rocks, slid over the side of the lifeboat and swam into the cave where he found the trio to be uninjured. With great expertise and using all his boat-handling skills, Nigel Crang counted the waves and, judging there be a flat period in the swell every third or fourth wave, placed the D boat on top of a rock, allowing Simon James to thrust one of the youths on board. The boat refloated on the next wave. Nigel Crang repeated the move for a second time, allowing the remaining two youths and Simon James to scramble into the craft. Nigel Crang later commented:

*Time was always against us, and darkness was setting in. It was tricky getting Simon James into the cave, then taking the three on board, one by one. It was gusting Force five to six and it was difficult to avoid our boat smashing onto the rocks as the waves took us above the cave entrance.*

An RNLI spokesman commented, at the time:

*Through skilfully manoeuvring the lifeboat they were able to enter the cave and recover the three boys minutes before they would have been swamped by the fast rising tide. With six people on the small inflatable, Nigel Crang*

*managed to turn into the sea just as a particularly large swell broke through the boat. The wave would certainly have capsized the boat if it had not been head to sea.*

Paul Jennings, Deputy Divisional Inspector of Lifeboats (South) said:

*This rescue saved the lives of three young men. It was conducted on the very edge of operating conditions. Calm thinking, excellent application of local knowledge and fine boat-handling skills all contributed to this successful service. They showed teamwork, persistence, seamanship and courage.*

For their outstanding courage and skills shown in this rescue, helmsman Nigel Crang and crew member Simon James each received the RNLI's Special Thanks on Vellum. Crewman Nick O'Brien received a framed Letter of Appreciation from the RNLI.

Many of the launches carried out by the ILBs may be seen by some to be 'routine' and the crews of these craft are often unsung heroes. The crews of the ILBs are, and will continue to be, an integral part of the Royal National Lifeboat Institution's team. Whether crewing the inshore lifeboats or taking their place aboard the ALB, the crews carry out the duties required of them with pride and dedication.

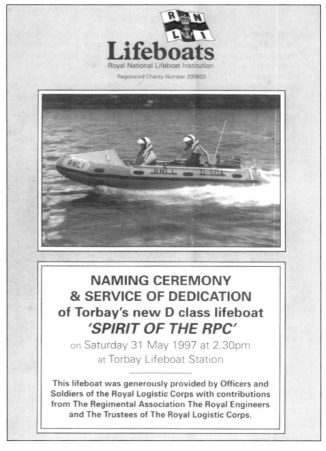

**NAMING CEREMONY
& SERVICE OF DEDICATION
of Torbay's new D class lifeboat
'SPIRIT OF THE RPC'**
on Saturday 31 May 1997 at 2.30pm
at Torbay Lifeboat Station

This lifeboat was generously provided by Officers and Soldiers of the Royal Logistic Corps with contributions from The Regimental Association The Royal Engineers and The Trustees of The Royal Logistic Corps.

*The inshore lifeboat A-512, in support of RAF rescue helicopter, off Pilchard Cove. IRB crew Dud Stone and Ken Gibbs.* RNLI

# 'PROVIDENT'
## By Name & By Nature

For the crew of the battleship HMS *Formidable* on New Year's Day, 1915, the 51-ton Brixham ketch *Provident* (BM 291) certainly lived up to her name. In the early hours of that fateful morning, HMS *Formidable*, a member of the Fifth Battle Squadron, was cruising in the English Channel under the Flagship HMS *Nelson*. Built at Portsmouth in 1898 and commissioned in 1901, she was a 1st Class Battleship of 15,000 tons. She was fitted with 15,000hp triple-expansion engines, which produced a top speed of 18.5 knots. Her armaments comprised four 12-inch guns, a dozen 6-inch guns, sixteen twelve-pounders, six three-pounders and four torpedo tubes. Commanded by Captain Loxley, she had a complement of 780 men. HMS *Formidable* had left Sheerness on 30 December 1914 as part of the Channel Fleet, under the command of Admiral Sir Lewis Bayley. Six destroyers had escorted the fleet from Sheerness to Folkstone but the escort had withdrawn upon the Admiral's orders, leaving the *Formidable* with two cruisers, HMS *Topaze* and HMS *Diamond*.

Unbeknown to the squadron, for most of the day they had been shadowed by the German U-Boat, *U24*, under the command of Kapitanleutnant Rudolph Schneider. The *U24* carried two bow- and two stern-torpedo tubes. At 03.12 hours the squadron was at a point some 12 miles south-east of Berry Head, Brixham, when, at a range of 360 metres, the *U24* fired both stern tubes striking the *Formidable* on the starboard side, abreast of her foremost funnel. Whilst able to maintain a slow forward course, the battleship started to list to starboard.

One hour after the first torpedo struck, the *U24*, which had now surfaced, closed to within 160 metres of the *Formidable* and fired a torpedo into her port side, demolishing her three boilers. The accompanying cruisers, HMS *Topaze* and HMS *Diamond* went to her immediate assistance, but a sudden deterioration in the weather accompanied by a severe increase in the sea state drastically hampered their efforts.

Many of her crew, dressed only in night attire, had taken to her cutters. One pinnace containing 40 men, having been at sea for nearly 24 hours, found landfall at Lyme Regis, Dorset. A dozen of the shipmates, including the Coxswain, had died from hypothermia and exposure. The bodies had been reverently 'buried at sea'.

The *Provident* was returning from a fishing trip in weather conditions described as a severe storm. Her skipper was William Pillar, aged 32 years, who by good fortune was also the Second Coxswain of the Brixham lifeboat, the *Betsey Newbon*. William Carter was *Provident's* mate, and John Clarke the second hand; a 'boy', 15-year-old Dan Taylor completed the crew.

It was a little after 09.00 hours that Carter sighted a cutter displaying a distress flag. Pillar trimmed and reduced sail in an attempt to close on the cutter but lost sight of the vessel in the 30ft seas that were running. Carter went aloft to spot the cutter, which he subsequently located. With exceptional skill and navigation, Pillar approached the cutter on a further three occasions in an attempt to have a line thrown to the crew, but each attempt failed. The fourth attempt proved more successful as he manoeuvred the *Provident* and approached upwind on the vessel. A line was thrown to the leeward side of the cutter and securely fastened to the *Provident*. William Pillar successfully manoeuvred the *Provident* up to the cutter and rescued the complement of 71 men, two of whom were officers. Showing exceptional courage, with outstanding skill and seamanship, together with acts of exceptional bravery by his crew, it took a further two hours to get the rescued men aboard the smack. After fighting the teeth of the gale, the *Provident* eventually reached her home port of Brixham with the survivors at 19.00 hours.

A contemporary report in the *Bridport News* of Friday 8 January 1915, recorded the words of one of the rescued sailors who stated that they all sang 'Auld Lang Syne' as the *Provident* berthed at Brixham:

*We all fell in love with little Dan, the cabin boy, who was untiring in his efforts to get us coffee and tea. We cheered the captain and crew to the echo for their gallant deed.*

The *Topaze* and *Diamond* rescued a further 80 men between them. Of the 780 crew of HMS *Formidable*, only 233 men survived this terrible ordeal. An official report on the incident records:

*The rescue was only effected by careful and splendid seamanship, and not without danger to the smack. An error of half the ship's length would have swamped or crushed the boat which was already holed in several places and kept afloat by bailing with boots while clothing and even legs and arms were stuffed into the holes. The small boat was cut adrift and sank almost immediately.*

In recognition of William Pillar's gallantry, on 6 February 1915 at Buckingham Palace, His Majesty King George V conferred upon him the Albert Medal for Gallantry. William Pillar also received a reward of £250, Carter and Clarke each received £100 and Dan Taylor £50.

The *U24* survived the war and was subsequently broken up for scrap in a British South-coast port. In 1917, whilst on submarine patrol in the North Sea, Kapitanleutnant Rudolph Schneider was washed overboard; although rescued, he died four hours later from hypothermia.

HMS *Formidable* rests in 60 metres of water the position 15°13'.14N 03°03'.99W. She lies completely upside-down with her hull almost broken in half just forward of the bridge structure. The wreck of HMS *Formidable* is designated as a war grave.

Whilst fishing on 28 November 1916, the *Provident* was challenged and stopped by a German submarine. Her crew were given time to leave the vessel before the submarine sent her to the bottom.

*The crew of the* Provident *outside Buckingham Palace following their Investiture* (COURTESY OF THE IMPERIAL WAR MUSEUM) *and the certificate awarded to William Pillar following the rescue of 71 members of the crew of HMS* Formidable, *1 January 1915.* GRAHAM PARNELL

# ARUN CLASS

The RNLI's experiment with an entirely different concept of lifeboat in the Waveney Class proved to be an unqualified success and the Institution turned its attention to a larger, faster boat capable of extended service offshore. The Waveney had not been considered a true all-weather lifeboat although time proved this to be an incorrect assumption and the committees felt there was a need for a boat at least 50 feet long, capable of speeds in excess of 18 knots.

As had been the case numerous times previously, G.L. Watson were commissioned to prepare the hull design and they drew a 52ft transom stern, semi-displacement hull with soft bilges and multiple spray rails at the waterline. Model tests indicated the need for changes to improve sea keeping and performance and the RNLI's staff re-drew the lines to incorporate extra beam and tunnels to allow for larger propellers. The multiple spray rails were also removed as they produced, rather than suppressed, the spray.

The prototype boat was commissioned from William Osborne of Littlehampton, a company that has a long history of RNLI prototype work, and launched in 1971. She was given the official number ON 1018 and the operational number *54-01*; she was named *Arun*. The material chosen for the first of the class was laminated wood, three skins of agba on laminated frames. A period of extensive evaluation then followed during which *Arun* travelled the length and breadth of the country. Many coxswains tried her and all were highly enthusiastic about her sea keeping and handling. A few old hands were initially sceptical about the change of shape when compared with the old traditional lifeboat and worried about the exposed screws and rudder. However, a short trip soon removed any doubts.

With the success of *Arun* a second boat was commissioned incorporating significant changes above the waterline. On *54-02*, the sheer line was cut down to give barely 3 feet of freeboard amidships and a redesigned wheel-house gave two separate cabins above deck. An inflatable shallow-water rescue boat, the Y Class, was carried on a gantry over the afterdeck with its own launching crane. The engines were also up-rated to enhance performance.

The second boat in the Arun Class, ON 1025, *Sir William Arnold*, was launched in 1973 and after initial trials stationed at St Peter Port, Guernsey.

The third boat, ON 1037, *Edward Bridges*, was then built, incorporating a further change to the hull. Her transom corners were radiused to produce an elliptical stern which, it was felt, would give better handling in following seas and also make the corner of the transom less vulnerable. The construction material was again laminated timber, identical to ON 1018 and 1025. She was launched in 1975 as *54-03* and stationed at Brixham as the Torbay lifeboat.

With the launch of the third wooden boat, thoughts turned to production. It had always been the RNLI's intention to build the bulk of the Arun Class from glass reinforced plastic (GRP) and a mould was now constructed, based on the hull of the latest boat, ON 1037, slightly modified to suit the new material. Since the users of the boat could still not decide which stern configuration was best, the mould was given a removable stern section to allow 52ft and 54ft boats to be built as required. This mould has been used for every Arun hull since, with a single exception. All mouldings have been produced by Hulmatic at Havant near Portsmouth. The first GRP-hulled boat, *54-04*, the *Tony Vandervell*, ON 1049, was launched in 1976.

To complement the GRP hull, Hulmatic developed a GRP superstructure that was almost identical in shape to the aluminium alloy house fitted to 1037. In general the change was successful, but the GRP superstructure proved slightly heavier and there were problems with radio interference as GRP has little or no 'shielding' effect. A decision was therefore taken to revert to an aluminium house for boat 9, *52-09*, *Spirit of Tayside*, ON 1056, and the shape has remained constant.

With the boat number *52-08*, *Joy and John Wade*, ON 1053, the 52ft hull with transom stern was re-introduced and the hull shape then remained unchanged through to the final boat, *52-46, The Duke of Atholl*, ON 1160, which was completed in 1990.

All of the Class, except the three wooden prototypes and one other mentioned briefly above, have been built in GRP. The exception is ON 1100, *Snolda*, that has a steel hull with aluminium alloy decks – her number is *52-030*, carrying the extra zero to denote steel or aluminium construction. Fairey Marine built this boat in 1985 as part of an investigation into a serious consideration for building the remaining boats from this material.

The experiment proved a complete success and many coxswains consider ON 1100 to be the best Arun for comfort and handling, although cost defeated any chance of more steel-hulled boats being built as future boats would have cost almost half as much again as a GRP-hulled vessel.

## SPECIFICATION SUMMARY

| | |
|---|---|
| Introduced: | 1971 |
| Designed by: | G.L. Watson |
| Number Built: | 46 |
| Crew Number: | 6 (7 for later boats) |
| Length Overall: | 52 foot/54 foot |
| Beam: | 17 foot |
| Displacement: | 25.25 tons (prototype) |
| | 32.25 tons (steel) |
| | 31 tons (GRP) |
| Engine Details: | |
| *52-01* | Caterpillar 336–375hp |
| *52-02* to *52-14* | Caterpillar D3433–460hp |
| *52-15* to *52-46* | Caterpillar 3408 TA |
| *52-15* to *52-41* | 485hp |
| *52-42* to *52-46* | 500hp |
| Maximum Speed: | 18 knots |
| Radius of Action: | 115 nautical miles |
| Total Range: | 230 nautical miles |

## DEVELOPMENT STAGES

*52-01* ON 1018
1971 first of class – wood – high sheer line

*52-02* ON 1025
1973 wood – low sheer line

*52-03* ON 1037
1975 wood – round transom – 54 foot

*52-04* ON 1049
1976 first GRP boat – GRP hull and wheel-house – round stern

*52-08* ON 1053
1977 transom stern reintroduced

*52-10* ON 1057
1978 aluminium alloy wheel-house reintroduced

*52-11* ON 1058
1979 wheel-house layout redesigned – open plan

*52-15* ON 1067
1980 engines changed from D343 (6 cylinder) to D3408 (8 cylinder) and up-rated to 485hp

*52-030* ON 1100
1985 only steel hull built – standard wheel-house

*52-43* ON 1149
1988 hull laminate changed to epacryn resin

*52-46* ON 1160
1990 last Arun built

*The* Edward Bridges *undergoing a refit at Mashfords Yard, Cremyll.* A. CURNOW

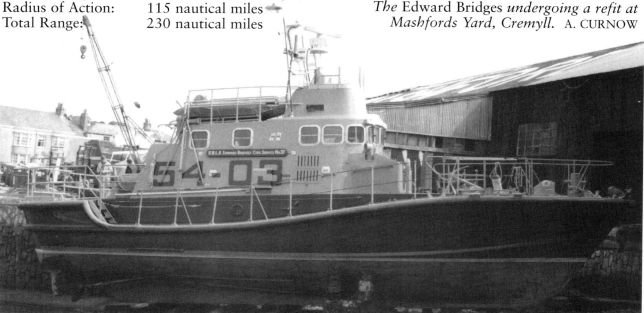

# DISTRIBUTION OF ARUN CLASS LIFEBOATS AS AT OCTOBER 2001

| Op.No | O.N. | Built | Lifeboat | Stations |
|-------|------|-------|----------|----------|
| 52-01 | 1018 | 1971 | *Arun* | St Peter Port 1973; Barry Dock 1974–97 |
| | | | | Sold to private owners |
| 52-02 | 1025 | 1973 | *Sir William Arnold* | St Peter Port. Sold to private owners |
| 54-03 | 1037 | 1974 | *Edward Bridges* | Torbay 1975–95 |
| | | | *(Civil Service No.37)* | On display Chatham Lifeboat Museum |
| 54-04 | 1049 | 1975 | *Tony Vandervell* | Weymouth 1976 |
| | | | | Sold to Finnish Lifeboat Society |
| 54-05 | 1050 | 1975 | *B.P. Forties* | Aberdeen 1976–98 |
| | | | | Sold to Icelandic Lifeboat Society |
| 54-06 | 1051 | 1976 | *Gough Ritchie* | Port St Mary 1976–98 |
| | | | | Sold to Chilean Lifeboat Society |
| 54-07 | 1052 | 1976 | *City of Bradford IV* | Humber 1977–87; Thurso 1988–89; |
| | | | | Ballyglass 1989–90; Tobermory 1991–98; |
| | | | | Southampton |
| 52-08 | 1053 | 1977 | *Joy and John Wade* | Yarmouth (IOW). Unallocated |
| 52-09 | 1056 | 1978 | *Spirit of Tayside* | Sold to Australian Lifeboat Society |
| 52-10 | 1057 | 1978 | *Soldian* | Relief Fleet |
| 52-11 | 1058 | 1979 | *Elizabeth Ann* | Relief Fleet |
| 52-12 | 1059 | 1979 | *Walter & Margaret Couper* | Relief Fleet. Unallocated |
| 52-13 | 1061 | 1980 | *George & Olive Turner* | Tynemouth. Unallocated |
| 52-14 | 1062 | 1980 | *Edith Emilie* | Sold to private owners |
| 52-15 | 1067 | 1980 | *Hyman Winstone* | Relief Fleet |
| 52-16 | 1070 | 1981 | *Richard Evans (Civil Service No.39)* | Relief Fleet |
| 52-17 | 1071 | 1981 | *Sir Max Aitken* | Relief Fleet |
| 52-18 | 1073 | 1981 | *Robert Edgar* | Weymouth |
| 52-19 | 1076 | 1981 | *Marie Winstone* | Relief Fleet |
| 52-20 | 1077 | 1982 | *Duchess of Kent* | Relief Fleet |
| 52-21 | 1078 | 1982 | *The Davina & Charles Matthews Hunter* | Relief Fleet |
| 52-22 | 1081 | 1982 | *Ralph & Bonella Farrant* | Relief Fleet |
| 52-23 | 1082 | 1982 | *Margaret Frances Love* | Barry Dock |
| 52-24 | 1085 | 1982 | *Mabel Alice* | Penlee |
| 52-25 | 1086 | 1983 | *A.J.R. & L.G. Uridge* | Relief Fleet |
| 52-26 | 1092 | 1984 | *St Brendan* | Rosslare Harbour |
| 52-27 | 1093 | 1984 | *Charles Brown* | Buckie |
| 52-28 | 1098 | 1984 | *Sir Max Aitken II* | Longhope |
| 52-29 | 1099 | 1984 | *Joseph Rothwell Sykes and Hilda M.* | Relief Fleet |
| 52-030 | 1100 | 1985 | *Snolda* | Poole – Training Craft |
| 52-31 | 1103 | 1984 | *Newsbuoy* | Relief Fleet |
| 52-32 | 1106 | 1985 | *Keith Anderson* | Hartlepool |
| 52-33 | 1107 | 1986 | *City of Belfast* | Donaghadee |
| 52-34 | 1108 | 1986 | *Margaret Russell Fraser* | Relief Fleet |
| 52-35 | 1113 | 1986 | *City of Dublin* | Howth |
| 52-36 | 1118 | 1987 | *Roy & Barbara Harding* | Castletownbere |
| 52-37 | 1123 | 1987 | *Kenneth Thelwell* | Holyhead |
| 52-38 | 1134 | 1987 | *City of Glasgow III* | Troon |
| 52-39 | 1135 | 1987 | *Mickie Salvesen* | Relief Fleet |
| 52-40 | 1136 | 1988 | *City of Plymouth* | Plymouth |
| 52-41 | 1143 | 1988 | *Ann Lewis Fraser* | Tobermory |
| 52-42 | 1144 | 1988 | *Murray Lornie* | Lochinver |
| 52-43 | 1149 | 1989 | *The Queen Mother* | Thurso |
| 52-44 | 1150 | 1989 | *Hibernia* | Relief Fleet |
| 52-45 | 1159 | 1990 | *Mabel Williams* | Relief Fleet |
| 52-46 | 1160 | 1990 | *Duke of Atholl* | Relief Fleet |

*The Brixham lifeboat crew re-enact the landing of William of Orange during the William &
Mary celebrations, July 1988.*  Among the crew are: *Steve Bower, Derek Rundle,
Ernie Fradd and Arthur Curnow.*  RNLI

*The* Edward Bridges *crosses the bow of the Cunard liner,* Queen Elizabeth II, *anchored in
Torbay, August 1992.*

# THE TORBAY LIFEBOATS RNLI GALLANTRY AWARDS

| Date | Recipient | Lifeboat | Casualty |
|---|---|---|---|
| | | | |

### Albert Medal
| | | | |
|---|---|---|---|
| 1 Jan 1915 | 2nd Coxswain William Pillar | | HMS *Formidable* |

### RNLI Gold Medal
| | | | |
|---|---|---|---|
| 6 Dec 1976 | Coxswain Keith Bower | *Edward Bridges* | MV *Lyrma* |

### RNLI Silver Medal
| | | | |
|---|---|---|---|
| 9 Dec 1939 | Coxswain William Mogridge | *George Shee* | *Channel Pride* |
| 16 Dec 1939 | Coxswain William Mogridge | *George Shee* | *Henrietta* |
| 17 Dec 1944 | Coxswain Frederick Sanders | *George Shee* | *Empire Alfred* |
| 7 Dec 1959 | Coxswain Henry Thomas | *Princess Alexandra of Kent* | *Cycloop* |
| 22 Dec 1964 | Coxswain Harold Coyde | *Princess Alexandra of Kent* | MV *Northwind* |
| 5 Oct 1973 | Motor Mechanic Barry Pike | *ILB 18-03* | Person in sea |

### RNLI Bronze Medal
| | | | |
|---|---|---|---|
| 30 Dec 1935 | Coxswain William Mogridge | *George Shee* | *Satanicle* |
| 23 Jan 1937 | Coxswain William Mogridge | *George Shee* | *English Trader* |
| 16 Dec 1939 | 2nd Coxswain William Pillar<br>Bowman Frederick Sanders<br>Motor Mechanic Richard Harris | *George Shee* | *Henrietta* |
| 17 Dec 1944 | Motor Mechanic Richard Harris | *George Shee* | *Empire Alfred* |
| 24 Dec 1946 | Coxswain Henry Thomas | *George Shee* | *Ayreshire Coast* |
| 7 Dec 1959 | Motor Mechanic Richard Harris | *Princess Alexandra of Kent* | *Cycloop* |
| 22 Dec 1964 | Motor Mechanic Richard Harris | *Princess Alexandra of Kent* | MV *Northwind* |
| 16 Dec 1973 | Coxswain Kenneth Gibbs | *Princess Alexandra of Kent* | *Petite Michele* |
| 26 Aug 1976 | Lifeboat man John Dew | *Princess Alexandra of Kent* | Persons stranded |
| 6 Dec 1976 | Motor Mechanic Stephen Bower<br>Asst. Mechanic John Hunkin<br>Lifeboat man John Dew<br>Lifeboat man Michael Mills<br>Lifeboat man Nicholas Davies<br>Lifeboat man Richard Brown | *Edward Bridges* | MV *Lyrma* |
| 19 Feb 1978 | Coxswain George Dyer | *Edward Bridges* | *Leslie H* |
| 2 Dec 1978 | Coxswain Arthur Curnow | *Edward Bridges* | *Fairway* |

## TORBAY LIFEBOAT STATION HONORARY SECRETARIES

| | | | |
|---|---|---|---|
| 1866–91 | The Revd Elrington | 1983–88 | Lt Commander R.H. Bew JP, MNI, RN retired |
| 1891–1905 | Alfred H. Kendrick | | |
| 1905–20 | The Revd R.W.P. Circutt | 1988–92 | G. Anthony Smith |
| 1920–24 | W.H.K. Brewer | 1992–93 | Ron Littlewood |
| 1924–48 | H.M. Smardon MBE | 1993–96 | Capt. A. Paterson RN |
| 1948–75 | Fred W.H. Park MBE | 1997–2001 | Capt. H.D. East |
| 1975–83 | Capt. B.J. Anderson CBE, JP, ADC, DL-Devon. R.N. | | |